Photoshop Made Simple

Rod Wynne-Powell

LONDON AND NEW YORK

First published 1999 by Butterworth-Heinemann

2 Park Square, Milton Park, Abingdon, Oxon OX14 4RN
711 Third Avenue, New York, NY 10017, USA

Routledge is an imprint of the Taylor & Francis Group, an informa business

First issued in hardback 2017

British Library Cataloguing in Publication Data
A catalogue record for this book is available from the British Library

ISBN 978-0-7506-4334-4 (pbk)
ISBN 978-1-138-43627-5 (hbk)

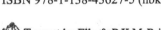

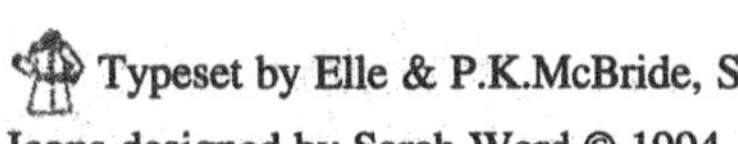

Icons designed by Sarah Ward © 1994
Transferred to digital printing 2006

Contents

Preface

Photoshop 5 is the latest incarnation of the premier cross-platform image-manipulation software, beloved of Designers, Photographers, Retouchers, Printers, and Animators. Feature-packed, powerful, yet surprisingly simple. There can be few users who find working with it a chore. The authors' task is how to give you this power, simply.

The program has undergone one change that is more fundamental than all others. It has brought in a Colour Management System. The aim was to define a standard of Colour whereby what you create on your computer can be understood by another on theirs, even though you do not know what computer the other is using, and be able to store this independent standard within your file for all to access. The basis is defined by the International Colour Consortium (ICC). It involves working in a known Colour Workspace, and profiling the characteristics of all devices from there.

The second major change is History. A very powerful form of Multiple Undo. This offers far more safety to novices and experts alike, giving great scope for experimentation and correction. The implementation allows the user to step back into the past, then take a completely different way forward from that point, yet paint a small portion of that earlier future into their picture. The true power of these features will only come from use. There could be frustration with the colour side, but it is worth the perseverance, (I am tempted to say "Trust Me;...").

The Multiple Undo will be a joy.

1 Getting started

Installation

Installation from the CD is automated, simply follow the instructions for your type of computer. Photoshop uses both RAM and hard disc space. The areas of the hard disc memory, Photoshop uses to work on your pictures is called a Scratch disc. Photoshop allows up to four of these to be set.

You can page through the Preferences in a continuous cycle. It is here that you make choices for:

- The Plug-Ins folder, which stores the program's filters;
- The type of cursors displayed; crosshairs or brush size;
- Adding lower-case extensions for PC filenames;
- Whether to allow the export of the clipboard;
- The position of the palettes at startup;
- Whether to show tool tips;
- Your scratch disks settings

Basic steps

1 After installation, open File–Preferences to allocate memory, set the location of your scratch disks and Plug-ins.

2 See pages 3 & 4 for individual procedures for Mac & PC.

Tip

If you do work for web pages on a Mac, you can choose the HTML color picker from Preferences.

1 Work through the Preferences

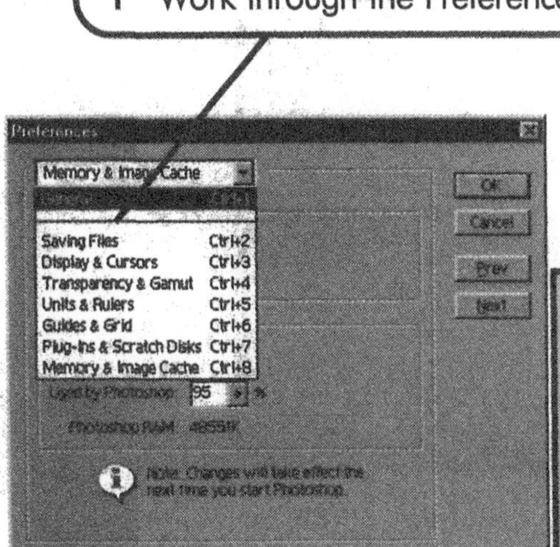

Tip

Only check 'Export Clipboard' if you need to copy to another program such as Quark Xpress. This will avoid delays when closing Photoshop, whilst it converts its clipboard contents to the system clipboard format.

Basic steps

Memory allocation – Mac

1. Go to the Apple menu and select 'About this Compu-ter' to see the free memory available.
2. Select Photoshop, then choose Get Info from the File menu ([Com-mand]/[Ctrl]+[I]).
3. In Memory Preferences, enter the Preferred Size first.
4. Set the Minimum size.
5. Click the close button; top left of window and launch Photoshop.

To decide how much memory to set for Photoshop, go to the Apple Menu–About this Computer, and note how much free memory is available; the maximum you can safely set is 10% less. Ideally, Photoshop needs between 3 and 5 times your normal file size in megabytes, but if you need other programs open at the same time, you may not be able to give this amount.

Set the preferred and minimum memory sizes in the Get Info box with Photoshop closed.

If you need PageMaker or Quark Xpress open as well, then set their memory allocation and open them before opening Photoshop, leaving 10% free.

1 Open 'About this Computer'

5 Click Close

4 Set Minimum Size

3 Set Preferred Size

Tip

Avoid using the system's virtual memory, as this will slow Photoshop.

Memory allocation – PC

Unlike the Mac, Photoshop for Windows has its memory set as a percentage of available free memory, from the preferences.

Another subtle difference is that status information is displayed in the Windows status bar not the Photoshop window.

Plug-Ins folder selection and scratch disk setup both require you to quit the program then restart it,to take effect.

Basic steps

1 From the File menu select Preferences.

2 Choose Memory & Image Cache and set the memory to be used by Photshop.

3 Choose Plug-Ins & Scratch Disks.

4 Click on the arrow to select the first hard drive, and so on...

5 Click OK.

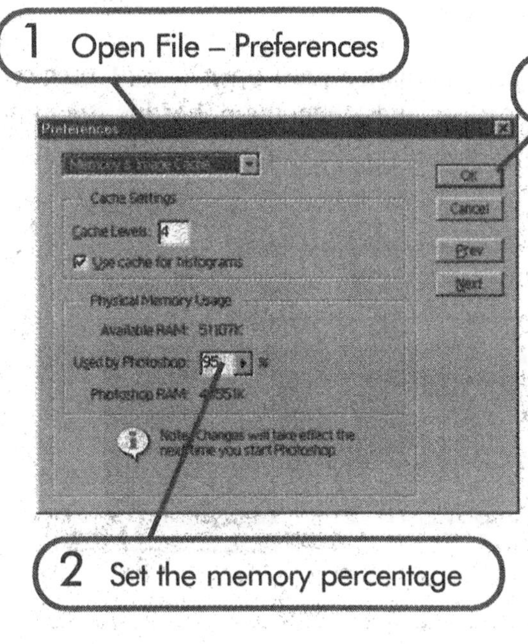

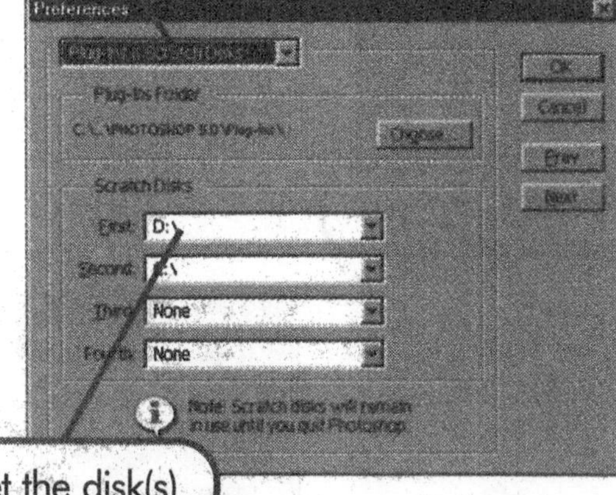

Status bar showing Info options

Tip
Keep plenty of contiguous free 'disk space' on your hard disc.

Getting Help

Typical contextual menu, showing relevant operations for the selected tool

Help is provided from the Help menu, contextual menus and from Adobe Online, for which you will need a modem, an Internet connection and a Web browser. This will also give access to other Plug-ins and updates.

Windows users have access to context-sensitive help by using the right mouse button; similar access on the Mac is found by holding down the Control key at any stage.

Tool tips are another form of help which you set in File/ Preferences. These small yellow tabs appear if you wait a second or so with the mouse over a tool in the toolbox. They show the tool's name and shortcut letter.

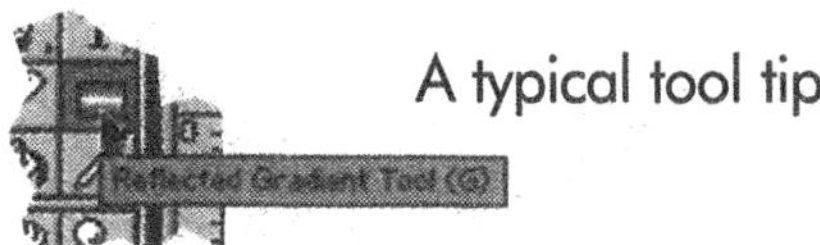

A typical tool tip

If you hear a beep and see this icon: ⃠ it means you cannot perform the task you attempted; double-click to see why not!

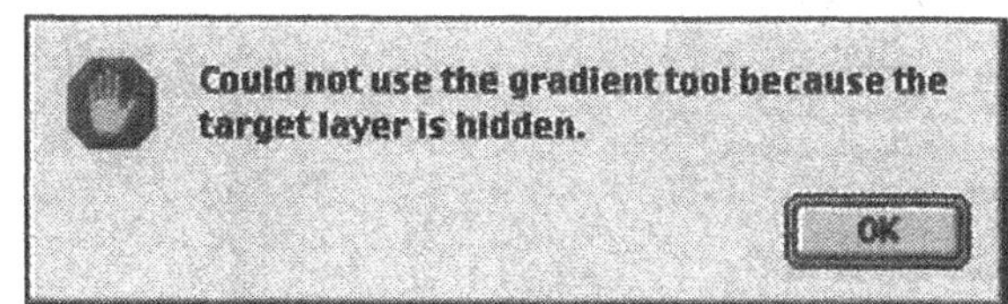

Take note

Keyboard shortcuts on a PC use the Control key; the Mac has a specific Command key.

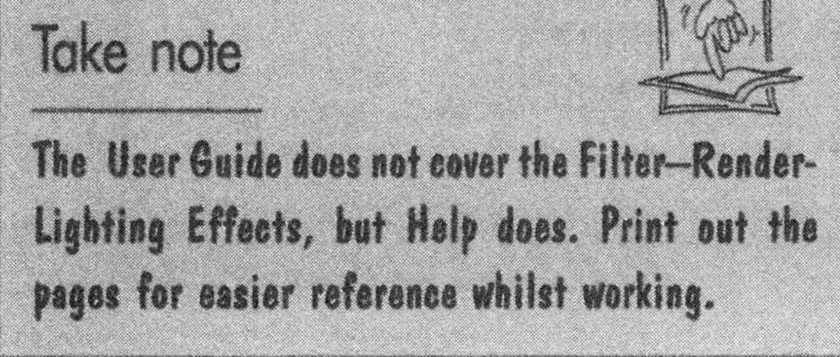

Take note

The User Guide does not cover the Filter–Render-Lighting Effects, but Help does. Print out the pages for easier reference whilst working.

The Help system

There are a number of options for getting help with Photoshop, to understand the program better or troubleshoot problems. Obviously you have the Adobe user guide and books like this one to refer to, but before dialling up the Customer support line, there are other options available which might answer your questions more quickly and effectively.

Contained in the Adobe Photoshop Help menu is a Help index. Here you can search in a number of ways: by listed topics or use the comprehensive index in the Topics window, or enter a keyword in the other window shown here. As you type, the Help program will guess the full title and suggest a topic. Press Enter to get the contents displayed.

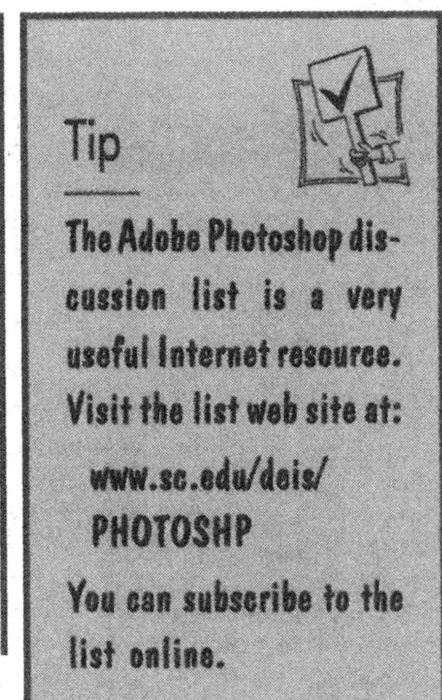

Tip
The Adobe Photoshop discussion list is a very useful Internet resource. Visit the list web site at:
www.sc.edu/deis/PHOTOSHP
You can subscribe to the list online.

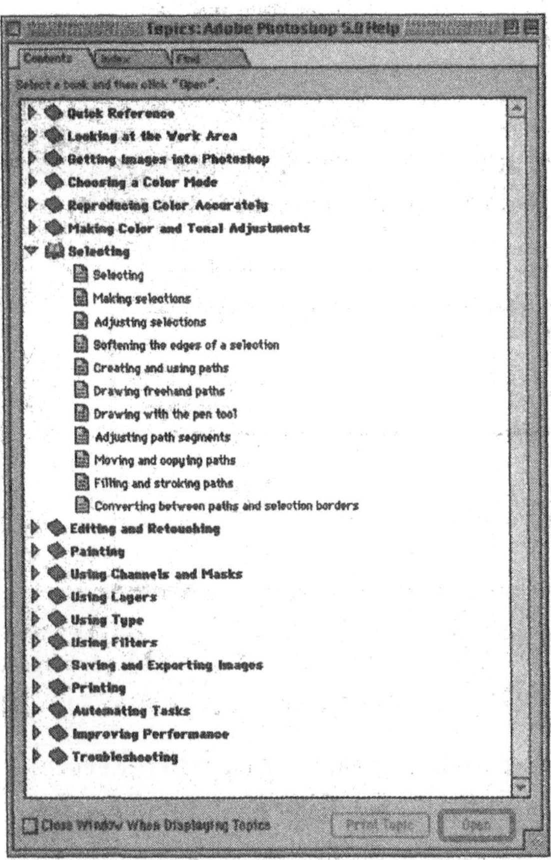

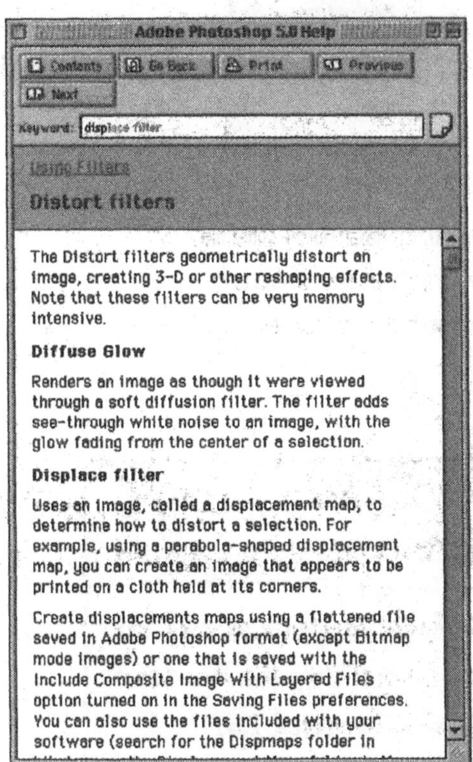

Basic steps

Online support

1 Click on the image area at the top of the tools palette.

2 Click the Update button the first time you use Online help.

3 Select from options to access the relevant section on the Adobe site.

For further information on Photoshop, updates, top tips and access to the Adobe Web forums, use the Adobe Online service. For this, you must have an Internet connection.

The Customer Support databases contain the most detailed papers, addressing some of the most common issues. This is often better than calling tech support as they will be using the same resources themselves to answer your queries and this way you can print the information out to digest and refer to again in the future. Whilst connected, check out the top tips, where you can download lots of illustrated PDF Photoshop tutorials.

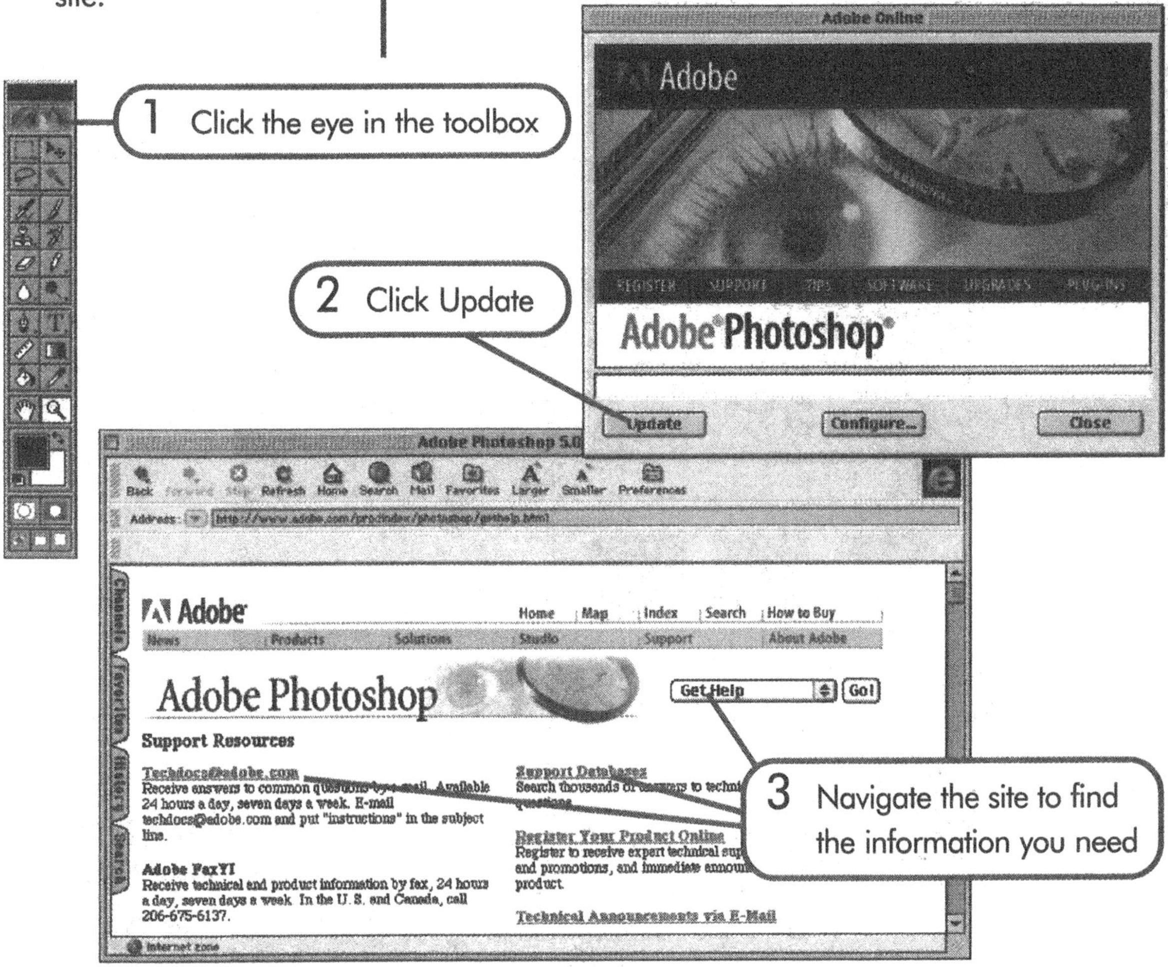

1 Click the eye in the toolbox

2 Click Update

3 Navigate the site to find the information you need

Adobe Gamma

The Adobe Gamma/Monitor Setup Utility control panel is for adjusting your monitor to give a neutral colour balance and provide an ICC (International Colour Consortium) profile. This sets how your monitor displays the full RGB colour range.

Gamma is the relationship between the data signals and the displayed brightness. If you feel daunted by what is being set here, use the step-by-step Wizard to make the adjustments.

By checking the box marked 'Use as Default' this profile is adopted as the system-wide monitor profile on an Apple Macintosh computer, but is Photoshop specific on a Windows PC.

When setting a value for Gamma, the only two figures generally needed are 1.8 for print-related work, and 2.2 for Business graphics and screen-based work.

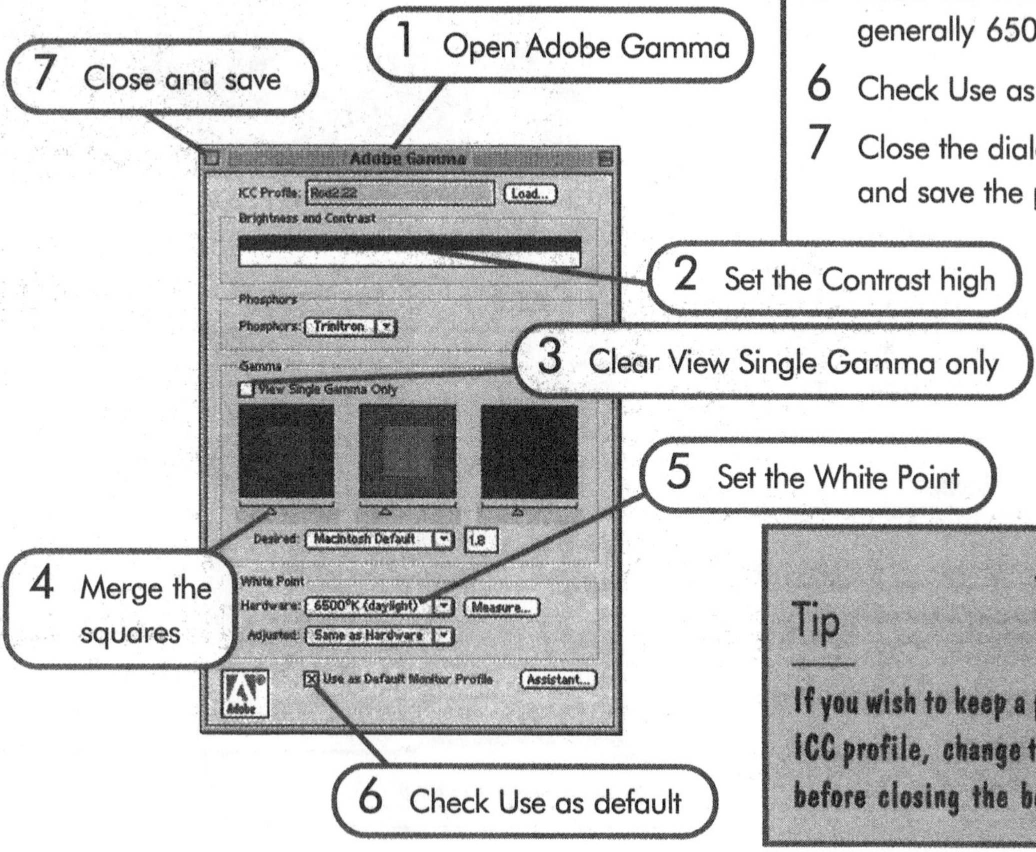

7 Close and save

1 Open Adobe Gamma

2 Set the Contrast high

3 Clear View Single Gamma only

5 Set the White Point

4 Merge the squares

6 Check Use as default

Basic steps

1 Open Adobe Gamma.

2 Turn the Contrast to almost maximum – the squares in the top bar should not be quite black.

3 Uncheck the box View Single Gamma only.

4 Move the sliders till the inner square merges with the outer.

5 Select the White Point, generally 6500°K.

6 Check Use as default.

7 Close the dialog box and save the profile.

Tip

If you wish to keep a previous ICC profile, change the name before closing the box.

Basic steps

The colour workspace

1 Calibrate the monitor, with Adobe Gamma.

2 Go to File – Color settings – Profile Setup.

3 Choose your colour workspaces –*Adobe RGB* for pre-press (see page 10); *sRGB* for Web/ screen work; *ColorMatch* if using PressView monitors, etc.

4 Set up how to respond to a Profile Mismatch. (Set to *Ask when opening*, if in doubt.)

Adobe has made significant changes to how colour is handled in Photoshop 5. It can now be tied to defined standards, and is independent of the hardware it is operating on. This defined area of colour in which your files reside is known as the colour workspace.

This means that your monitor needs to be calibrated to give the correct colour response to the digital data supplied from that workspace. After that you will have greater control over the quality and consistency of colour you achieve. Files from other people in the same or different Workspaces can be matched with accuracy.

In the update, Version 5.0.2, the procedure for setting the workspace is handled as part of the installation procedure.

2 Go to Profile Setup

Profile Setup

Embed Profiles

RGB CMYK Grayscale Lab

OK

Cancel

Assumed Profiles

RGB: SMPTE-240M

CMYK: Ask When Opening

Grayscale: None

Profile Mismatch Handling

RGB: Ask When Opening

CMYK: Ask When Opening

Grayscale: Convert to Grayscale

3 Choose your workspaces

4 Select the Profile Handling

Take note

Try to remain in RGB till the end of editing, but if the starting point is CMYK, try to remain in CMYK mode. See page 11.

Adobe RGB(1998)

Adobe RGB (1998) is an excellent all-round RGB workspace, ideally suited for work that is to be converted to CMYK in which a wide gamut of colours can be faithfully recorded.

As the workspace is an independent standard, you must decide:

- Does the incoming file match this space?
- If it does not, how do you make it do so?

These decisions are handled in Profile Setup.

- Can you assume where these files originate?
- Are they all scanned from your own scanner?
- Are they from Photoshop 5, or 4 or earlier?
- Are they profiled?

If the source varies wildly the best setting will be to 'Ask when opening'. In this way, if no profile embedded, you can choose 'Apple RGB' or 'Monitor RGB' as the assumption, then convert to your workspace. Any file direct from your scanner can be brought in without conversion. Profiled files can be converted to RGB. They will only be altered if they were from a different workspace.

Once you have set the Profile handling, any mismatch will show the message 'Converting Colors' as you open a file.

A pre-press workspace

Opening files in Photoshop 5, created in versions without ICC profiles assumes they were assessed by the monitor, so set 'Assumed Profile' to Monitor RGB/Apple RGB.

When the file is not what the program is expecting, a mismatch will occur. The program uses the Profile Setup information to make the correct changes. In this dialog box you also decide whether to embed a tag defining your workspace when saving. These are the checkboxes along the top of the box. With the workspace set to Adobe RGB (1998), a tagged file for another

Basic steps

1 Select File–Color Settings–RGB Setup.

2 Click on RGB, and select the workspace *Adobe RGB (1998) / SMPTE-240M.*

3 Check Display Using Monitor Compensation, and close box.

4 Open File–Color Settings–Profile Setup.

5 Check the RGB box – your file will be tagged for the Adobe RGB (1998) workspace.

6 Set the Profile Mismatch Handling to *Ask when Opening.*

Take note

The default workspace is sRGB, which is suited to screen-based work, and home-based printers. It clips too many colours to be ideal for pre–press.

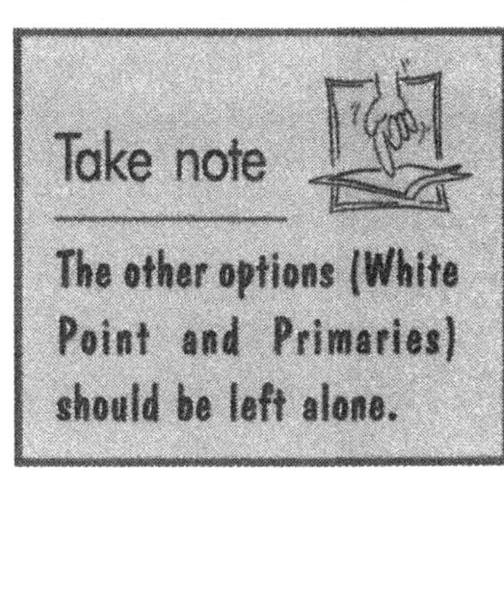

workspace will alert you to the options of bringing the file in with no change, or asking you to convert the file to conform to your chosen workspace.

Until the most files contain an ICC profile for the originating workspace, any assumptions are likely to be individual. It is to be hoped that ultimately all files will have this information, so that any conversions are made from a known stable base. SMPTE-240M or Adobe RGB (1998) can then be made the assumed profile, and thus the ‘Converting Colors’ message will be seen less frequently.

A CMYK file is specific to the intended printing process, so care should be taken if it is to be converted, as it already has a restricted gamut. Returning a CMYK file to RGB, will not restore any lost colours, and so is less suitable for high quality output processes, such a colour transparency. It is not recommended that a CMYK file created for a newspaper should be converted to CMYK for subsequent use in a glossy magazine.

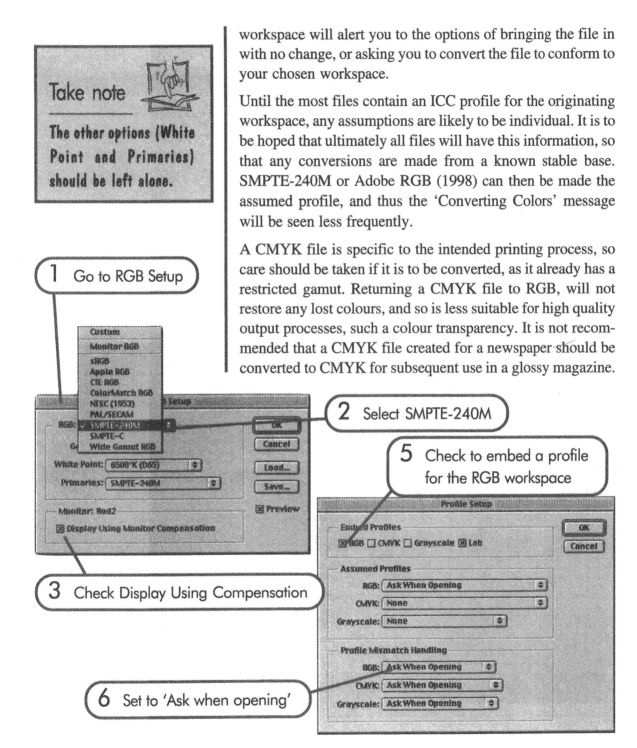

1 Go to RGB Setup

2 Select SMPTE-240M

3 Check Display Using Compensation

5 Check to embed a profile for the RGB workspace

6 Set to ‘Ask when opening’

Colour gamut

Colour gamut is the collection of colours available for display or reproduction. The RGB colourspace has a wider gamut than CMYK. To help in showing which colours can be preserved and which ones are lost, Photoshop shows out-of-gamut colours with a default overlay of grey. The Gamut warning colour, set in Preferences is used as an indicator for colours within an RGB image which would fall outside the CMYK gamut when converted. The colour indication is user-definable.

To see whether a colour would go out of gamut on conversion from RGB to CMYK, you turn it on via the View menu.

Not only can your image be shown with this feature, it can be particularly helpful when choosing a colour from the palette, to have this feature switched on, so that you are aware of the limitations from the outset.

Basic steps

1 In the View menu, turn on Gamut Warning to show out-of-gamut colours.

2 Click on the Foreground Swatch in the Tools palette to bring up the Color Picker.

- You can now see very graphically which colours are not going to reproduce correctly in CMYK.

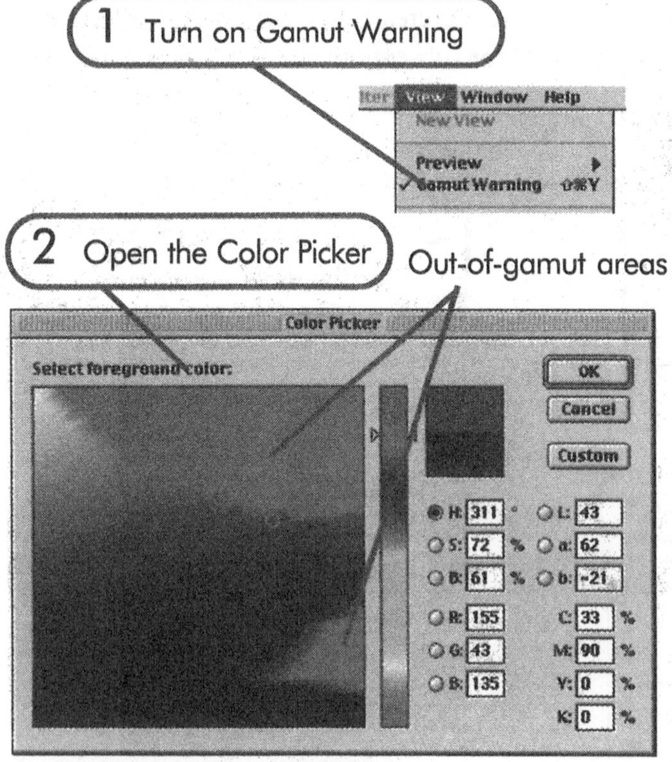

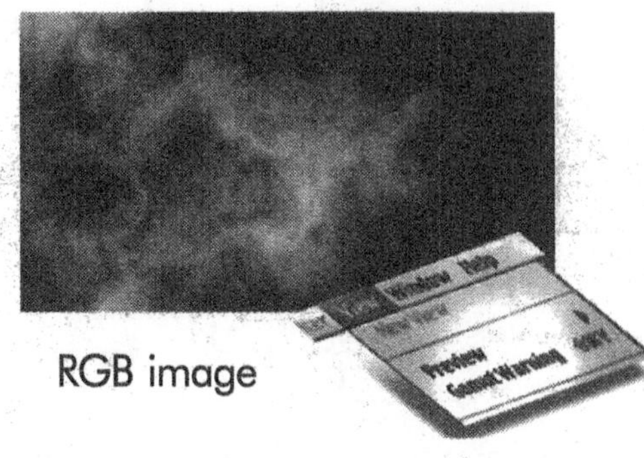

RGB image

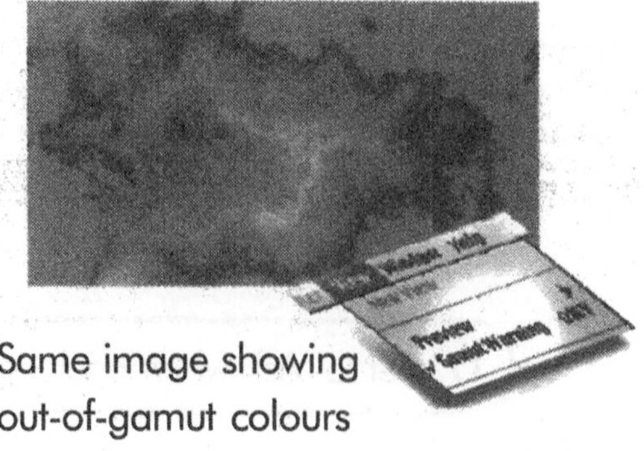

Same image showing out-of-gamut colours

Background

- To change the Background to transparent

1 Double-click the Background in the Layers palette.

2 The name will change to become *Layer 0* – this can be renamed if needs be.

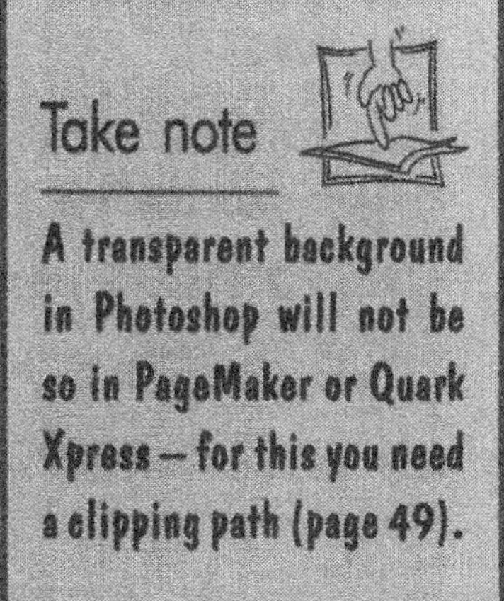

Take note

A transparent background in Photoshop will not be so in PageMaker or Quark Xpress – for this you need a clipping path (page 49).

The structure of Photoshop allows the user to have a series of images each on a layer of its own, which can be more or less solid (opacity); can react in various ways with each other (blend modes); and can be affected individually (layer masks); adjusted in colour, contrast, saturation, etc (adjustment layers). See also page 68.

However, the original (background) layer will be opaque, unless the file was opened as transparent, reacting differently to true layers. If you use Edit–Clear on the background it will take on the background colour defined in the Tools palette, whereas a Layer would become transparent, shown by default, as the checquerboard effect.

If you start your session in Photoshop by placing an EPS file from a vector drawing package such as Illustrator or Corel Draw, it is best to start with a transparent background and build the image from there. When you Place a file it will have a rectangular bounding box with crossed diagonal lines. This can be resized and rotated and transformed generally before being rendered into the file. This is where the Grids and Guides can be extremely helpful in assessing how various items are positioned, aligned or sized.

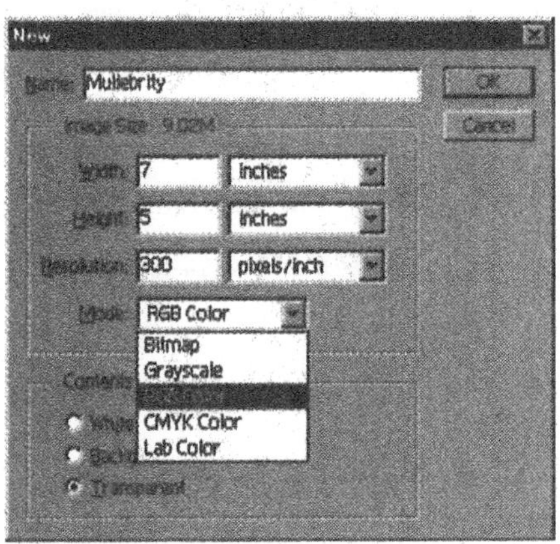

WithTransparency set in the Open dialog box, the bottom layer will be Layer 0

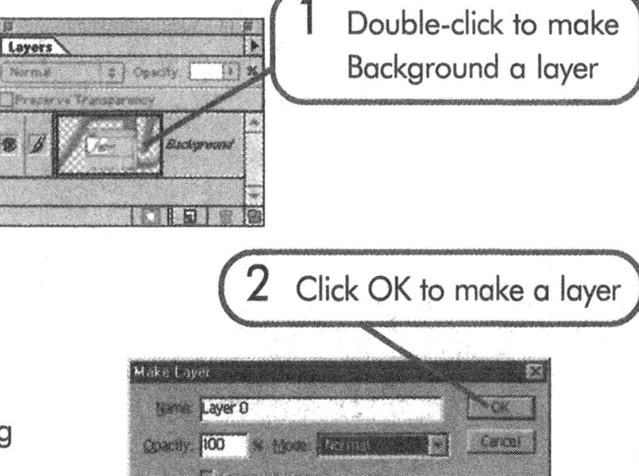

File formats

Photoshop opens a range of file formats other than its own native one. The complete list appears in the Open dialog box, by clicking on Show All Files, and then on Formats which is revealed. (see page 24).

The cross-platform formats, TIFF, EPS, Photo-CD and JPEG are the most important. GIF, with its restricted number of colours, is ideal for Web work. Any format Photoshop can open can also be saved; however avoid resaving a compressed file when this is a lossy format such as JPEG; recompressing a lossless formatted file is fine.

When saving files containing Layers, Channels or Paths, remember that if these are to be edited at a later date, you should save in native Photoshop format (.psd). EPS and TIFF files are best for use in DTP (Desktop Publishing). CMYK files can be saved in DCS 2.0 format which saves each colour channel separately, as well as keeping a composite channel; this allows the creation and saving of channels for Spot Colours, varnishes or bump plates (specialist means for applying precise colours, not available to CMYK, or a shiny coating to selected parts of an image, or the creation of raised text or objects in a picture).

Photographic images needing compression for efficient Web use or transmission are suited to JPEG, whereas graphics for buttons and cartoon-style illustration are more suited to the GIF format. This is lossless, using the LZW (Lempel-Ziv Welch) format.

Mac and PC have their own internal formats of PICT, BMP and PCX, these should be reserved solely for platform-specific use, such as icons or screensavers. As yet you can only open, not save to Photo-CD format, and can only save back to Scitex and Targa files from files of those origins.

- ❑ Keep the native Photoshop file for editing.
- ❑ Use EPS if clipping paths are needed – for cutouts and runarounds.
- ❑ Use EPS or TIFF files for cross-platform work in Quark Xpress and PageMaker.
- ❑ Use DCS 2.0 for spot-colours and 'specials'.
- ❑ Use JPEG, FlashPix and GIF for the Web.

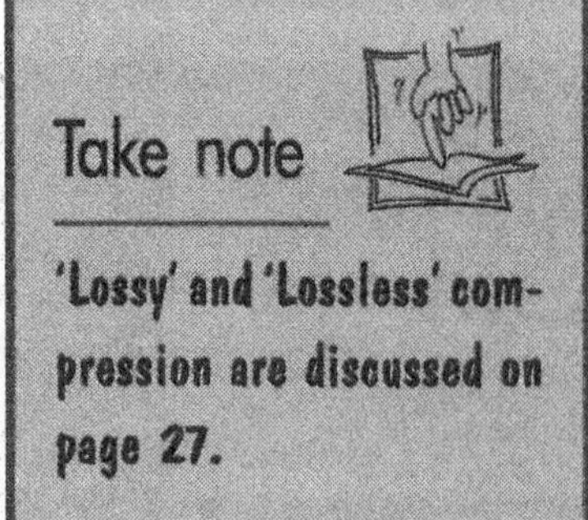

Take note
'Lossy' and 'Lossless' compression are discussed on page 27.

Miscellany

- ❑ Flatbed scanners are ideal for prints.
- ❑ Negatives and transparencies are best scanned using dedicated slide scanners.
- ❑ Import vector art from other programs, such as Corel Draw, Illustrator, FreeHand or Canvas using Place, or simply drag and drop (if both programs are open at the same time).

Here are some helpful hints worth bearing in mind when starting to use Photoshop, since the startpoint could be any of:

- a transparency or print to scan in;
- a file from a colleague or client;
- a digital camera or camcorder;
- an idea in the user's head!

If you are working to a specific size, then setting your units of measurement is important. This is done in Preferences, and apart from inches and centimetres there is also a percentage setting which can be extremely handy for use in Actions (see page 147). A shortcut for this is to double-click the ruler. If the ruler is not present it can be summoned with **Command/Ctrl + R**.

To assist with layout a grid can be set in Preferences. Click-drag from the ruler area into your picture to draw a guide.

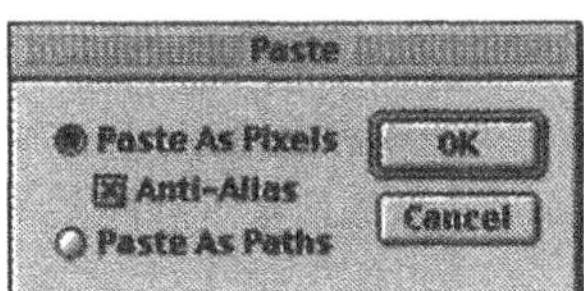

Using Paste from Illustrator can paste the Paths, or turn them into pixels

Pasting twice, once for each setting, adds a new path (which appears in the Paths palette); as well as the image itself

Save files as Photoshop EPS to use File–Place when you need to resize and rotate them in a montage.

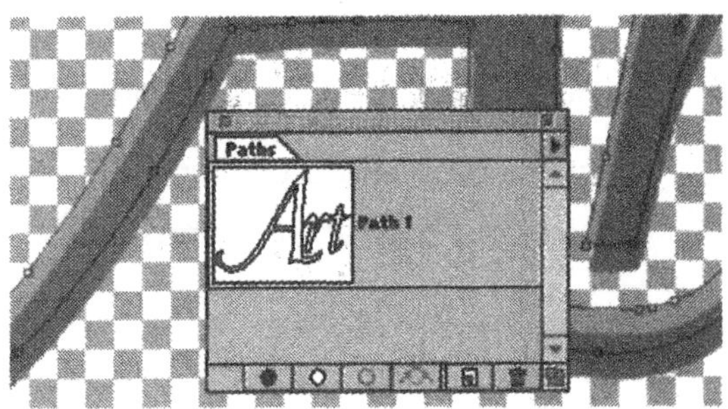

Summary

- ❑ Installation is largely automatic, but you do need to set the memory allocations when you first start. Photoshop needs free memory of between 3 and 5 times the file size to work efficiently.
- ❑ You must have more space on your hard disk than the RAM you allocate or you will not be able to use even the full RAM you do have.
- ❑ When you see the Prohibition sign and are beeped, simply double-click to find the reason.
- ❑ If you cannot find what you are looking for, and have tried the Help menu, try going Online and looking on the Adobe Web site.
- ❑ Use Adobe Gamma, ColorSync 2.5.1 or later, or ICM 2 to set your ICC monitor profile, via the wizard or Control Panel.
- ❑ Make sure you understand about colour workspaces; select the one appropriate to your type of work.
- ❑ If you are supplying work to others check to see whether they are using ICC profiling. If they are, which workspace do they use?
- ❑ If you have entered valid CMYK conversion data, and want to see how the RGB colours might fare when converted, turn on the CMYK Preview from the View menu, and/or the Gamut Warning.
- ❑ Files can be opened and saved in a variety of formats. Choose the format which best suits the job.

2 Fundamentals

The tools palette

Positioned at the top left of your screen, you will see the tools palette. This contains all the tools necessary for editing, selecting, painting and navigating your way around Photoshop. To select a tool, click on its icon. In Photoshop 5.0, there are some 46 tools to choose from – all the extra tools are nestled in fly-out menus. The illustration opposite shows all of these, as well as the keyboard shortcut to use. The hidden tools are accessed using any of the following methods:

- Mouse down on the tools palette icon and move the cursor across to the new tool icon.
- Hold down the Option/Alt key as you click on the icon. This will allow you to toggle or cycle through the options available for that tool.
- Use the Shift key plus the key shortcut to toggle the tool selection or cycle through the available options.

Once a tool has been selected, you will see the cursor icon change to become that of the tool type, whenever the cursor is inside the image window. At the bottom of the window it is possible to select the Show Tool option (see page 20). The current tool name will then be displayed.

Most tools have different operating modes. Tool behaviour can be modified by changing the settings in the Options palette.

The lower section of the palette displays the foreground and background colours, below that are two buttons which enable you to switch between selection border and Quick Mask mode and finally there are buttons for the three screen display modes.

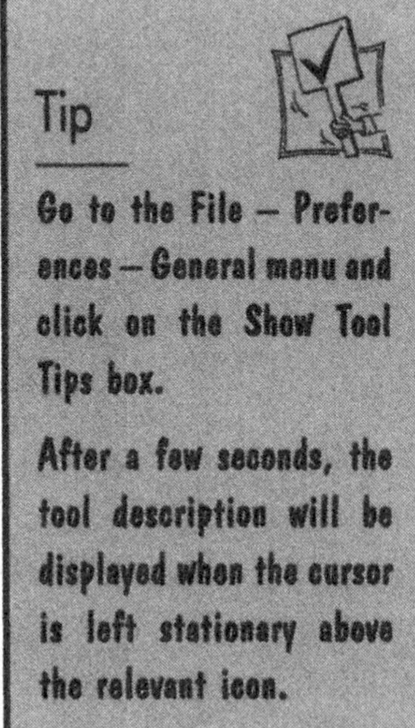

Tip
Go to the File – Preferences – General menu and click on the Show Tool Tips box.
After a few seconds, the tool description will be displayed when the cursor is left stationary above the relevant icon.

When the rubber stamp tool is selected, for example, further tool options are made available in the Options palette. Here one can choose the opacity, blending mode and whether the tool will operate in aligned or nonaligned mode.

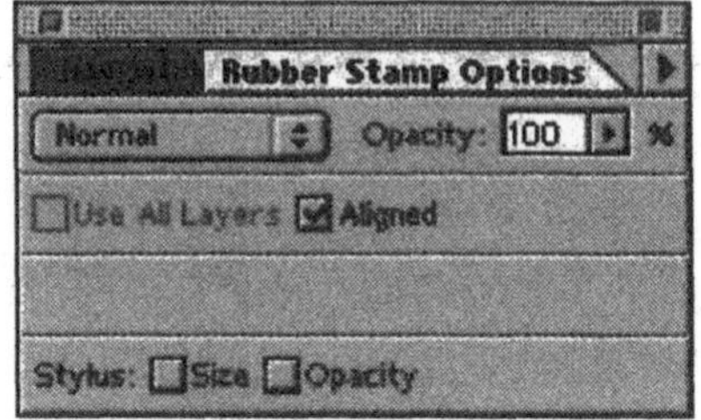

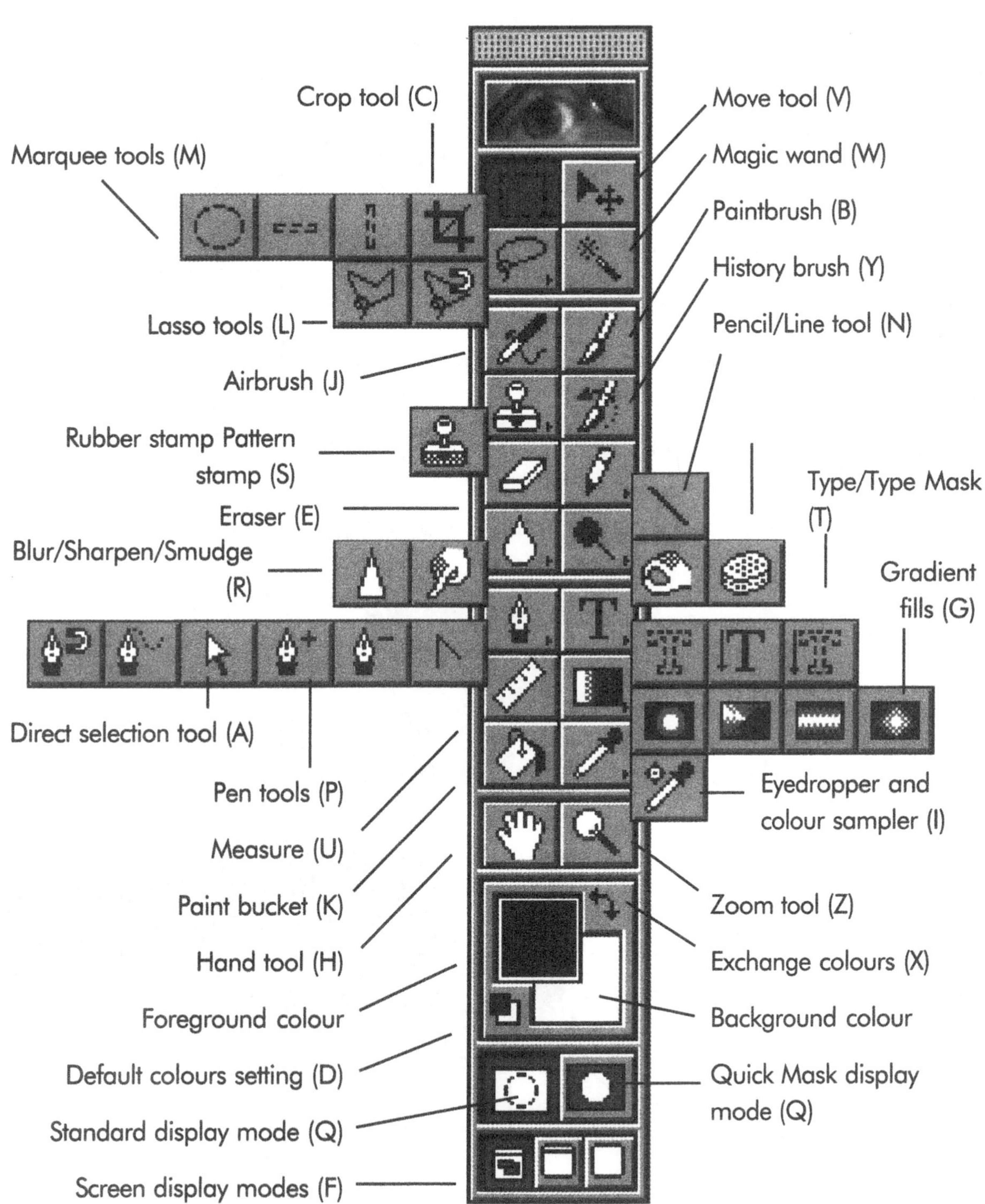
Crop tool (C)
Move tool (V)
Marquee tools (M)
Magic wand (W)
Paintbrush (B)
History brush (Y)
Lasso tools (L)
Pencil/Line tool (N)
Airbrush (J)
Rubber stamp Pattern stamp (S)
Type/Type Mask (T)
Eraser (E)
Blur/Sharpen/Smudge (R)
Gradient fills (G)
Direct selection tool (A)
Pen tools (P)
Eyedropper and colour sampler (I)
Measure (U)
Paint bucket (K)
Zoom tool (Z)
Hand tool (H)
Exchange colours (X)
Foreground colour
Background colour
Default colours setting (D)
Quick Mask display mode (Q)
Standard display mode (Q)
Screen display modes (F)

Image window

When you open an image, it appears inside a standard document window. In this default mode it is easy to manoeuvre the windows around the screen. The status boxes at the bottom of the image window provide valuable feedback information about the image's file size, or can be set to display other information, as listed below.

When displaying scratch disk size for example, the first readout represents the current scratch disk usage and the second readout the total amount of scratch disk space available.

- To toggle the ruler display on and off, choose **View – Show/Hide Rulers**.
- To show or hide guides, choose **View – Show/Hide Guides**.

Tip

Use the Tab key to toggle between the hiding and showing of all palettes.

Use Shift+Tab to hide/show all palettes but the tools palette.

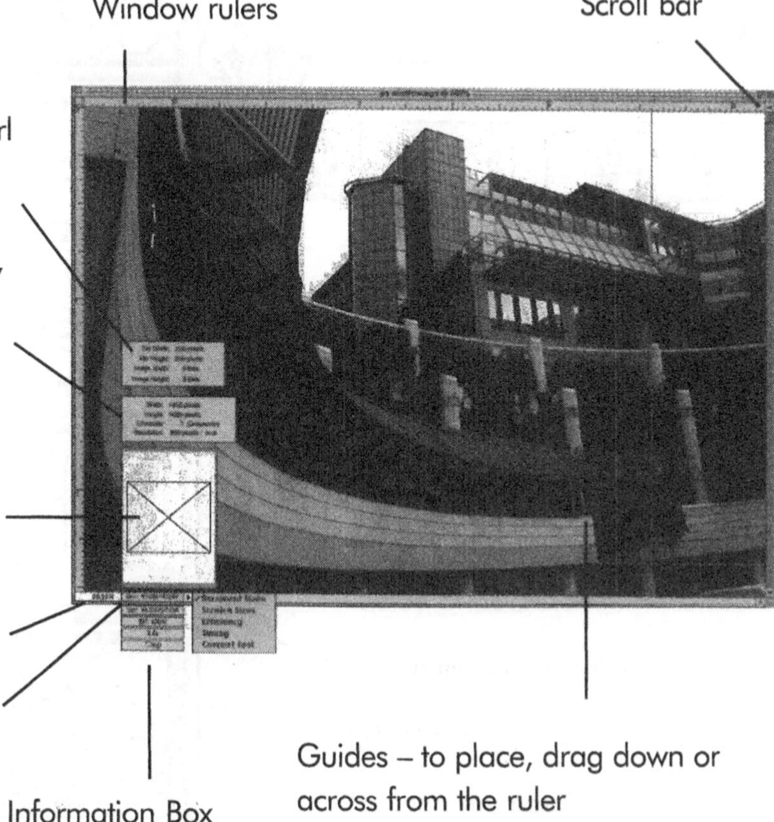
Window rulers
Scroll bar
Hold down the Command/Ctrl key to display the Tiling
Hold down the Option/Alt key to display the File size and resolution information
Mouse down to display a scaled preview of the size the image will print with the current page setup (see chapter nine)
Image scale
Document/scratch disk size
Information Box
Guides – to place, drag down or across from the ruler

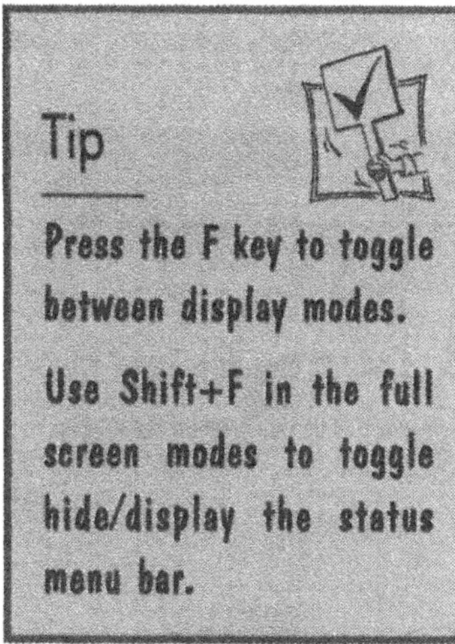

Tip
Press the F key to toggle between display modes.
Use Shift+F in the full screen modes to toggle hide/display the status menu bar.

Beware of using garish desktop patterns or strong colours for your desktop display. These will have an impact on how you evaluate the colour balance in an image. The display mode can be changed as shown below and the neutral grey pasteboard surround provides a clearer less cluttered view of the image.

It is always possible to have more than one window view of an image open at the same time. Choose Window – New Window to create a second window view. This means it is possible to have a full image window view and close-up view open simultaneously. Click to activate either window and switch quickly between the two views.

The bottom of the tools palette has three screen display buttons. Clicking on the these icons will alter the way the image window is displayed: from being shown within a document window to full screen with a neutral grey pasteboard surround or absolute full screen mode with a black background and the status bar hidden.

Import and opening

Basic steps

You open a file in Photoshop the same way as you would with any other type of document: double click the document icon, drag the document onto the application icon or use File – Open.

Double-clicking will not always open an image file into Photoshop. On a PC, the three character file extension will decide in which application a file is opened, and this amy be another application, such as a web browser program.

You can aAcquire an image from a scanning device. To do this, choose File – Import – (device driver). This will open the scan driver interface for whichever scanner device you are using.

1. Choose Open from the File menu.
2. Navigate through the folders to select a file's location.
3. Select the file and click on the Open button.

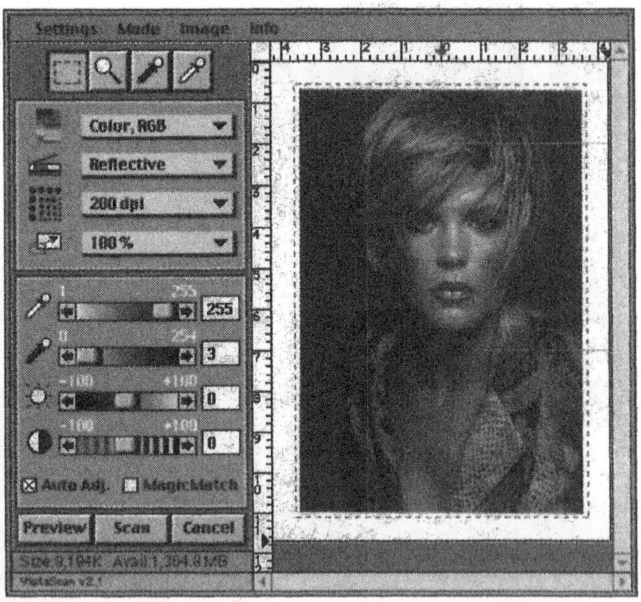

1 Use File – Open

2 Locate the file

3 Click Open

VistaScan flatbed scanner interface window, showing a preview image and scanning controls

Basic steps

Kodak Photo CD

1 Open the Photo_CD folder and select Images.

2 Select the image you require and click Open.

3 Choose the source profile matching your photograph, resolution and destination type.

4 Click OK.

It might seem logical to go to the Photos folder on the Photo CD disc and open the pictures directly as you would from any disk. However, to get the best quality, Kodak Photo CD images must be opened through the File – Open menu from within Photoshop. To determine which 'Source' profile should be used, click on the Image Info button. This will give you an indication of the emulsion type of the original. In the example, an Ektachrome E6 profile was selected as the source profile. All profiles are locate in the System ColorSync Profiles folder.

For destination, you can choose from any number of output profiles. If editing in RGB, you can select the Lab colour mode, then convert to RGB afterwards in Photoshop. The Cielab profile is conveniently identified by Kodak as 'pslabpcs.pf'!

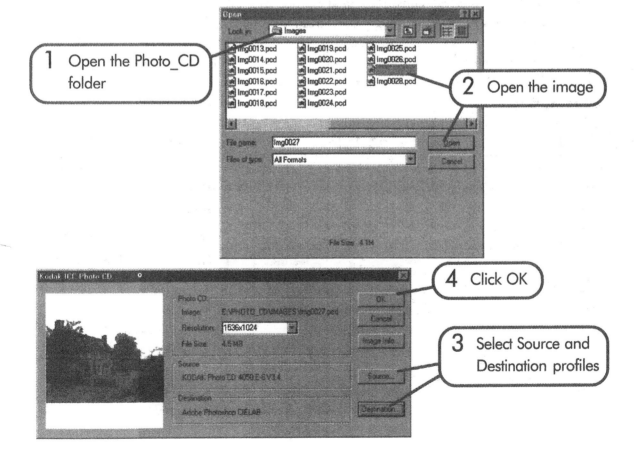

1 Open the Photo_CD folder

2 Open the image

4 Click OK

3 Select Source and Destination profiles

Saving

When saving an image, go to the File menu. Three options exist: Save, Save As... and Save a Copy... The first time you save a picture, the Save dialog will appear on the screen. Here you enter the destination of where to save the file, then choose the file format it is to be saved in and the name it shall be given.

Remember to save often. When working on an underpowered computer, you may find Photoshop has a habit of crashing whenever you edit a large image. And of course, all the work carried out since the last time you saved will be lost. Saving will automatically overwrite the last saved version. If you don't wish to overwrite, then choose File – Save As, to call up the Save dialog. Rename the image or choose a new folder location. If you don't rename, a dialog will ask if you wish to replace the original. Saving multiple versions of an image is one way of permanently recording different image states from a session.

Basic steps

1 Go to the File menu and choose Save.
2 In the Save dialog box, choose a location to save the file to.
3 Select a file format from the list.
4 Rename the file as necessary.
5 Click Save.

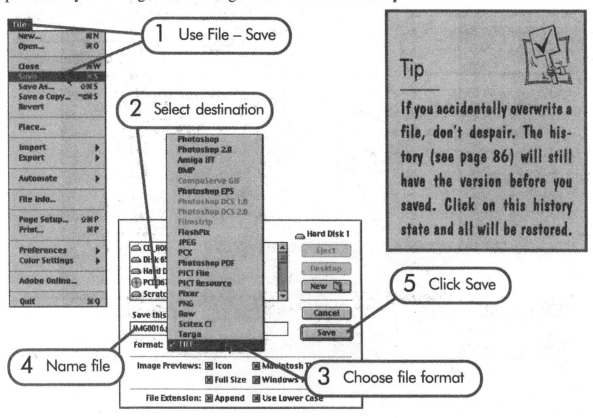

1 Use File – Save

2 Select destination

3 Choose file format

4 Name file

5 Click Save

Tip

If you accidentally overwrite a file, don't despair. The history (see page 86) will still have the version before you saved. Click on this history state and all will be restored.

To adjust the file saving options, go to the Preferences menu. The choices here are fairly obvious – when the *Append File Extension* option is checked, the file will automatically have the three-letter file type code added. The *Use Lower Case* option is especially important when saving files that are to be uploaded to an Internet server. Some servers are case-sensitive and you cannot therefore name files using capital letters.

The Save a Copy... option will automatically append the word 'copy' at the end of the original file name. If for example, the original master is layered, you can choose to flatten and save as a TIFF and the original will remain intact. Best of all, the original file remains throughout in its original format.

Of the many file formats available, the most relevant for everyday use are: the native Photoshop format, TIFF, EPS and DCS. For as long as the image is open, live in Photoshop, you can alter an image however you want. It is only when you come to save, that the issue of the format in which it was created, comes into play. So if a layer is added to an original TIFF file, you have to accept either to flatten it first, or save in the Photoshop format.

Set the options for saving in the File – Preferences – General menu. The settings here are reflected in the Save dialog box.

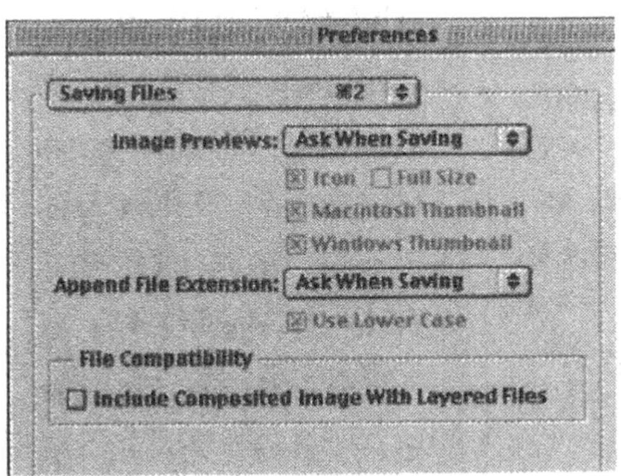

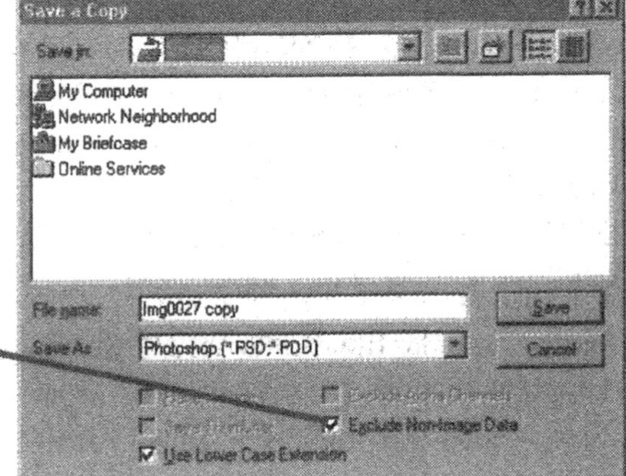

Checking the Exclude Non-image Data option in the 'Save a Copy... dialog will strip out all icon previews and ICC profiles from the file.

File formats

The native Photoshop format is the most versatile of all because it allows you to save in any colour mode, include layers, channels and paths, and it compresses the file data as efficiently as possible without any loss. The Photoshop 2.5 format always stores a simplified, flattened version of the image and can be used to send files to users of this older software which does not support layers.

TIFF and EPS are the most popular formats used for the placement of image files in graphic design layouts. The TIFF format will support alpha channels and clipping paths, but not layers. Most word processing and all page layout programs should all recognise these formats too. You can save in both RGB or CMYK colour modes, but remember, mostly you will be required to place an image in CMYK. If a file is intended to go to a professional press, you will generally be required to use CMYK. Desktop ink jet printers like the Epson series however, prefer to handle printing images from RGB. Channels, which might be used for spot colours are not supported by the EPS format, they are though by DCS 2.0. Normally, you should flatten your image, remove all alpha channels and save as a TIFF or EPS and place the image in a layout program.

JPEG is a 'lossy' format which compresses image data into a much smaller size, making it possible for example, to archive an 18 Mb image onto a floppy disk. To achieve such a level of compression, image data is inevitably and irrevocably degraded. You can see the effect for yourself by examining in close-up a JPEG image which has been heavily compressed. The compression options are available on a sliding scale, with 1 providing the most and 10, the least amount of compression. JPEG is most commonly used on the Web as a means of distributing images in a more manageable size.

Another popular file format used in web page design is the GIF (Graphics Interchange Format). This is suited for web graphic logos and similar images designed for display on a web site.

Tip

If the file format you want to use is dimmed or not showing, check to see if the image needs to be flattened or if it still contains a layer or alpha channel.

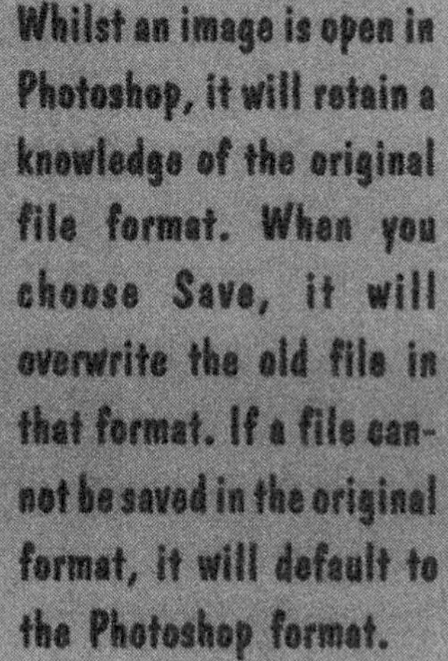

Take note

Whilst an image is open in Photoshop, it will retain a knowledge of the original file format. When you choose Save, it will overwrite the old file in that format. If a file cannot be saved in the original format, it will default to the Photoshop format.

Basic steps

1 Convert the image to Index Color mode.

2 Choose File – Export GIF 89a.

3 Set the options and click OK

4 Name the file, choose the destination where to save and click Save.

Rather than simply choose the CompuServe GIF format option when saving, try Exporting with the GIF 89a format following the instructions shown here. The GIF 89a format includes useful extras like the ability to interlace an image, so when viewed on the Web, the picture downloads a low resolution version first and gradually builds up the image detail.

You'll need to convert the image to Index Color mode first though and work destined for the web is best converted using the Web 216 colour palette. Leave the **Dither** option set to *Diffusion* for images. In the Export dialog you can set one or more colours to appear as transparent. Click on any of the colour swatches or shift click to select more than one colour.

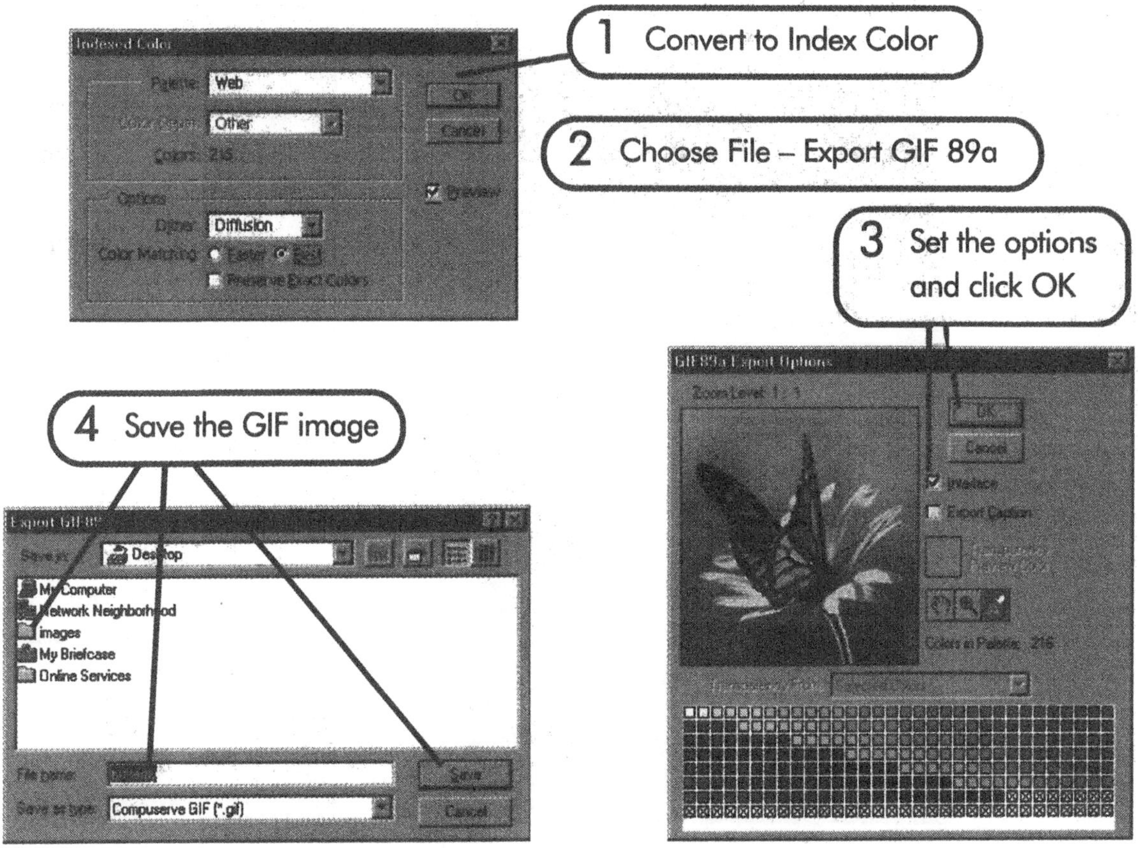

1 Convert to Index Color

2 Choose File – Export GIF 89a

3 Set the options and click OK

4 Save the GIF image

Zooming in and out

You can use any of the zooming methods described here to reduce or magnify the image view displayed on the screen.

It is easy enough to reposition the image window as you would with any open window on the desktop.

There are several ways of navigating around an image that is open in Photoshop. One method is to select the hand tool from the tools palette, or use the keyboard shortcut of holding down the Spacebar. The hand tool enables you to scroll around the image window – mouse down with the hand tool and shift the image view around within the window area.

Basic steps

1 Select the Zoom tool from the tools palette.

2 Click on the image, or marquee an area with the zoom tool to enlarge.

3 Hold down the Option/ Alt key and click to zoom out.

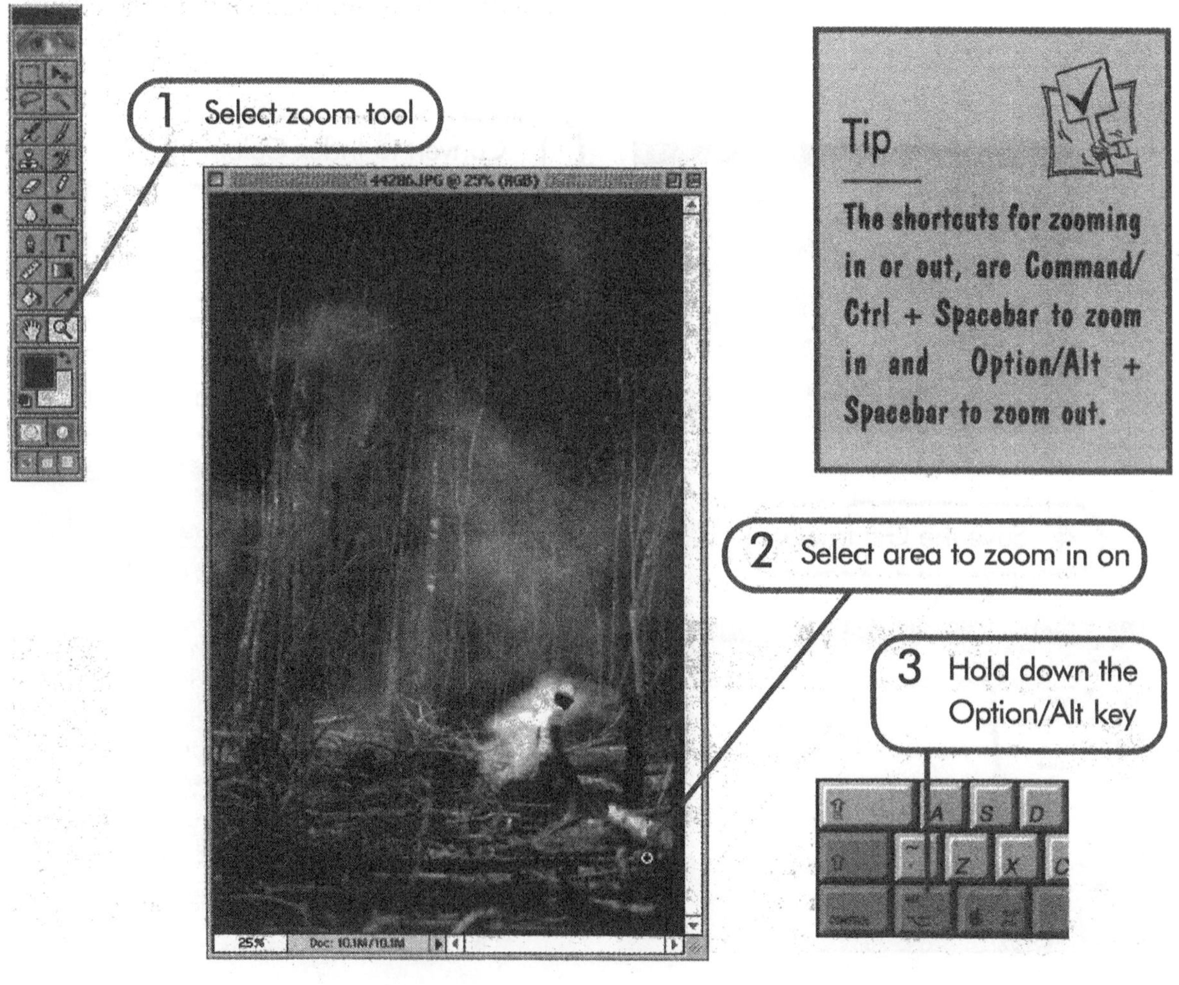

Tip

The shortcuts for zooming in or out, are Command/ Ctrl + Spacebar to zoom in and Option/Alt + Spacebar to zoom out.

Navigator

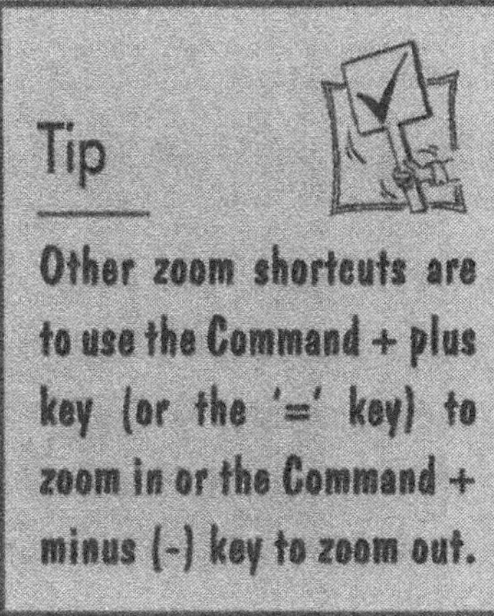

Tip
Other zoom shortcuts are to use the Command + plus key (or the '=' key) to zoom in or the Command + minus (-) key to zoom out.

The Navigator palette (shown below left) is usually grouped with the Options and Info palette and is normally found at the top right of the screen area. The Navigator offers an alternative, easy and direct method of scrolling and zooming in and out of an image. It is possible to resize the palette by dragging the bottom of the palette window out. This will let you see a larger preview. The coloured rectangle indicates the current view selection as seen in relation to the whole image. Other rectangle colours can be selected via the palette fly-out menu options.

Drag inside the rectangle border to scroll the image. Hold down the Command/ Ctrl key and drag the mouse to define an area to zoom in to.

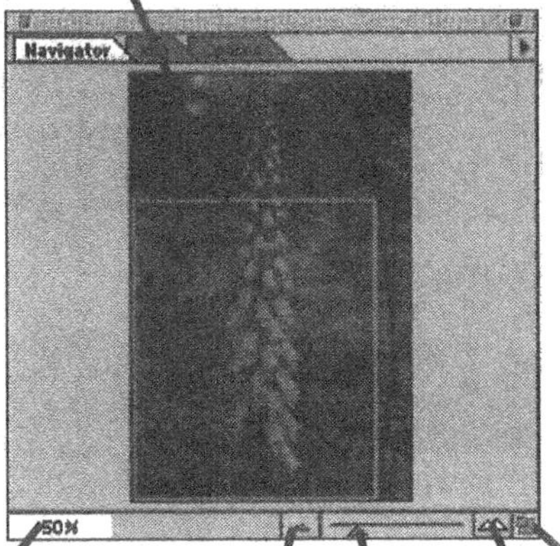

Type a zoom percentage here and press [Enter]

Drag here to enlarge palette view

Click to zoom in

Click to zoom out

Drag slider to rapidly zoom in or out

Palette display

As was pointed out earlier, the Photoshop palettes can be toggled between Show/Hide, using the Tab key or Shift+Tab to Show/Hide everything except the tools palette. The individual palettes can be positioned anywhere on the screen.

- To restore all palettes to their original position, choose File – Preferences – General and click Reset Palettes to Default Positions.

Palettes can be grouped in any order – just drag a palette tab outside of the palette group to separate it or across to another group. Double-click the palette tabs to collapse the palette window. When a palette or palette group is positioned an the bottom of the screen, the palette will collapse down to the bottom edge.

Each palette has a fly-out menu providing extra options associated with it, e.g. resetting the palette tools or resetting all tool options.

> **Tip**
>
> **If your system will allow, add a second small monitor and use this to display all the palettes, keeping the main monitor for displaying the image window.**

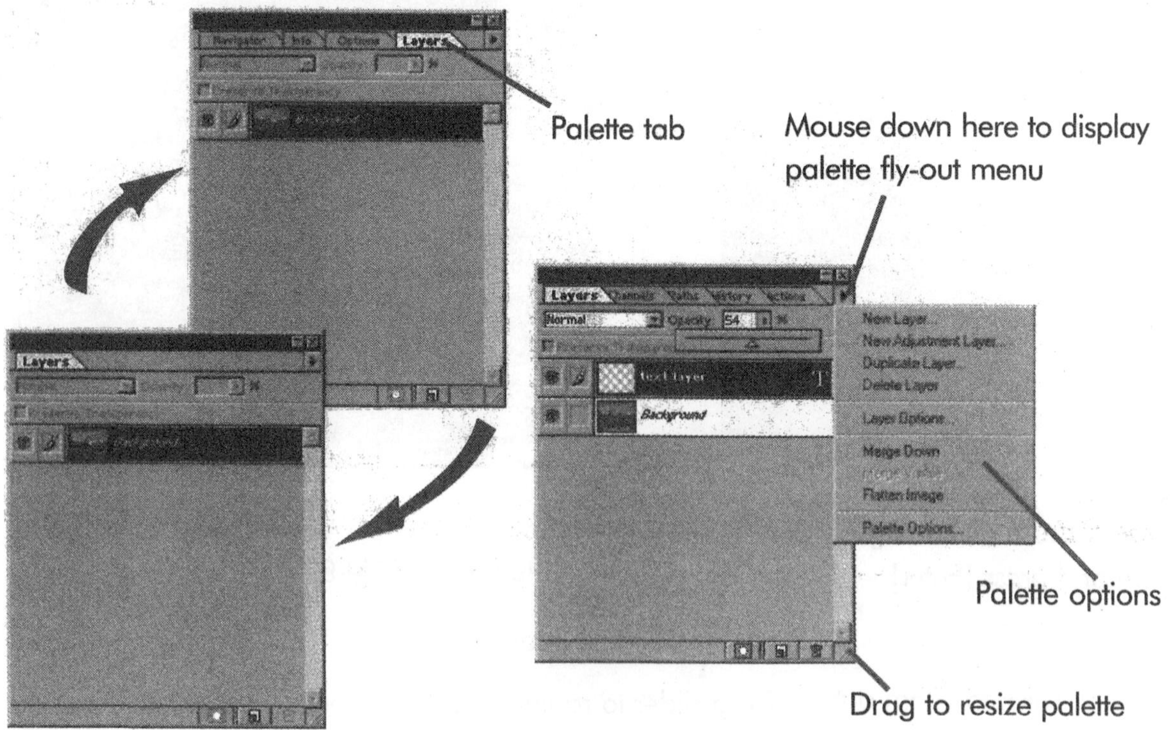

All the palettes to be found in Photoshop 5. These will be referred to throughout the book.

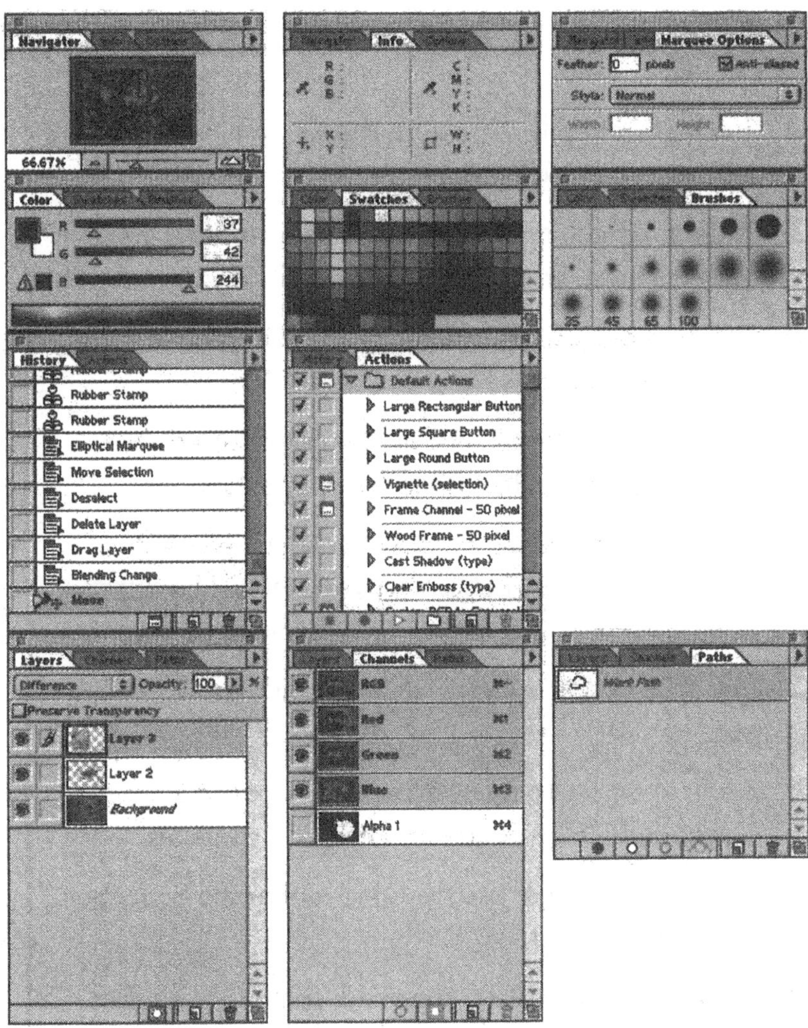

The palettes are grouped in twos or threes. You can select an individual palette by clicking on the palette tab at the top. You can rearrange the palettes as demonstrated on the page opposite.

Use the Window menu (shown left) to show or hide individual Photoshop palettes, or use the function keys which act as shortcut, hot keys for displaying/hiding palettes: F5=Brushes, F6=Color, F7=Layers, F8=Info, F9=Actions

Summary

- All the Photoshop tools can be accessed via the tools palette.
- A quick way to select a tool is to learn the keyboard shortcuts.
- The tools and palettes can be shown or hidden using the Tab and or Tab+Shift keys.
- There are three image window display modes. Switch between these by pressing the letter 'F' key.
- Kodak Photo CD files should always be opened from within Photoshop.
- Other files can be opened via the File menu or by double-clicking a Photoshop file image icon.
- The native Photoshop format is the most efficient format to use. Print publishing work should be saved using either the TIFF, EPS or DCS formats.
- Use JPEG or GIF formats when saving files for on-line use.
- Zoom in on an image with the zoom tool or learn the Command/Ctrl + Spacebar keyboard shortcuts.
- To scroll an image, use the hand tool or the Spacebar keyboard shortcut.
- Palettes can be easily compacted, split or their order rearranged.

3 Editing

Marching ants

Basic steps

1. Select with marquee.
2. Choose Select–Color Range.
3. Use the eyedropper to sample the (red) tail.
4. Use Fuzziness to soften the edges.

Very often you need to define an area to work upon – Photoshop shows this as a shimmering line of 'marching ants'. Within is your selected area; the area beyond is masked from any action you take. You can select by several methods: freehand using the lasso; constrained to an ellipse or a rectangle with the marquee; by tonal values within a preset tolerance with the magic wand; conversion from paths; an alpha channel; QuickMask or Color Range, or a combination of any or all these methods.

When an area to be selected has a good colour contrast, but the colour exists elsewhere, you can subselect the area, by predefining it by loosely lassoing or marqueeing before using Select–Color Range.

A selected area can be modified in a number of ways. The Select–Grow command enlarges it into similar areas, at the boundaries. Select–Similar expands the selection into disconnected similar areas. Magic wand settings define the tolerance. Modify–Expand or Contract will add/subtract edge pixels, up to a maximum 16. The Select–Transform Selection permits all the standard adjustments; Scale, Rotate, etc.

Take note

For accurate curve-fitting in selections, use the pen tool (see page 45).

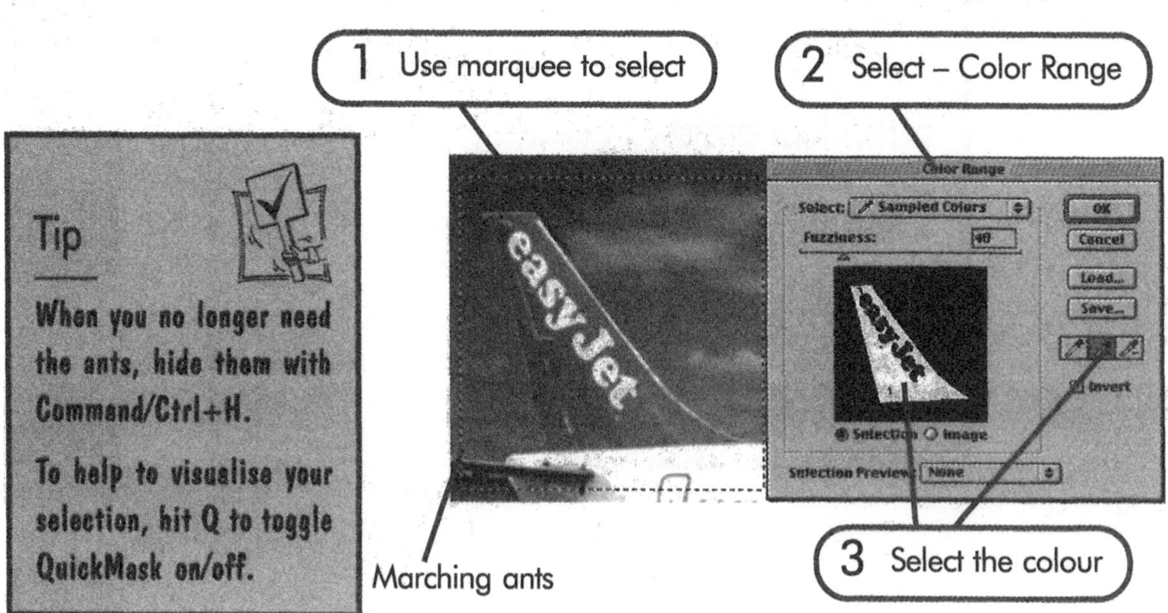

Tip

When you no longer need the ants, hide them with Command/Ctrl+H.

To help to visualise your selection, hit Q to toggle QuickMask on/off.

Basic steps

1 Open two files, e.g. *Clouds* and *Windmill Sail.*

2 With the Move tool, click and drag Sail to Clouds, it will arrive as a new layer.

Tip

Take care when dragging an image to a file with a selection active—any subsequent moving of the incoming image will be cropped by that selection.

Here the image of the sail in a bland sky was dragged from its file and dropped onto the far more dramatic sky for subsequent layer masking (see page 38).

Drag 'n' drop

A selection, either the bounding envelope or contents, or a layer (see page 68) can be moved from one open window to another, without involving copying and pasting.

To move the envelope (the marching ants) from one document to another, just click and drag from the current document to the other using a marquee or lasso tool. Use the Shift key to place it in the centre of the target document.

To move the contents or an entire layer, use the move tool; dropping with the Shift key held ensures the selection/layer is centred.Both images must have the same resolution to keep the same size, and be in the same mode; RGB, CMYK, etc.

Paths can also be dragged and dropped, provided all their points are selected. A path takes priority over a marching ants selection in the moving process, so should be deselected in the Paths palette, when moving the ants selection. A path dropped into another document retains the name it had in the source document, unless an existing path is already selected.

Multipe layers can be moved if they are linked. They keep their order, and can be treated in the standard way once in the new document. Click in the blank box to the left of the image icon in the Layers palette to link a layer to the selected layer.

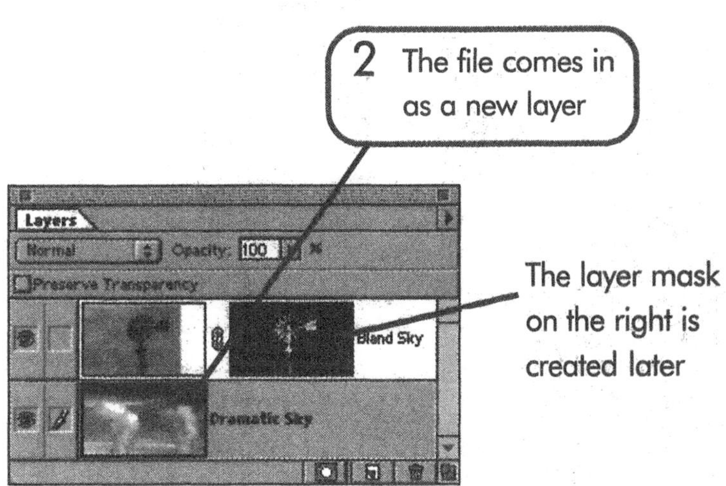

Selecting by colour

Basic steps

If an object to be masked or cut out from its background is very different in colour to its surroundings then use Select–Color Range. Double-click the background in the Layers palette; this will change the name to Layer 0, enabling masking the layer later.

The display options for this selection are in the pulldown at the bottom of the palette. If you need to repeat the operation, save the settings. Having made your colour range selection, it can be refined by entering QuickMask mode. QuickMask is simply a temporary channel, similar to a saved selection (with eye icon clicked). Its default colour is red.

Painting with black adds to a mask, white removes it. Zoom in to improve the mask where necessary. Beyond the selected area – the poppy in this example – may be other selected colours, which can be lost by painting with black. Hit Q to make the selection, then save it.This adds a new channel in the Channels palette and names it Alpha 1.

1 Choose Select–Color Range.

2 Select the left eye-dropper and click on the main colour in the area to be selected.

3 Select the middle eyedropper and click additional colours to add to the selection.

4 Click OK. You now have the outside of the mask.

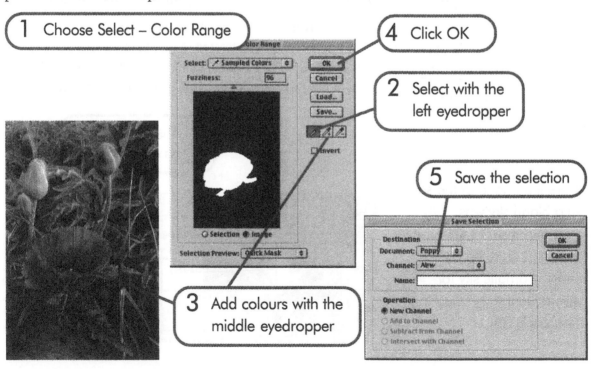

5 Save the selection.

1 Choose Select – Color Range

4 Click OK

2 Select with the left eyedropper

5 Save the selection

3 Add colours with the middle eyedropper

Basic steps

1 Paint out the unselected bits in the centre of a saved selection in the Alpha 1 Channel.

2 Select–Load Selection, choosing Alpha 1, and add a layer mask (click left icon at base of Layers palette)

3 Click the middle icon to add a Layer, and drag beneath the selection layer.

Tip

To change the QuickMask colour, double-click the right hand QuickMask box, then choose a new colour with the Color Picker.

Improving a selection

Double-click Alpha 1 in the Channels palette. The mask appears as black with a poppy-shaped white hole, but with a bit still black. Hit **Command–Ctrl+D** to deselect. Paint with white in the poppy's centre, to add to the selection, or with black beyond, to lose unwanted selections. Note the similarity to QuickMask to understand what is happening. Click on RGB in the Channels palette to return to the full-colour image, then Select–Load Selection, or **Command–Ctrl-click** the Alpha 1 channel in the Channels palette to select your new channel.

Create a layer mask by clicking the left icon at the bottom of the Layers palette, with the selection active to clear the background from the poppy. Create a new layer, by clicking the middle icon and drag it beneath Layer 0; the poppy will be cut out on top.

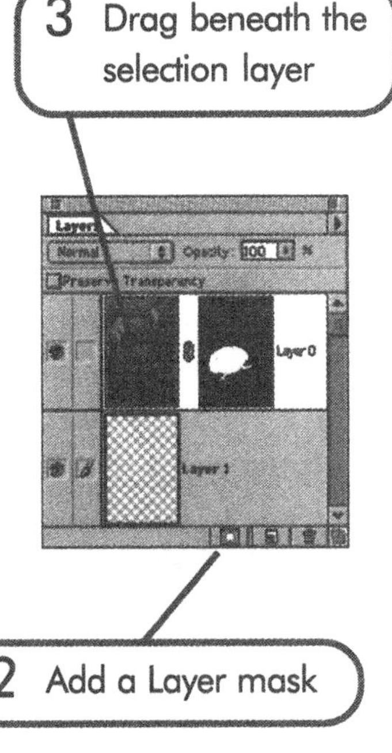

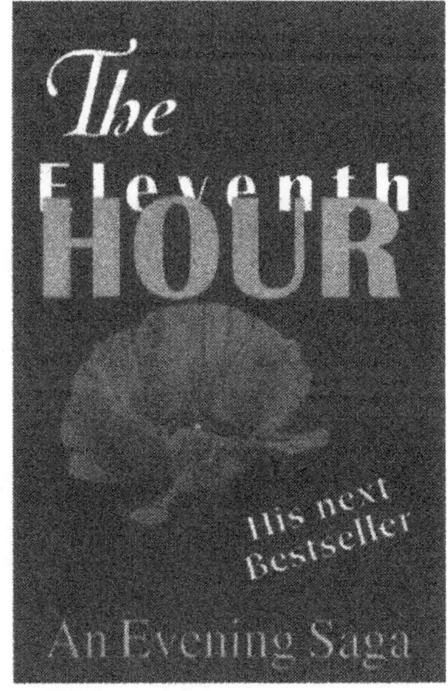

Poppy isolated in new background, then text added to complete the picture.

Selections using contrast

Sometimes there is a fair contrast between an image and the background. By clicking in the channel with most contrast, creating a duplicate, this can be made into a black-and-white mask by using Adjust/Levels – move the right and left triangles there, inwards. This Channel can be selected; Select/Load Selection, or Command/Ctrl clicked in the Channels palette.

It is used here to drop out the plain sky to reveal the more dramatic one in the layer beneath.

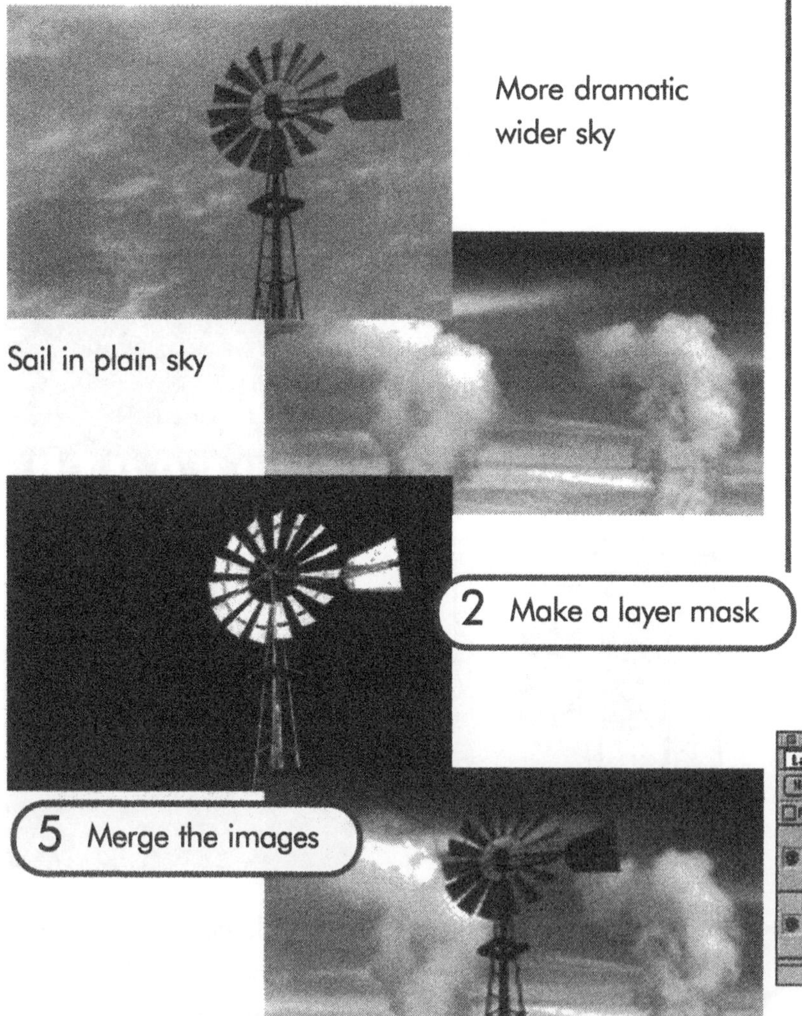

Basic steps

1 Open *Sail* and the *New sky* with transparent backgrounds.

2 Drag the best defined Sail channel to third icon along bottom of Channels palette to create a new one (Alpha 1).

3 Go to Select/Load Selection. Check Invert and choose Alpha 1.

4 Click Layer 0, in Layers palette, then the left icon at the bottom, this masks the sky.

5 Use the Move tool to drag the *Sail* image to the *New sky* and drop into position.

4 Mask the sky

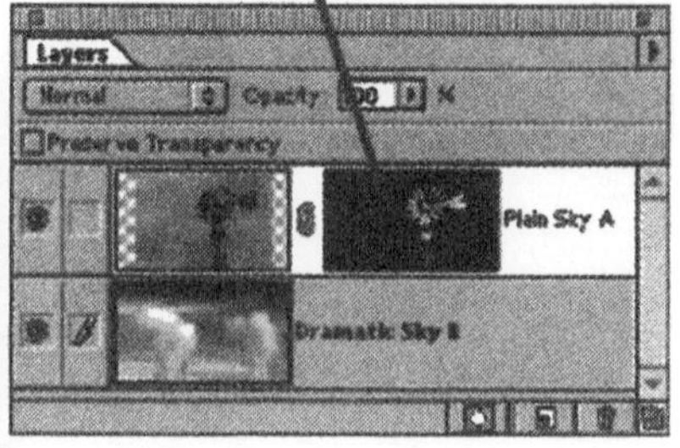

Basic steps

1. Click edge to start.
2. Follow around your edge without necessarily holding the mouse button down.
3. If the path is not following the edge well, just move back, and come forward again.
4. When a small circle appears beside the cursor, you are back at the start.
5. Click to close.

Use paths where there is fine detail.

Use Lasso when edge is to be softened.

Magnetic tools

New to this version of Photoshop are the magnetic tools, which cling to edges. The settings for these tools seem complex, but the principle is to set a circle that is large enough to cover both sides of the edge, so the tool plots the path or selection to the boundary. There are two important options:

- **Frequency** defines the control points made as it follows the edge; you decide how accurate it should be. The more accurate it is, the longer it will take to calculate.
- **Edge contrast** defines the minimum value needed to find the edge. A faint edge may need an adjustment layer to enhance that edge, or try a channel with more contrast.

A small dot appears next to the cursor as you near the end of your selection to help you close it.

The rules governing how you use the magnetic tool variants are identical, only the end result is different; marching ants from the magnetic lasso, or a path from the magnetic pen tool. You can be convert either one to the other. (see also page 48)

The last item, **pressure**, is an option only available to users of a pressure-sensitive digitising tablet, but it allows you to set a large circle, which narrows as you press harder for finer detail.

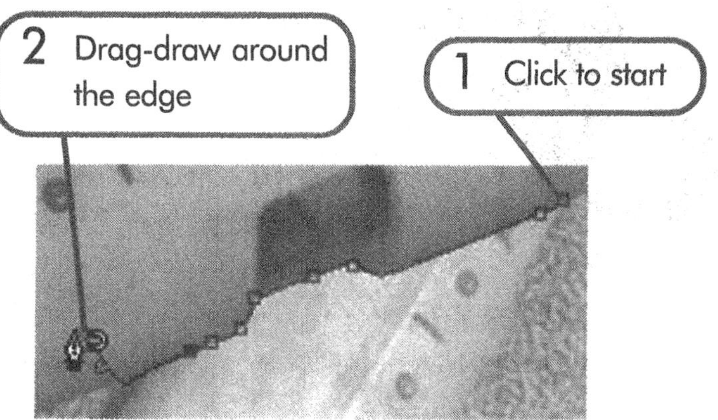

Moving a selection

There are two ways of moving a selection: you can move its outline, the envelope; or its contents. The file must be at least greyscale or colour. The example ampersand character starts as black on clear, making selection easy. Use the magic wand or the shortcut of Command/Ctrl+clicking on a Channel in the Channels palette.

The idea behind checking Preserve Transparency in the Layers palette is this confines the work to the opaque parts of the image. So, once the initial selection has been inverted you are lightening from the hard outer edge to the feathered edge of the selection. This gives the highlight.

By moving the envelope further in the same direction, and working beneath the ampersand, you create the shadow with its softer edge because your feather is greater.

Remember the shortcuts:

- Command/Ctrl+I invert the Selection
- Option/Alt+Delete fill with the foreground colour
- Command/Ctrl+L for Levels.

Outline envelope moved

With highlight and shadow

Basic steps

1 With the magic wand click in the black.
2 Change to the lasso.
3 Click inside the image and drag the cursor down and right – only the envelope moves.
4 Check Preserve Transparency, and invert the selection.
5 Select–Feather about 5-pixels, and in Levels, move the lower black triangle inwards.
6 Invert the selection.
7 Feather 7-pixels, and move it down further.
8 Create a new layer, then click and drag it beneath the '&'.
9 Fill with grey. You have a rounded ampersand with a soft shadow.

Take note

Use the marquee or lasso variants to move the envelope, NOT the move tool.

The Move tool

- Use the move tool for dragging and dropping an image from one file to another.
- Whilst working with other tools, hold the Command/Ctrl key to access the move tool.

Take note

To keep all the image layer or mask when moved beyond the current canvas, do not have a selection live.

If a layer or channel is moved beyond the visible boundary, the canvas can be increased to bring it back, provided it was not moved with the whole canvas selected.

The previous example showed the less obvious moving of only the Selection envelope.

The move tool can move either the entire layer (when no selection has been made) or the selected contents of a layer. This is done by Click-dragging and letting go when positioned. Movement can be constrained to 45° increments by holding down the Shift key when dragging within the same image.

To drag and drop a selection to the same position in another image whose canvas is identical, hold the Shift key down as you drop. If the canvas is a different size, the selection will be centred.

Arrow keys nudge selections or layers, a pixel at a time. Hold the Shift key to move 10-pixels at a time.

In the Layers palette, click the icon to the left of the image of unselected layers to be able to move all of them as a group. A layer or grouped layers can be moved beyond the image boundary, without being lost, unless you Select All and move the visible area at any time or save the file. Any such action will crop the image to the canvas.

If you hold the Option/Alt key down while moving a selection, you will move a copy, this is almost like creating a temporary Custom cloning brush. Having a feather to the edge can be very useful to ensure a good blend.

Click here to group

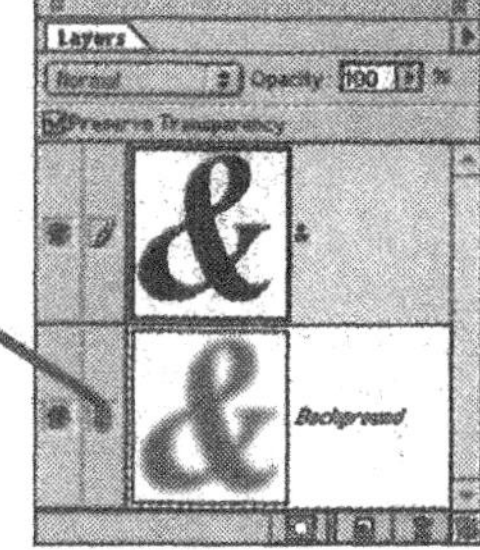

Tip

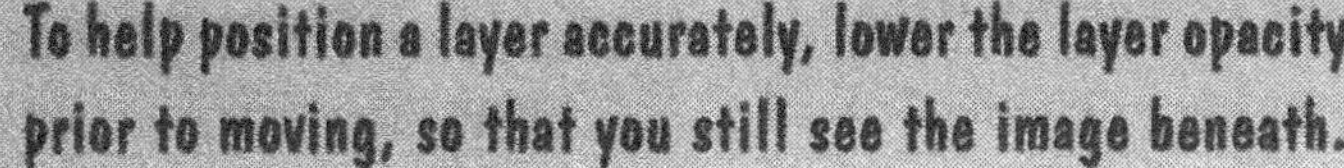

To help position a layer accurately, lower the layer opacity prior to moving, so that you still see the image beneath.

Cropping

To crop an image, select the crop tool from the top left of the toolbox. Select a point and drag the rubber-banded rectangle to the opposite corner, it need not be too accurate. There are four corner points and four midpoints which can be used to refine the crop area. The movable centre point defines the centre of rotation, and can even be outside the rectangle. The cursor changes as it passes over an editing point to show the directions it controls. Click and drag outside the selection to rotate.

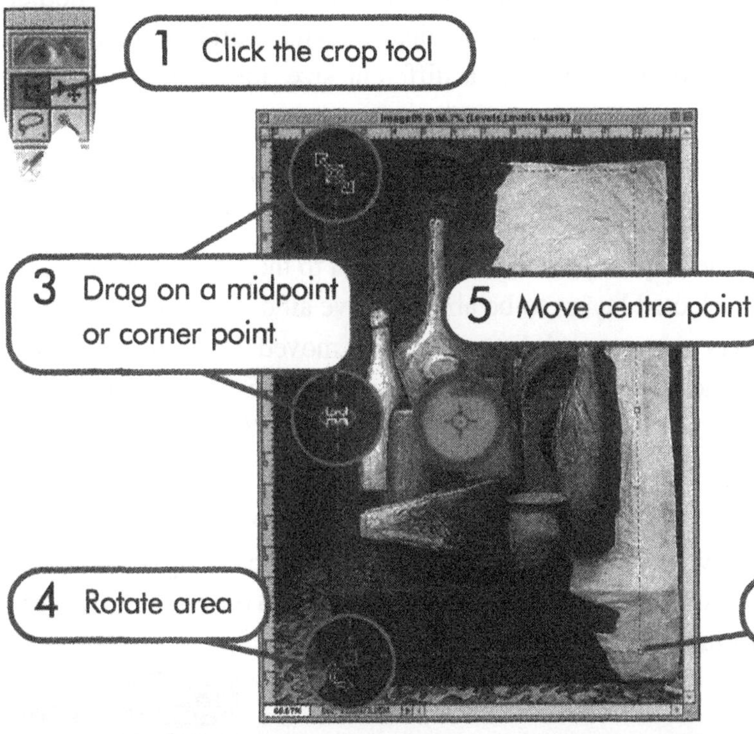

Basic steps

1 Select the crop tool.
2 Click top left, and drag to bottom right.
3 Click on a midpoint to move a side, or a corner point to move in both directions at once – and drag to new position.
4 To rotate about the centre, move the cursor outside the box and click and drag.
5 Move the centre point to rotate about a new position.
6 Double-click within the box or hit [Enter] to finish.

Tip

Use the ruler tool or a known horizontal or vertical for a misaligned scan, then use Image–Rotate Canvas–Arbitrary. The amount will be set – check the appropriate radio button.

Tip

Hold Command/Ctrl down to adjust crop close to an edge. This disengages the snap-to-edge effect.

Basic steps

1 Select the entire Image (Command/Ctrl+A).
2 Select Edit–Transform–Skew.
3 Move the top midpoint and top left to the right.
4 Go to Edit–Transform–Scale and move the top midpoint downwards.
5 Go to Edit–Transform–Rotate and drag outside anti-clockwise.
6 Hit [Enter] when it looks right.
7 Add reality with a shadow.

Transform

The Transform or Free Transform tool can distort a flat object to give the effect of it lying along a plane in perspective. In the example shown a snapshot has been made to look as if it lies on a ribbed surface.

Free Transform becomes easier when you understand the modifier keys:

- Shift constrains the aspect ratio
- Option/Alt controls symmetry – both sides move equally
- Command/Ctrl allows independent movement
- Command/Ctrl+Option/Alt+Shift controls perspective
- Clicking and dragging outside rotates

Straight view of Hescwm Felin

Transformed postcard view

Control points when first locked to image

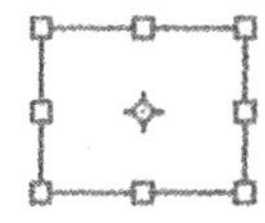

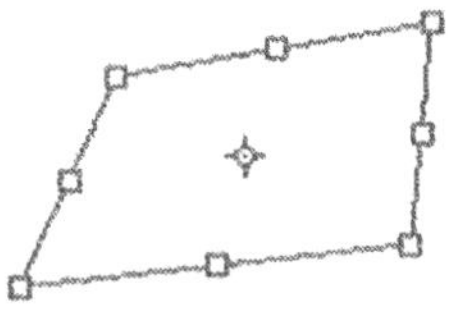

After dragging into shape for the transformation

Uses of paths

Paths are used either for the creation of selections, or for providing a track for the range of painting tools.

Edit by moving anchor points or their handles. By using modifier keys this can take place before the path is closed. The Command/Ctrl key gives the edit points hollow arrows, the convert points tool appears using the Option/Alt key.

Hold down the Shift key to constrain the movements of paths, anchor points or Bezier handles to 45° increments.

If a grid or guide is present and Snap-to-point is selected, paths are attracted in the same way as selection tools.

As you cross an existing path with the standard pen tool a plus will appear showing that a click will add a point. Conversely, a minus will appear over an existing one to be deleted. So you rarely need to choose the variants to the basic pen tool from the Tools palette.

To create a selection from a path, open the fly-out menu on the Paths palette, and choose Make Selection. When the dialog box appears, choose the amount of feather to apply to the edge, and whether to anti-alias or not (anti-aliasing is averaging of the pixels at the edge). If a selection is active, you may add, subtract or intersect with that selection.

Paths can also be scaled, rotated or skewed, either as a whole or by groups of selected points.

To blur along a path, stroke the path or subpath with the blur tool selected. Clone pixels along a path by using the rubber stamp tool, or a custom pattern stamp as in the Dollar image (see page 47), or simply run the airbrush or paintbrush along an edge. Set the brush size before stroking a path, then select the required tool from the list shown here.

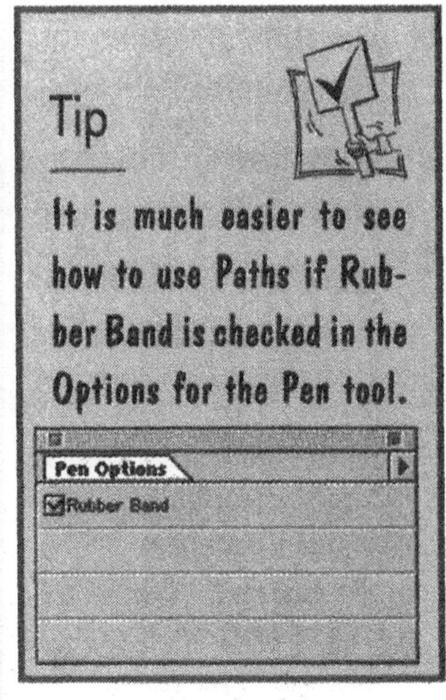

Tip
It is much easier to see how to use Paths if Rubber Band is checked in the Options for the Pen tool.
Pen Options
Rubber Band

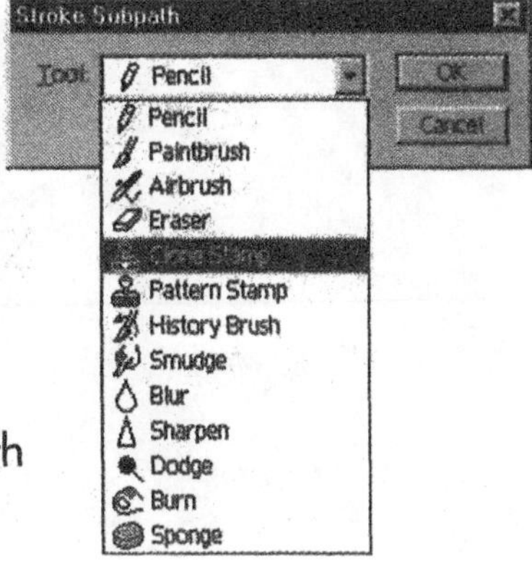

Tools you can use along a path

Basic steps

- To make a path around an object:

1 Click the pen tool on the edge to start.

2 Move to where there is a change of direction then click and hold down. As you drag away a curve will appear behind. Move around till it fits and let go.

3 Move again and click and drag.

4 Repeat till you return to the start; a circle appears by the cursor.

5 Click here to finish.

Tip

For a fuller description of Bezier curves, see the Adobe User Guide (pages 153-160)

Pen tool basics

The pen tool creates paths, a mathematical way to describe curves, often used in Photoshop. Also called vectors, or Bezier curves, they are more normally found in drawing programs.

Pull out the handle from a point and move away from the origin; this exerts a pull on the curve you create and this reacts with the pull from the previous handle, if you are creating a path, or with the handles either side, if you are editing an existing path.

As you open a new point, both handles will be linked and move equal distances either side of the control point. This means the two handles are at a tangent to the curve. If you rotate the handles the curve will become S-shaped around the point. If you break this relationship by using the > tool you create corners as you now only control the direction from one side of the point at a time.

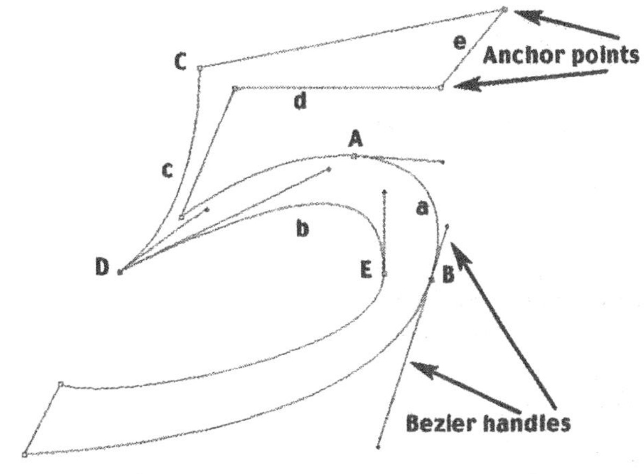

Curve 'a' is affected by the handles A and B.

Curve 'b' is defined by handles D and E.

Curve 'c' is defined by handles C and D.

The straight lines 'd' and 'e' occur because there is only a direct pull from points at each end.

Using the pen tool

Basic steps

The basic pen tool is the most versatile of the group and is very intuitive in use. Start by clicking at a suitable point on the edge of an image, then click and drag to let the path behind that point follow your edge, release and move along the edge. Do this till you arrive back at the first point, when a small circle will appear against the pen. Double-click on the first point, or press Enter, and your path will close.

To edit a point while drawing, hold down the Command/Ctrl key. The cursor changes to the hollow arrow for editing.

The path can also be editing after closing, either by changing the tool's properties bythe use of each separate function or by using a modifier key with the main pen. The + pen adds points, the - pen removes points, the > pen splits the handles allowing the shape to be controlled from one side of a point. The plus appears as you cross a line, the minus appears alongside when you are over an anchor point.

In the example, the pen tool is used to outline an eagle's head. The outline is then copied and turned into a shadow, and the two images are merged to give a 3-D effect.

1 Click on an edge.
2 Click and drag to follow shape.
3 Repeat back to start, double-click to close.
4 Double-click on the Background in the Layer palette to create Layer 0.
5 Click the Add Layer Mask button at the bottom of the palette.
6 Go to Select/Reselect. Offset the ants and feather, then fill with grey.
7 Choose a backround colour, add new layer, and move it beneath.

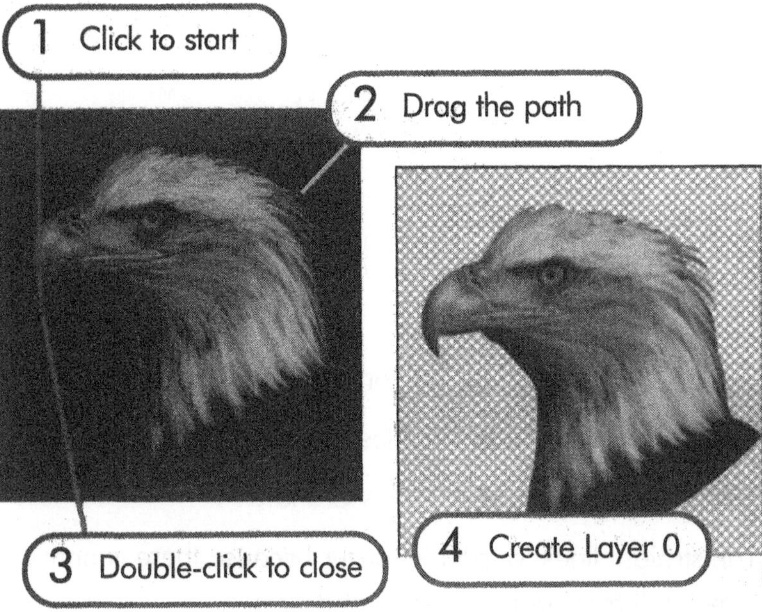

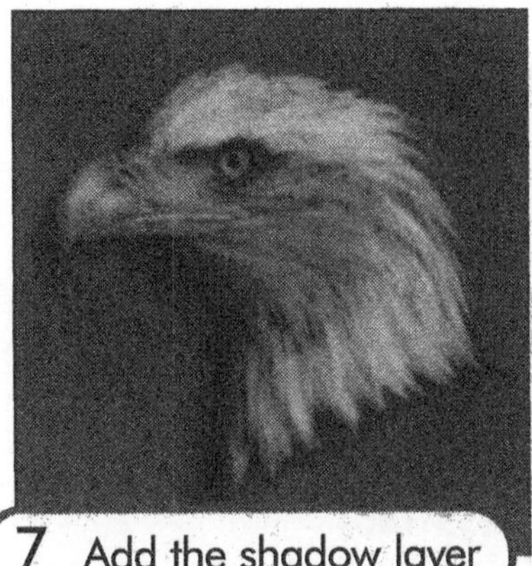

Basic steps

1 Select a rectangular area of 50-Dollar bill image.

2 Choose File – Edit– Define as Pattern.

3 Create text selection of Dollar sign.

4 Define as Brush.

5 Increase Spacing from default of 25% to 99%.

6 Create the path to be tracked.

7 Select pattern stamp and custom brush and select Stroke Path.

8 Click OK.

Tracking along paths

Paths can be used to provide a track for the painting tools.

In this example a pattern had been saved by making a rectangular selection in an image of a 50-dollar bill, then defining it as a pattern, using File–Edit–Define as Pattern.

A Custom brush was created by typing the dollar sign using the type selection tool with black as the foreground colour. This was rotated slightly. A rectangular selection was made around this black on white image, and defined as a new brush from the small triangle at the top right of the Brushes palette. The text selection was then deleted.

The path was then created in the shape of a dollar sign .

The Dollar custom brush was selected and the spacing reset to 99%.

The Paths palette was opened, and Stroke Path selected.

The tool was changed to the pattern stamp tool (the rubber stamp variant) and the newly created brush selected.

Hitting OK then stroked the pattern of small dollars along the large dollar path with the pattern from the 50-dollar bill.

The Stroked path with custom brush

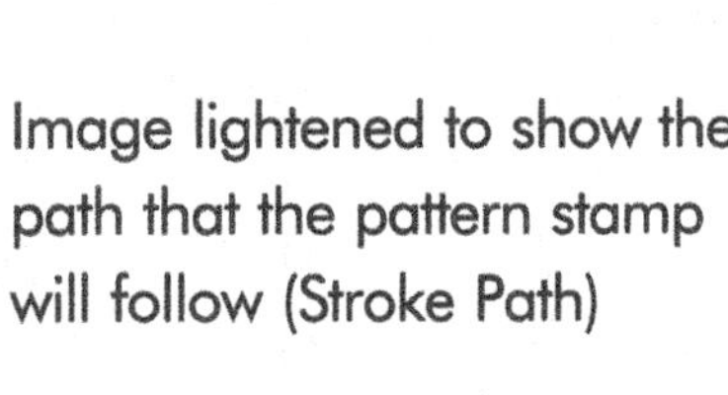

Image lightened to show the path that the pattern stamp will follow (Stroke Path)

Pen tool – other points

When a path has been closed it appears with the default name 'Work Path', in the Paths palette. To save a path go to the small triangle at top right of the palette and pull down to 'Save path...', if you are happy with 'Path 1', hit OK. Better practice is to name it meaningfully, 'Path 2' in a month's time is none too helpful!

A new tool to Photoshop 5 is the freeform path tool; having clicked once on the starting point, just follow around with the pen and it will automatically drop points along its path. This is ideal for creating quick outlines which may be edited once the path is closed.

Also new, the magnetic pen allows you to follow natural edges of colour or contrast once you have started. Click to start, then follow the edge with the circle – you do not need to hold the mouse down. If you are zoomed in, you can move the image within the window by holding down the Spacebar to get the hand cursor. When you return to the start, press Enter and the path is closed.

The options you set for this tool will be dependent upon the picture's edge.

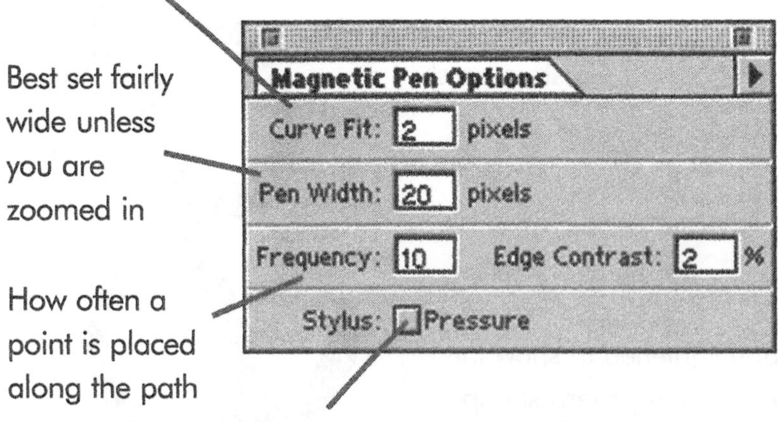
How close the edge is followed
Best set fairly wide unless you are zoomed in
How often a point is placed along the path
Magnetic Pen Options
Curve Fit: 2 pixels
Pen Width: 20 pixels
Frequency: 10
Edge Contrast: 2 %
Stylus: Pressure
Check if using a digitising pen, and set a large width, which will tighten with added pressure

- ❑ Enter a meaningful name when saving a path.
- ❑ Use the magnetic tool for fairly accurate edges when doing visuals.
- ❑ Use the Spacebar to interrupt the path creation and move beyond the edge of the current window.
- ❑ Use the freeform pen beyond soft edged cutouts, to make a clipping path.
- ❑ Make a clipping path from the Paths palette menu with the chosen path selected, for use in DTP Cutouts.

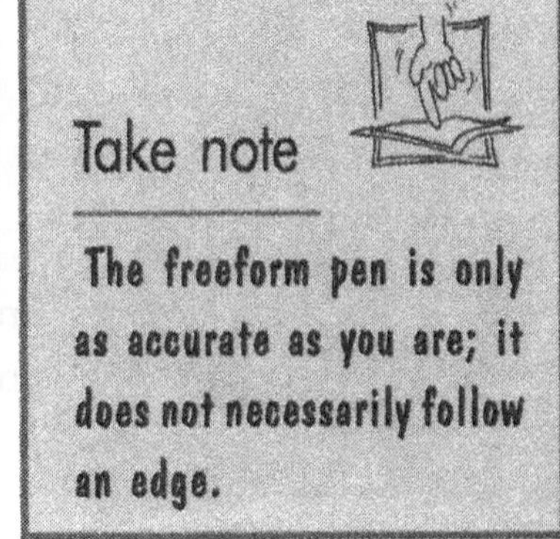
Take note

The freeform pen is only as accurate as you are; it does not necessarily follow an edge.

Basic steps

Clipping paths

1 Create and save a path around the object to be cut out.

2 Name it, for example, 'Clip'.

3 Go to the Paths palette menu, choose Clipping Path...

4 Select Clip, and leave Flatness blank.

5 Click OK and save file as an EPS.

Page layout programs make masks around images using clipping paths. It is important therefore to understand that the path must enclose the image. If you used the magic wand to select a background outside the image then invert this before going to the Paths palette menu to save the path, otherwise you save the background!

Clipping paths create hard edges. If you made a soft edge in Photoshop and you want the image to fall on white paper, then the selection must be expanded by at least half the existing soft edge using Select–Modify–Expand before creating the clipping path.

It is generally best to save in EPS format when using a clipping path. Though you can save in TIFF format, if this is recognised by your DTP/drawing application.

Take note

You can only make a clipping path from a saved path – not the Work Path

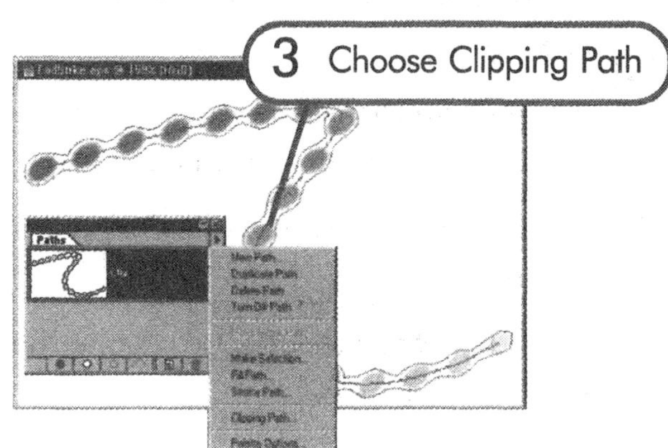

To show the spacing of fading brushstrokes, eliminate the background closely around the strokes

The effect of the clipping path shown by placing a tint behind the image. Against white paper, this allows text to be flowed around the image.

Summary

- ❑ By saving a selection, you create an alpha channel; this can be reselected by Command/Ctrl-clicking the channel in the Channels palette.
- ❑ Toggle the 'marching ants' between Hide and Show with Command/Ctrl + H.
- ❑ Use QuickMask mode to clean up selection masks (shortcut Q to toggle). When in QuickMask mode use shortcut X to toggle between black and white.
- ❑ Use the Command/Ctrl key to crop accurately without snapping to the edge of the image.
- ❑ Check the angle that a selection needs to be rotated with the ruler tool first, then go to Arbitrary Rotate, you will only then have to enter whether Clockwise or Anti-clockwise.
- ❑ Learn the modifier keys to make almost every change to a path with just the default pen tool.
- ❑ Learn the constraints offered by using the Shift and Option/Alt keys.
- ❑ Do not forget to check the Use Rubber Band box when using the the pen tool.
- ❑ Remember the curve behind the present control point is the portion of curve being fitted.
- ❑ Remember to set the Size/Opacity/Blend Mode of the chosen tool before selecting Stroke Path.

4 Image adjustments

Levels (basic)

Basic steps

Levels is the most basic of image adjustment tools. The Levels dialog box represents the tonal values of an image as histogram bars ranging from the darkest on the left (0) to the brightest on the right (255). The accompanying illustrations show low and high key photographic images with their histogram displays.

The Input sliders can be adjusted to reassign the shadow and highlight points. One basic method of levels adjustment is to drag the shadow and highlight sliders in as necessary, so that the shadow and highlight points just touch where the histogram bars begin and end. After setting these, the gamma slider in the middle can be adjusted to determine the relative brightness of the image. An Input gamma value higher than 1.00 will produce a brighter image, a lower value will produce a darker image.

The Output slider controls govern the output pixel value range. Normally you want this set between 0 and 255 of course. If the output values are adjusted as shown here, the darkest pixels will be re-mapped to a much lighter brightness value (here to 183) and all in-between values are compressed to compensate. This effectively allows you to vary the brightness and contrast with great accuracy from within the Levels dialog box.

This type of adjustment enables you to produce a faded image which could be used as a background in a printed or Web page.

1. Choose Image – Adjust – Levels.
2. Make sure the Preview box is checked.
3. Adjust the shadow and highlight Input sliders.
4. Set the gamma slider to adjust the overall brightness.

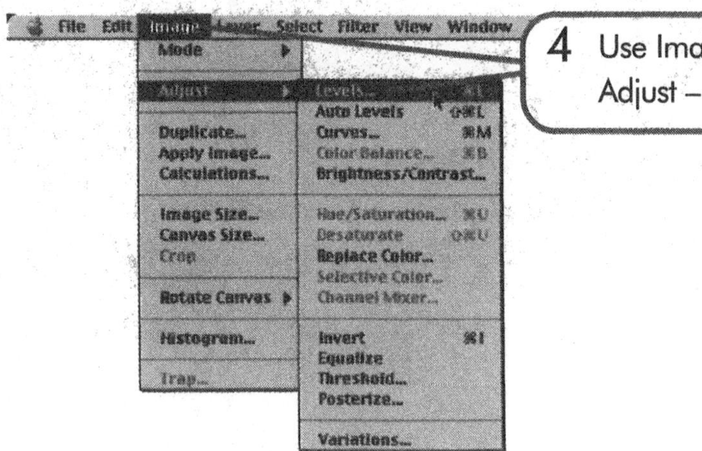

4 Use Image – Adjust – Levels

Tip

The Brightness/Contrast image adjustment is an alternative method for applying output levels slider adjustments. For precise contrast control, use Levels or Curves.

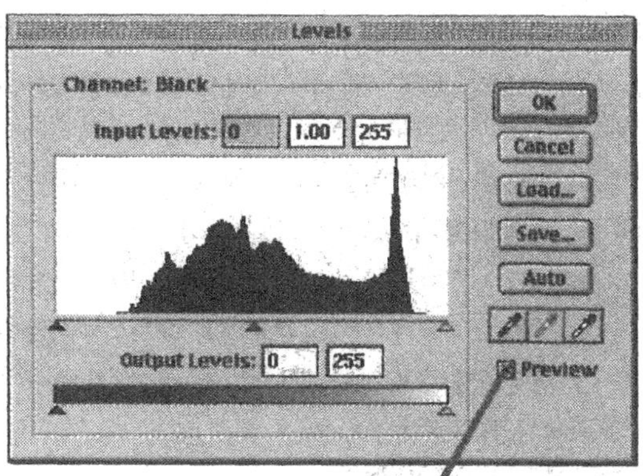

2 Turn on Preview

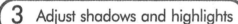

3 Adjust shadows and highlights

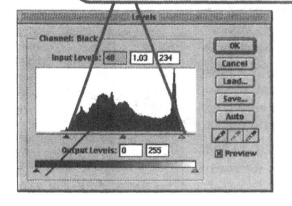

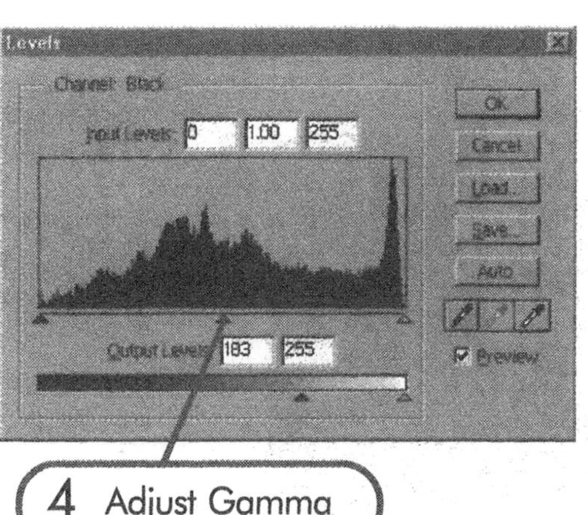

4 Adjust Gamma

Levels adjustment

If an image is in RGB mode and you switch off the preview box, then Option/Alt+mouse down on the shadow or highlight slider, you will see the monitor image change to a posterised display. Watch for the point where the shadows or highlights just begin to darken/lighten. You have then discovered the darkest or brightest portion of the image. Use this technique to set the shadows and highlights or to find where to click on the image with the eyedroppers. In the example opposite, you could use the eyedroppers to assign the shadows and highlights, and the posterised preview display will help to identify where those shadows and highlights are.

Another method is to assign shadows and highlights using the Levels dialog box eyedropper tools. First, they need to be configured – double-click the highlight eyedropper and set the brightness value to 96%, then double-click the shadow eyedropper and set the brightness to 4%. You can then select the highlight eyedropper – search for the whitest portion of the picture (not a bright shiny highlight) and click to set the highlight value. Repeat with the shadow eyedropper, searching for the darkest portion of the picture. The grey eyedropper is a really handy tool – you can click on any area of the picture which should be neutral and the colour balance will automatically be corrected.

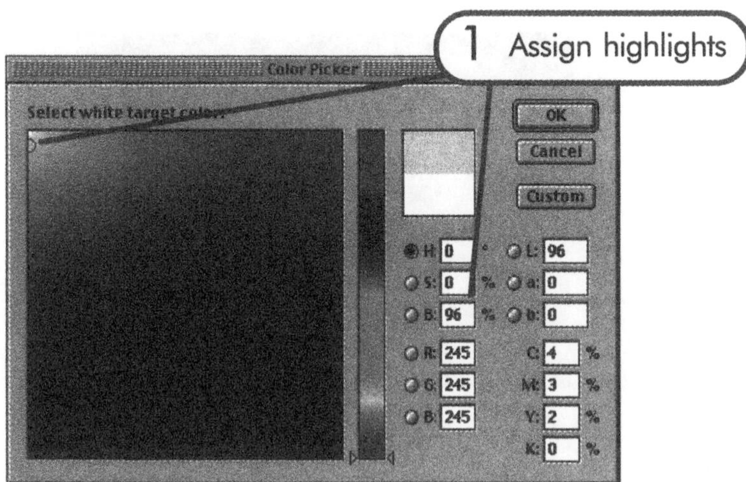

Basic steps

1 Double-click the highlight eyedropper in the Levels dialog box and assign a brightness value of 96%.

2 Double-click the shadow eyedropper, and set its value to 4%.

Take note

You do not ever want an image to contain 0% black or 100% white. The percentage figures given here are appropriate for print reproduction.

3 Select the shadow eyedropper button in the Levels dialog box and click on the darkest part of the picture.

4 Select the highlight eyedropper button and click on the lightest area.

5 Adjust the overall lightness using the gamma slider.

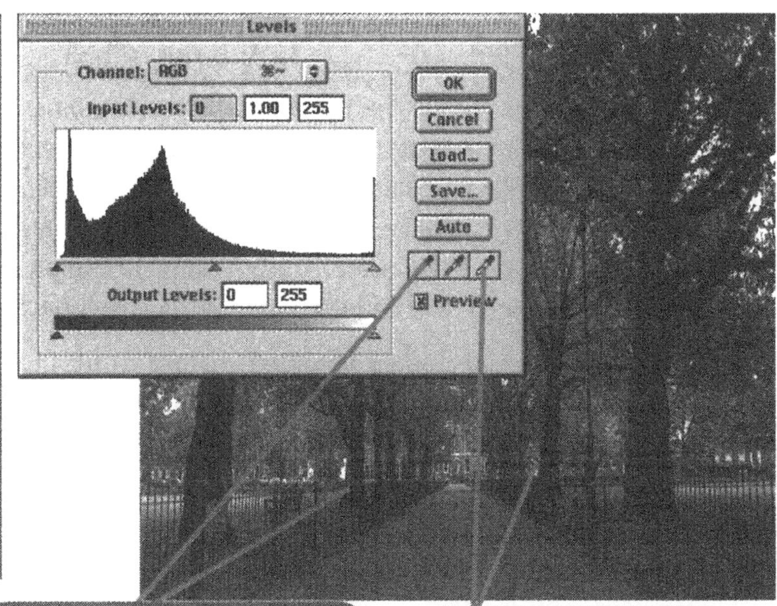

3 Set the shadows point

4 Set the highlights

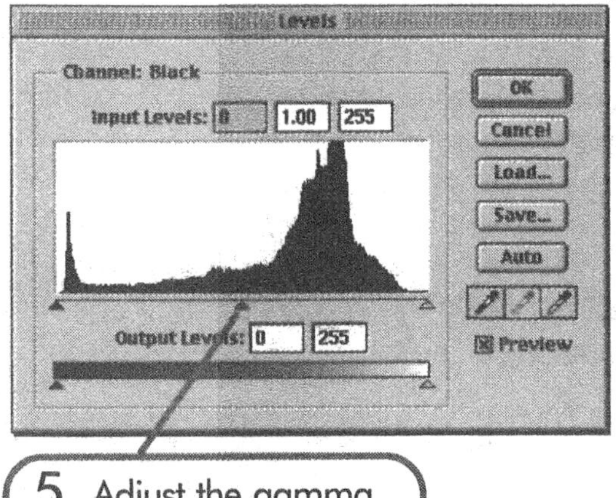

5 Adjust the gamma

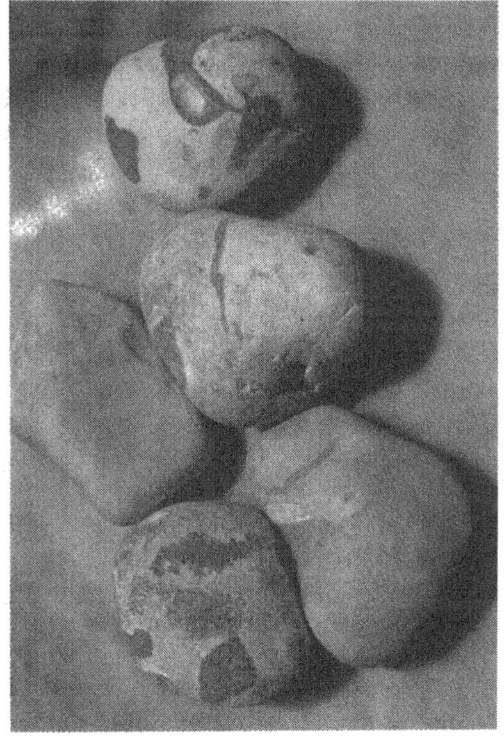

The histogram display for a low-key image will have most of the bars bunched around the left, shadow end, whereas the histogram display of a high-key image will have most of the bars around the highlight end. Moving the Input sliders inwards, will increase contrast.

Variations

Once the Levels have been set, the next thing to consider is the image's colour balance and colour saturation. **Variations** is the most intuitive of all the colour adjustment tools – it combines the power of Color Balance, Hue/Saturation and Levels Gamma adjustment all inside the one dialog interface. For this reason, it is recommended that beginners start learning to use Variations for their colour adjustments before progressing to explore the many extra features the other adjustment tools have to offer.

Notice how the Variations dialog window expands to fill the screen, displaying twelve image previews. The top two thumbnails show the before and currently adjusted versions of the image. On the right, we have three previews showing lighter, current and darker variations. Then in the middle we have the current adjusted image surrounded by six alternative colour shifted versions. This is a very good way to learn about colour theory, as the colour variations are shown opposite each other, i.e. red is the opposite of cyan and so forth. Clicking on the red preview, will make the colour of the central image redder and each of the surrounding previews will compensate to show what happens if you add more of another colour. If you next clicked on cyan, then the colour balance would revert to where it was originally.

The same rules apply to clicking on the lighter or darker windows. The colour wheel previews will simultaneously be refreshed as you do this. That's the basic principle of how the Variations adjustment works. Now look in the top right section. This is where you can selectively fine tune the variations, so that they will apply to the shadows, midtones or highlights only (as in Image – Color Balance). The Hue/Saturation button will switch the central display to three variants: current, less and more saturated. The degree of change is determined by the slider, which can be fine, coarse or one of the settings in between. When selecting OK, the combined tweaks are applied as a single adjustment.

Colour theory

The Variations dialog displays what are known as the additive primaries (red, green, blue) and subtractive primaries (cyan, magenta, yellow) in their complimentary positions on the colour wheel. Red is the opposite of cyan, green is the opposite of magenta and blue is the opposite of yellow.

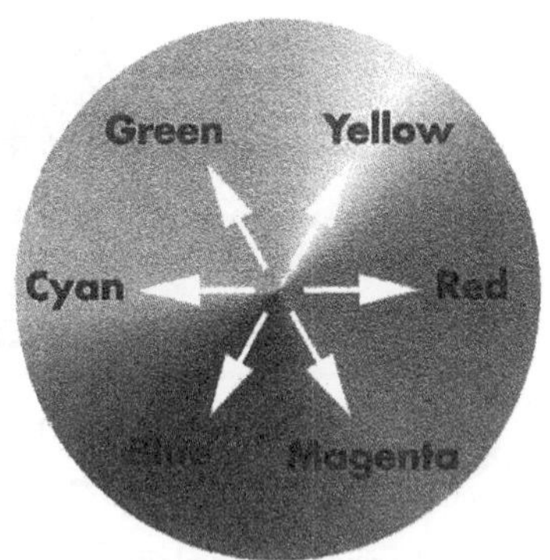

The colour wheel

Basic steps

1 Choose Variations from the Image – Adjust menu.

2 Click on the preview windows to change the colour balance, saturation or lightness.

Before doing so, you will want to check for clipping. The Show Clipping check box helps you to easily spot where an image adjustment will cause colour areas in the picture to go out of gamut. Where clipping occurs, this is shown by what is referred to as 'neon' colours in the previews. Take care not to exceed the recommended adjustment, otherwise this may cause the adjusted image to be degraded.

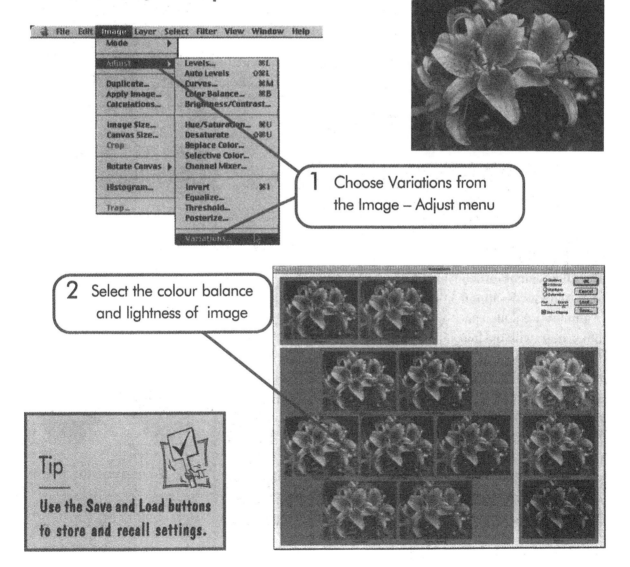

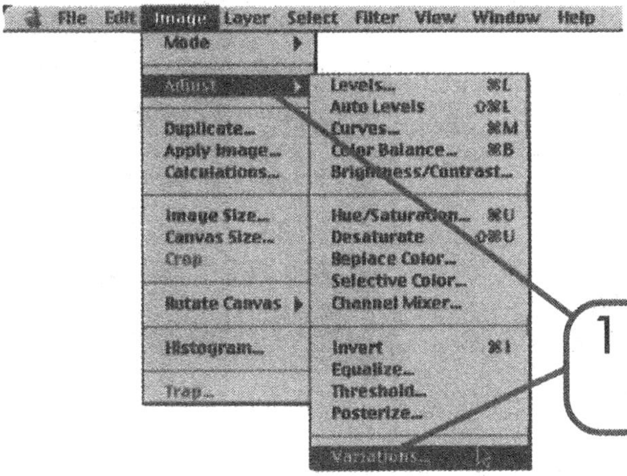

1 Choose Variations from the Image – Adjust menu

2 Select the colour balance and lightness of image

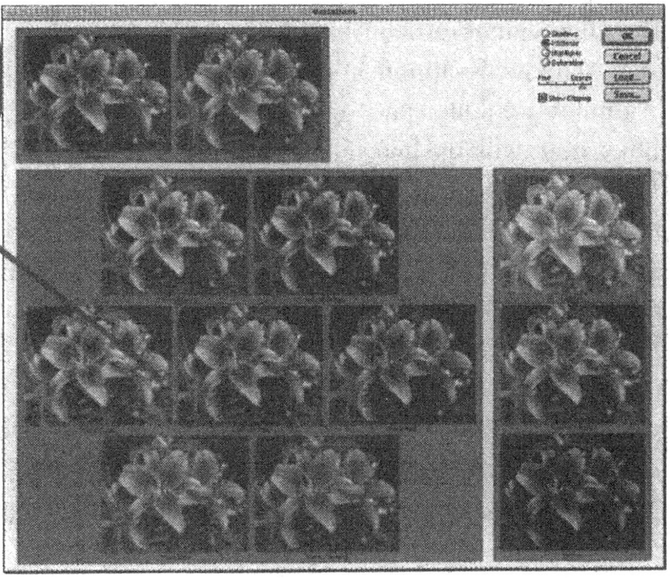

Tip

Use the Save and Load buttons to store and recall settings.

Other adjustment tools

Color Balance

Once familiarised with variations, you'll be ready to understand how to use the remaining adjustment tools. The Color Balance adjustment works exactly the same as Variations – you choose to add more of a particular colour or its opposite, using the slider controls. And just like with Variations, you can choose to apply the colour shifts independently to either the shadows, midtones or highlights. There is no gamut warning, so be aware of this when applying excessive colour shifts.

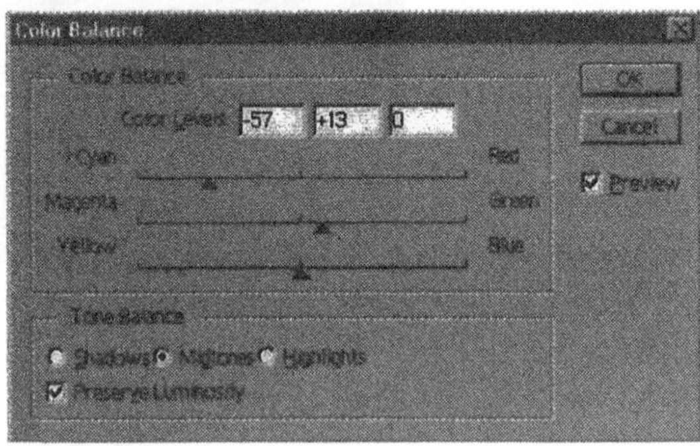

Tip

You can also make colour shift changes using the Levels adjustment. Under Channels, select from one of the individual colour channels and adjust the gamma slider. In the red channel, a lower gamma value will make the image more cyan. A higher gamma will produce a red shift.

Hue/Saturation

The Hue/Saturation adjustment gives you more than just the basic saturate/desaturate controls. The HSB (Hue, Saturation, Brightness) colour space can be thought of as having three dimensions with the hue values radiating in a circle, with red at 0 degrees. Colour is most saturated at the edge (+100) and desaturated at the centre (minus 100). In the remaining dimension, we have lightness values ranging from black (minus 100) to pure white. The hue slider needs a little more explanation. In the normal master channel mode, adjusting the hue will cause all the colour values to shift around the colour wheel. Try it yourself to see what I mean: reds will re-map to yellow, the yellows re-map to green and so forth. If you click on the Colorize button, the hue values are replaced with a single hue colour, which is determined using the hue slider.

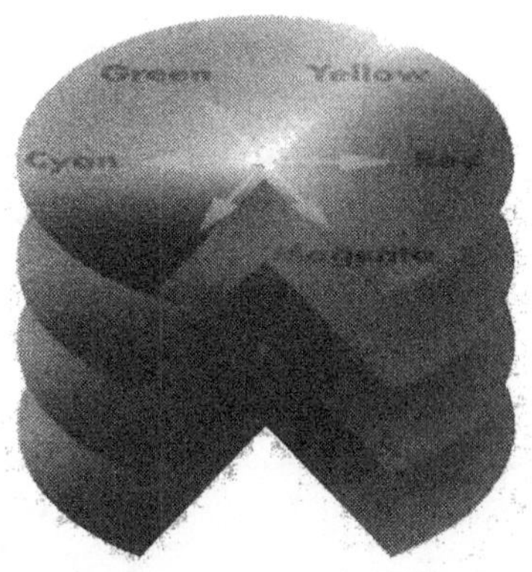

A 3-dimensional model of the HSB colour space, described in the text.

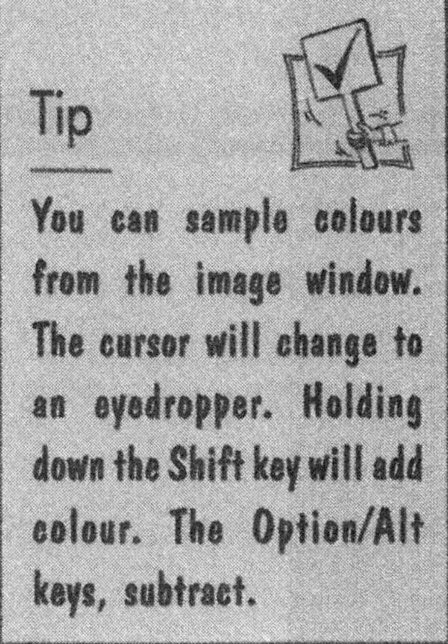

Now in the Edit pop-up menu, pick one of the listed colour groups. You'll notice that an adjustable set of sliders appear between the two colour chromaticity ramps. These represent the now restricted focus of any further Hue/Saturation adjustments. In this mode of operation, you can also use the eyedroppers to select, add or subtract more precise colours based on image samples. The central dark grey section represents the range of colours currently chosen and you can manually prescribe the colours selected by dragging the inner and outer slider handles. The lighter grey areas on either side represent the selection fade amount. When a colour selection is made, the hue adjustments will be represented by changes in the lower chromaticity ramp. If green is the colour selected, as shown here, a hue adjustment to the right will make the greens appear more cyan and a shift to the right will make them more yellow. When the Colorize check box is switched on, the colours in the image will be replaced with the single hue value setting.

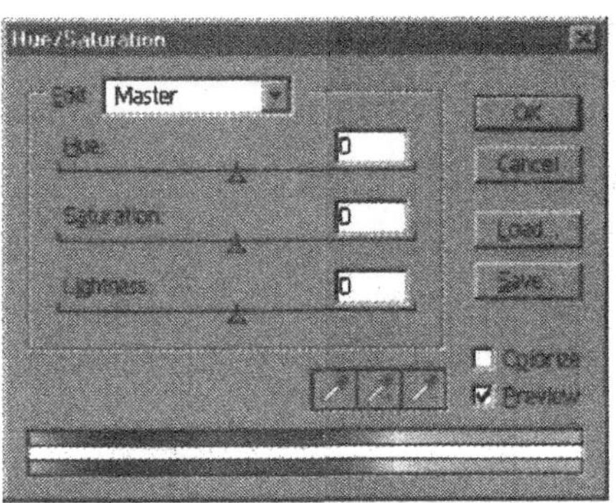

The Hue/Saturation interface

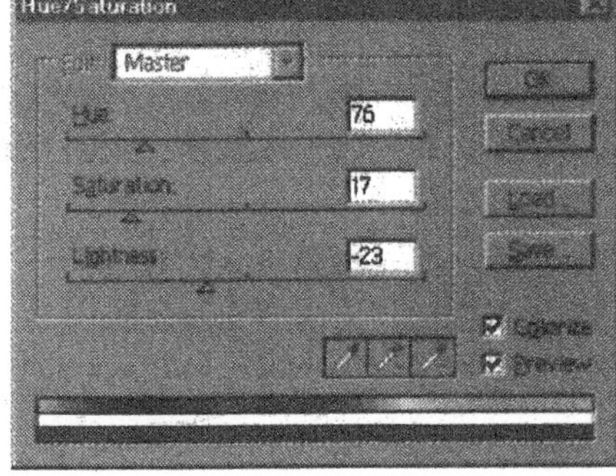

Hue/Saturation interface, with Colorize checked on

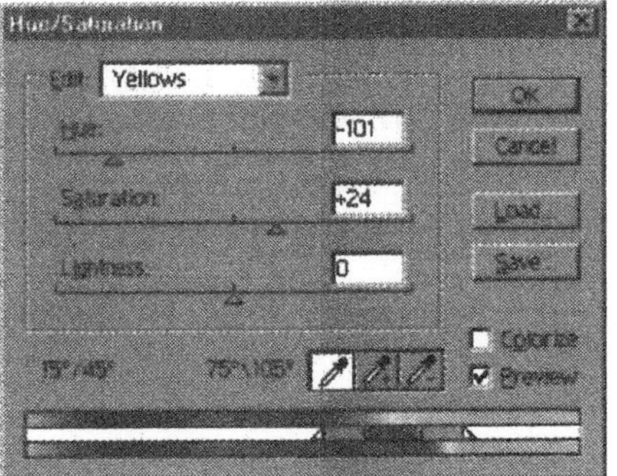

Hue/Saturation interface, showing an adjustment being made to the Yellows. The hue shift will make the yellow appear greener and with increased colour saturation.

Curves

The Curves adjustment is like an advanced version of the Color Balance adjustment. With Curves you can selectively adjust the colour at any specific point on the tonal scale. Moreover, you can boost or reduce overall contrast or modify the contrast in an individual colour channel. The pictures here show examples of before and after applying a simple curves adjustment.

The Curves dialog box graph has a line representing the relationship between the input and output tonal values. To start with, the graph line is always straight. As points are added (by clicking on the line) and the curve points dragged to change the shape, the relationship between input and output is changed. The figures in the Input and Output boxes found at the bottom left corner of the Curves dialog box, provide numeric feedback at any curve point, showing the before and after pixel values.

A common uses of Curves is to fine-tune the colour balance and image contrast. Only Curves give this degree of subtle control. You can if you like, create wild solarised effects, similar to using the Photoshop Stylize – Solarise filter. To achieve this, add multiple points and/or click on the arbitrary map mode button and draw freehand any line you like (see opposite, below). In arbitrary map mode, there is a Smooth button. Click on this to smooth out the sharp edges of the curve and create a gentler tonal adjustment. A solarised curve will be particularly effective when it is applied to a colour image in Photoshop.

Tip

Holding down the Option/Alt key at the same time as you select an image adjustment, calls up the last used settings.

Basic steps

1. Choose Image – Adjust – Curves.
2. Add a point to the curve graph.
3. Click on the arbitrary map button to make a freeform curve shape.

Tip

The Fade Filter command also works with image adjustments. Go to the Filter menu and choose Fade – Adjustment. From version 4.0.1 onwards, you can fade brush strokes too.

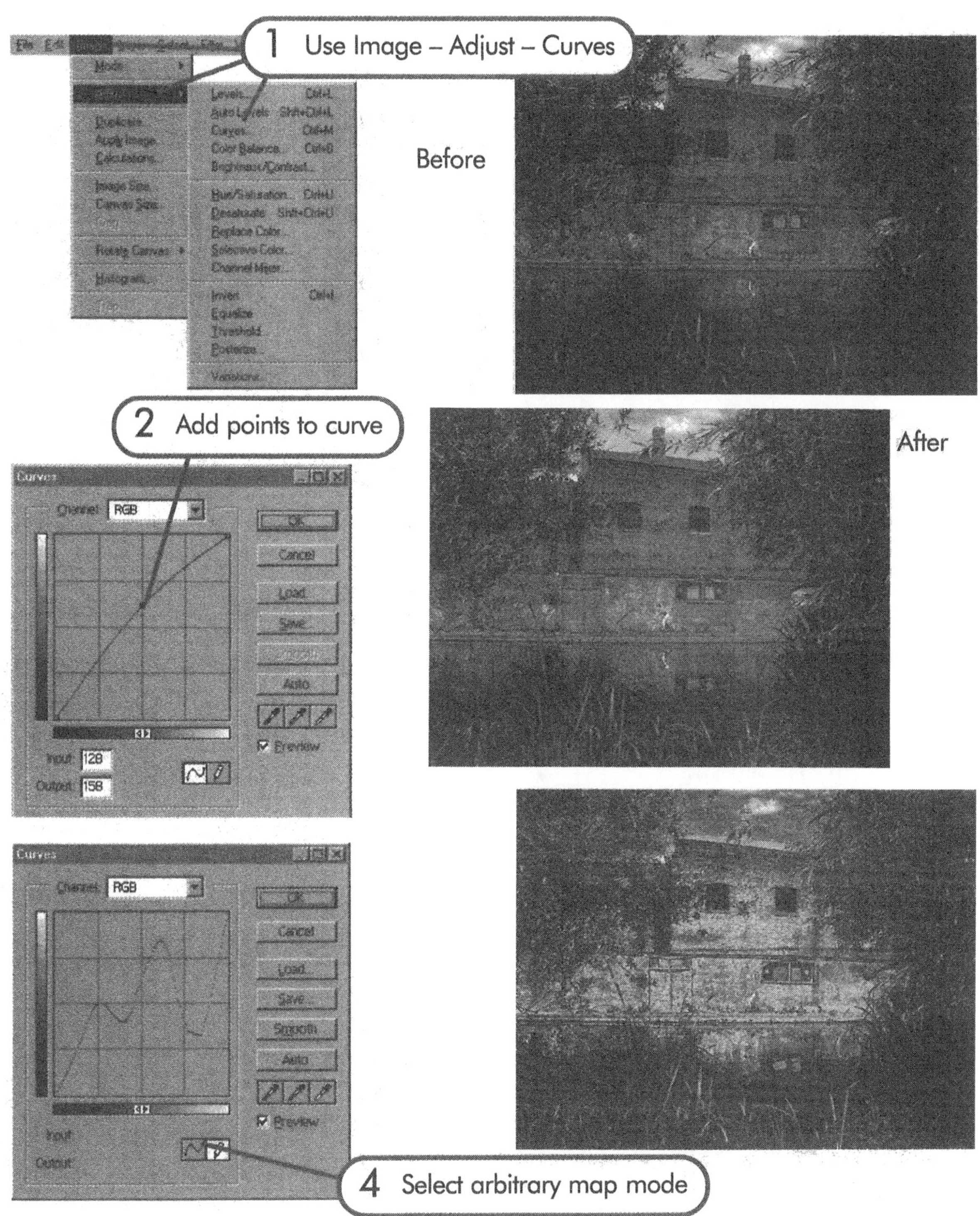
1 Use Image – Adjust – Curves
Before
2 Add points to curve
After
Curves
Channel: RGB
OK
Cancel
Load
Save
Smooth
Auto
Preview
Input: 128
Output: 158
4 Select arbitrary map mode

Info palette

The Info palette provides important data about the colour in the image. Advanced users, especially repro professionals, who edit entirely in CMYK colour, will rely heavily on the numeric feedback contained in this palette when judging the colour. The readout numbers show the pixel values at that point in the image; the X and Y show the coordinates of the reference point; W and H show the width and height of a dragging operation. These are displayed for all tools except for the measure tool, which has its own separate display for the Info palette.

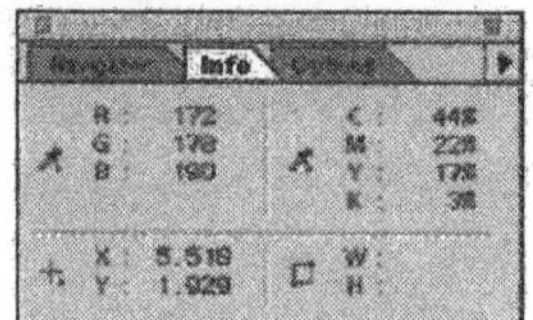

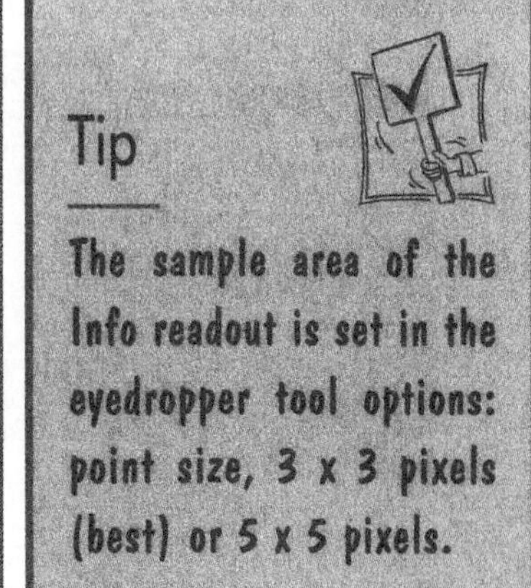

Tip
The sample area of the Info readout is set in the eyedropper tool options: point size, 3 x 3 pixels (best) or 5 x 5 pixels.

There are various options for the readout displays. For example, in the Info palette options you can choose the mode for the first and second colour readout. Having RGB and CMYK values side by side, is useful for RGB editing. The mouse coordinates set the measurement values for the Info palette.

Take note
CMYK greys are usually made up of even amounts of magenta and yellow and a higher amount of cyan.

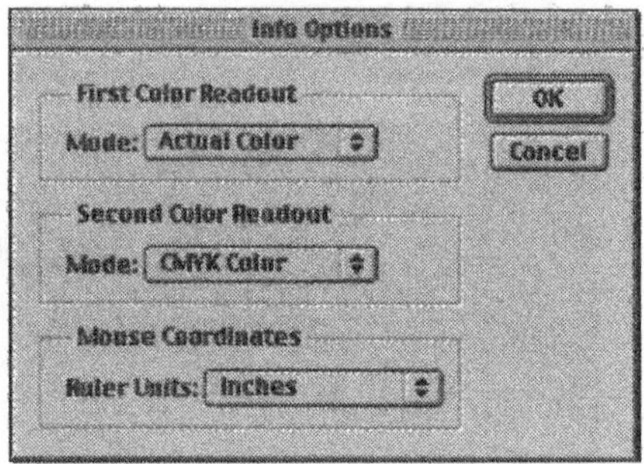

When the measure tool is selected, the Info palette will change to display the length and angle of a measurement (in whatever units chosen) and when followed by a protractor measurement (Option/Alt mouse down and drag from the end of a measurement line), the length of the two measurement lines are shown, and the angle between them.

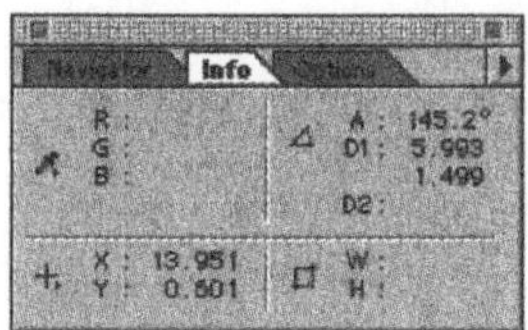

The Info palette shown using the measure tool to measure an angle

Basic steps

Colour samplers

1. Choose the colour sampler tool from the tools palette.
2. Position sample points in the image window.
3. Refer to the Info palette numbers when carrying out the image adjustment to read before and after values.

The new colour sampler tool is an extension of the eyedropper. Up to four colour samplers can be added anywhere in the image and the readout display will report back the image information of each simultaneously. This is especially useful when you want to colour correct an image using numeric feedback. In RGB colour mode, equal red green and blue values will equal neutral grey.

If there is a colour cast present in an area which should be grey, you can first place the sample points and correct accordingly using the curves adjustment. In the example below, the before and after numbers can be seen, relating to the numbered sampler positions in the picture.

1 Select the colour sampler

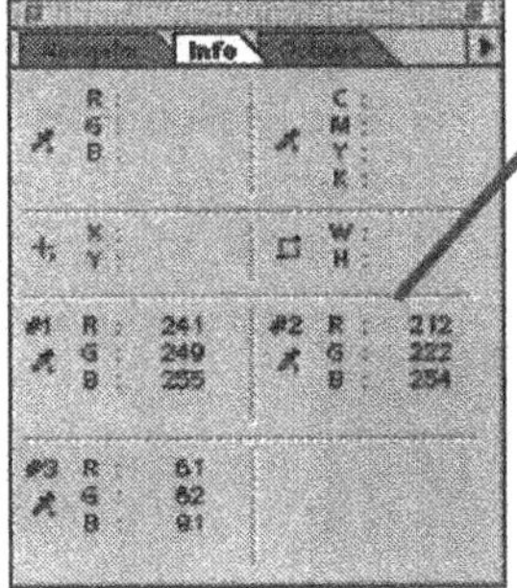

3 Check the Info palette readouts

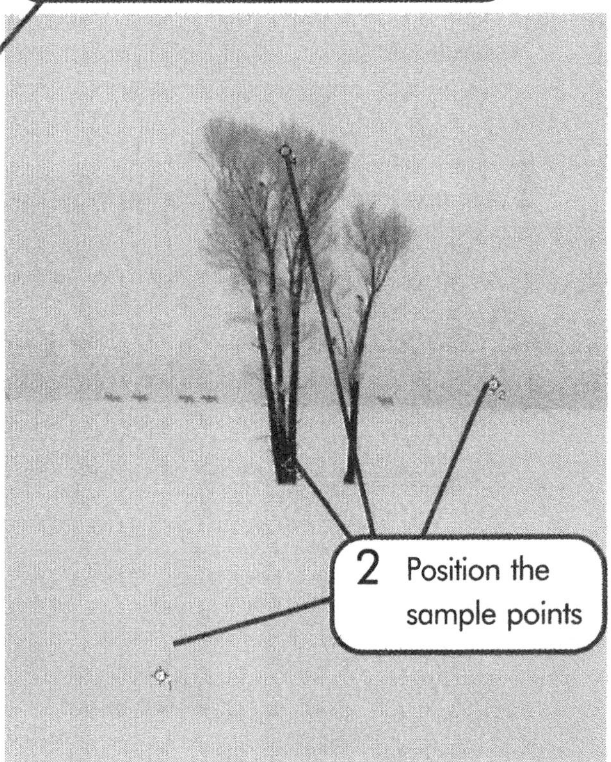

2 Position the sample points

Tip

Command/Ctrl dragging allows you to reposition the sampler.

Option/Alt will change the cursor to scissors to remove a sampler.

Contrast adjustment

Curves is the best tool to use when you wish to adjust the contrast of a picture. Most definitely do not use the Brightness/Contrast adjustment to do this. In the curves dialog box, if you create an 'S' shaped curve as on the left, it will soften the contrast. If the curve 'S' shape is drawn the other way round as shown on the right, the contrast will be increased. Here is a handy tip: when the Curves dialog box is open, and you drag the cursor inside the image window, you can precisely locate the tonal point on the curve, which is shown by a circle icon.

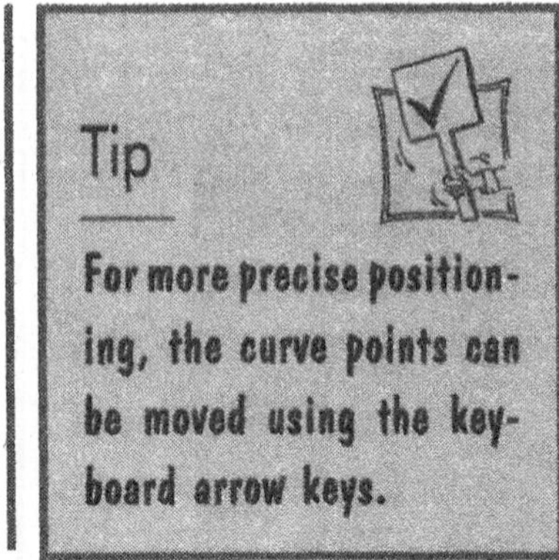
Tip

For more precise positioning, the curve points can be moved using the keyboard arrow keys.

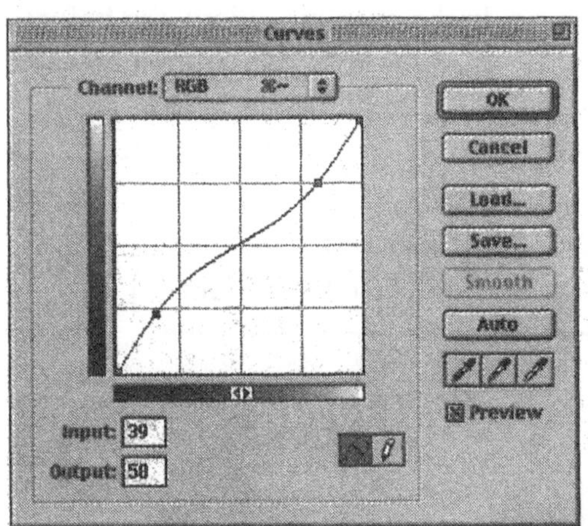

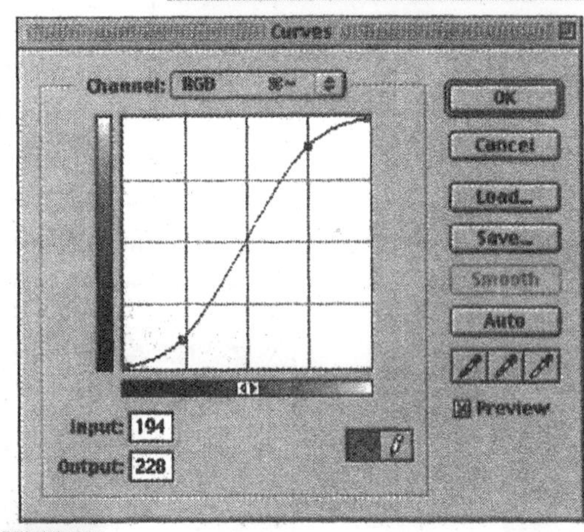

Less contrast

Normal

More contrast

Channel Mixer

Basic steps

1. Take an image in RGB colour mode and choose Image – Adjust – Channel Mixer.
2. Check the Monochrome box .
3. Adjust the colour channel mix. The blue sky will now appear darker.

This brand new Photoshop 5.0 feature enables the user to mix the colour channel contents. In RGB mode for example, the red channel naturally enough, is made up of 100% red, 0% green and 0% blue, but you can vary that mix by adding in the content of the other colour channels into the red channel. If you wanted you could have all the red channel in the blue channel and all the green channel in the red. The possibilities are endless but also rather futile, unless you know what you want to achieve with the Channel Mixer.

Switch to monochrome mode and you can mix the channels used to generate a grey scale image. Normally when you convert to grey, the colour channel values are averaged out in a fixed fashion, but working with this adjustment, you can alter this balance and consequently the grey scale conversion can be made of a custom mix of your own choosing. When mixing the channels in monochrome mode, try to make all the channel values add up to +100%.

1 Open the Channel Mixer

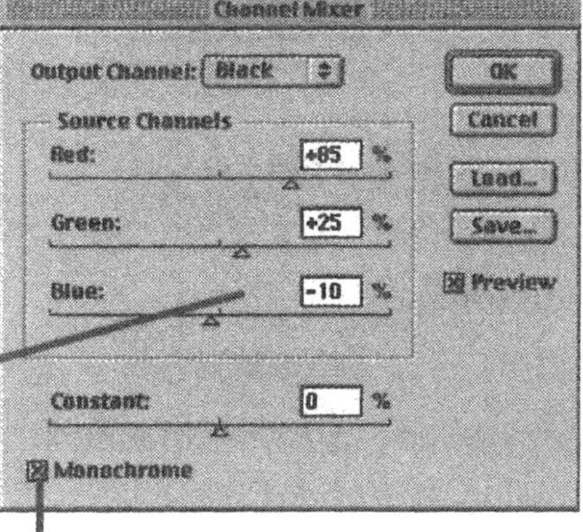

3 Adjust the mix

2 Turn on Monochrome

Reducing the Blue darkens the sky

Summary

- Use Image – Adjust – Levels to set the image shadow and highlight points.
- The Levels histogram represents the distribution of tonal values as a bar chart.
- The gamma slider is used to adjust the relative brightness of an image.
- The shadow and highlight eyedroppers can alternatively be used to assign the shadows and highlights within the image.
- Variations is an easy to use adjustment tool, incorporating colour balance, saturation and gamma correction all in one.
- The Hue/Saturation adjustment has the potential to accurately pinpoint specific colours to be altered and make global changes based on hue or saturation values.
- Curves are a sophisticated version of the Color Balance adjustment.
- The Info palette supplies numeric feedback of pixel colour values.
- Colour samplers can provide simultaneous Info feedback on up to four points in an image.
- Alter the tonal contrast of an image using Curves – don't use Brightness/Contrast.
- The Channel Mixer is a very powerful adjustment tool, but should be used with caution. It is an excellent way of converting a colour original to black and white.

5 Composites

Layers

Basic steps

Layers first made their appearance back in Photoshop 3.0, when for the first time it became possible to combine many elements together in a single image. One way to understand the concept of layers, is to imagine them as sheets of clear acetate overlapping the background image. A layer can contain part of an image or it can be a complete image layer. The main purpose of layers is to have the ability to position image elements separate from the background as well as the flexibility of being able to reorder or move these elements around.

Best of all, layers give you the opportunity to be creative and experiment with multiple image elements and also have the freedom to make alterations at any later date – one thing which History cannot do. The only drawback is that too many layers will impede Photoshop performance unless that is, you have enough memory to cope with the increased file size.

1 Select the area to made into a layer.

2 Use the move tool to drag the selection across to the new image window.

3 The new layer appears in the layers palette.

1 Make a selection of the area to be moved

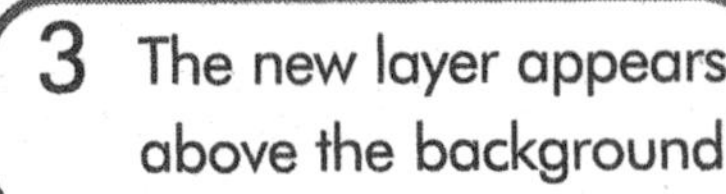
3 The new layer appears above the background

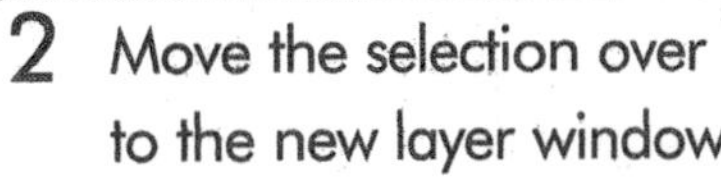
2 Move the selection over to the new layer window

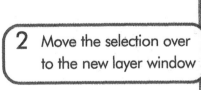

Ways to create new layers

Tip
A quick way to make a duplicate new layer based on a selection, is to use the keyboard shortcut: Command/Ctrl–J

- Clicking the **New layer** button in the **Layers** palette.
- Choosing **New Layer** from the **Layers** flyout menu.
- Going to the main **Layer** menu – this in itself will make a new empty layer only.
- If there is an active selection in the image window, **Layer – New Layer – Via copy**, will copy the selection contents and duplicate as a new layer in register with the source.
- You can also drag an image or active selection from another window across using the move tool, which is always quicker and more efficient than using the copy and paste method.

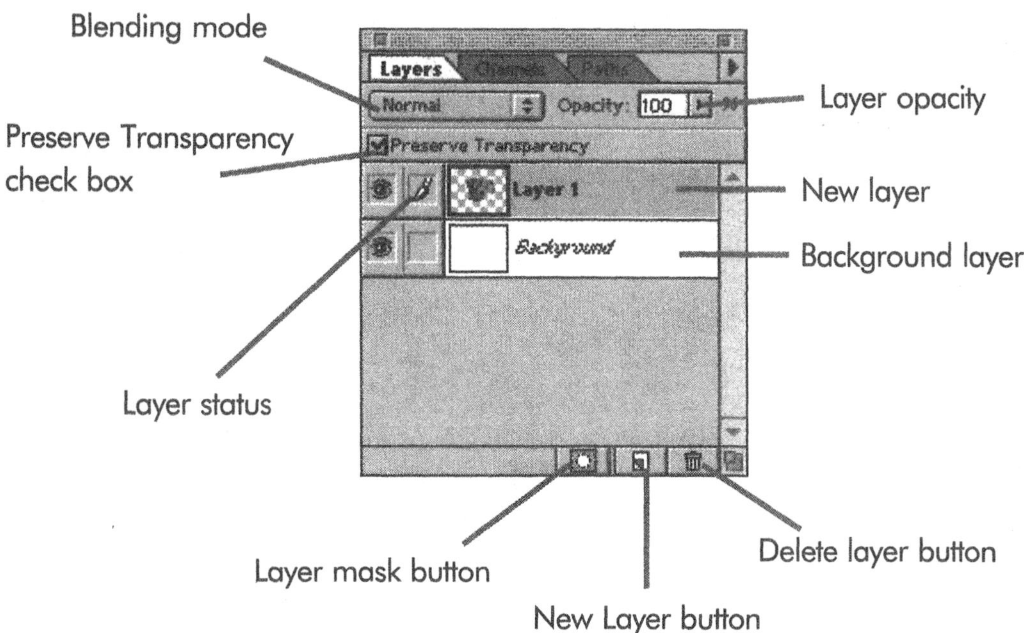

The Layers palette, identifying the main features. New layers are always added immediately above the currently active layer. The layer status is showing that this layer is currently active and editable. Linked layers are shown using the linked chain icon (see page 74)

Blending modes

The default 'Normal' blending mode will render pixels in a layer at 100% opacity on top of the underlying layer (see illustration on page 72). The Normal blending mode will probably suit most image composites, but there are more options available in Photoshop layers yet to explore. To start with, the opacity can be varied using the Opacity slider in the Layers palette. Drag the slider or highlight the percentage box and type in a number.

You can also set the blending mode in the pop-up menu. There are a good many options to choose from and it helps therefore to know what each one does. This is not a complete list, but these are some of the more useful modes to try out.

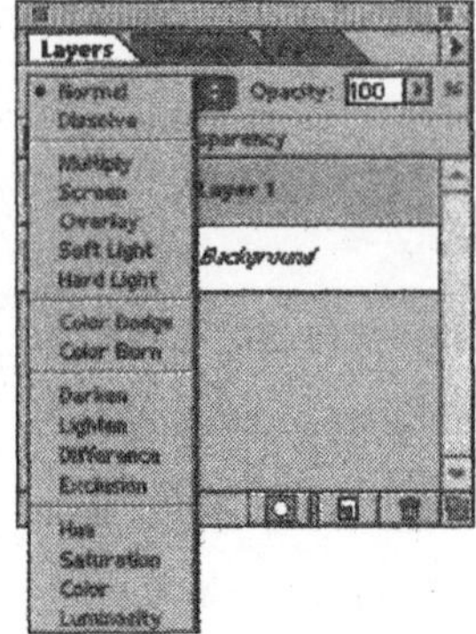

The Layers palette, showing the pop up menu of layer blending modes

Multiply

Multiplies the combined pixel values, always producing a darker colour. The effect is similar to viewing two transparent objects sandwiched one on top of the other.

Screen

The opposite to Multiply – the effect is similar to projecting one image on top of another

Overlay, Soft Light & Hard Light

These can be grouped together as variations on the theme of projecting one image on top of another. The **Overlay** blending mode is usually the most effective, multiplying or screening the colours depending on the base colour, while preserving the highlights and shadows of the base colour. **Soft Light** darkens or lightens the colours depending on the base colour, producing a more gentle effect than the Overlay mode. **Hard Light** multiplies or screens the colours depending on the base colour. Hard Light produces a more pronounced effect than the Overlay mode.

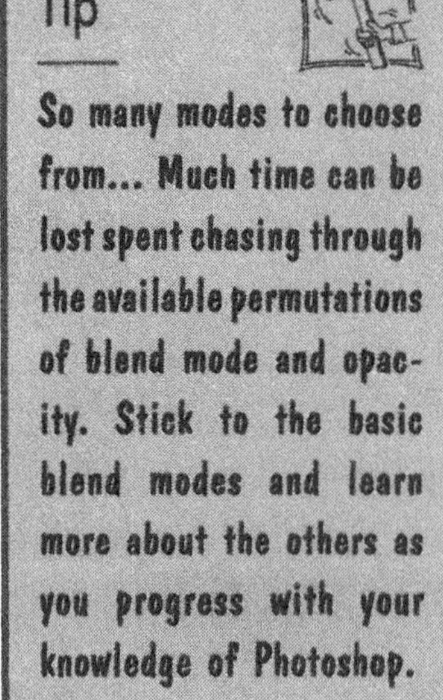

Tip

So many modes to choose from... Much time can be lost spent chasing through the available permutations of blend mode and opacity. Stick to the basic blend modes and learn more about the others as you progress with your knowledge of Photoshop.

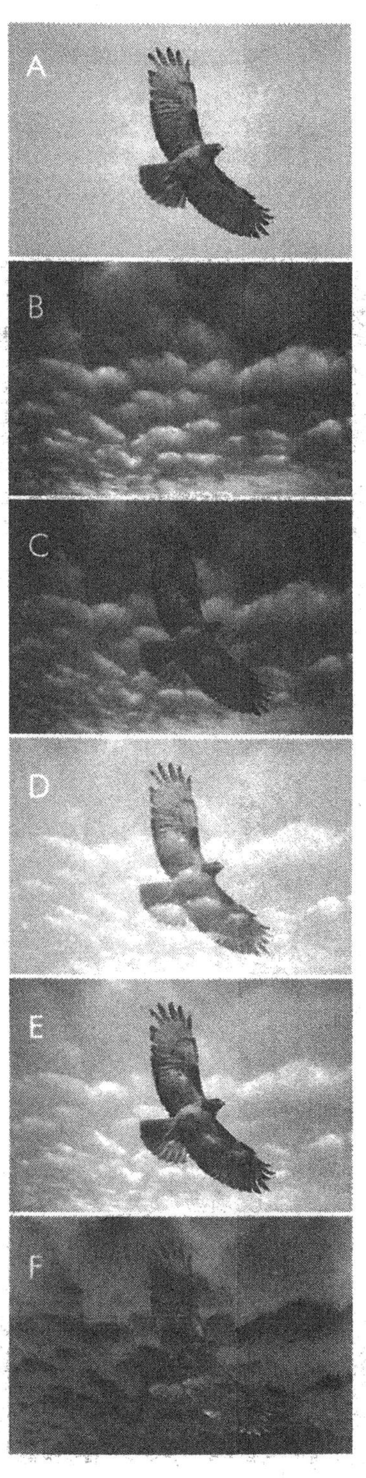

Darken & Lighten

Darken looks at the base and blending colours and selects whichever is darker and makes that the result colour. Lighten looks at the base and blending colours and selects whichever is lighter and makes that the result colour.

Difference

Subtracts either the base colour from the blending colour or the blending colour from the base, depending on whichever has the highest brightness value. In visual terms, a 100% white blend value will invert (i.e. turn negative) the base layer completely, a black value will have no effect and values in between will partially invert the base layer.

Hue, Saturation & Color

Hue preserves the luminance and saturation of the image, but replaces the hue of the blending pixels. **Saturation**, preserves the luminance and hue, but replaces the saturation of the blending pixels. **Color** preserves the luminance values, whilst replacing the hue and saturation values. Color mode is particularly suited for hand colouring photographs.

To illustrate some of the blending mode results, the eagle layer (A) was placed as a layer above the sky background layer (B) .

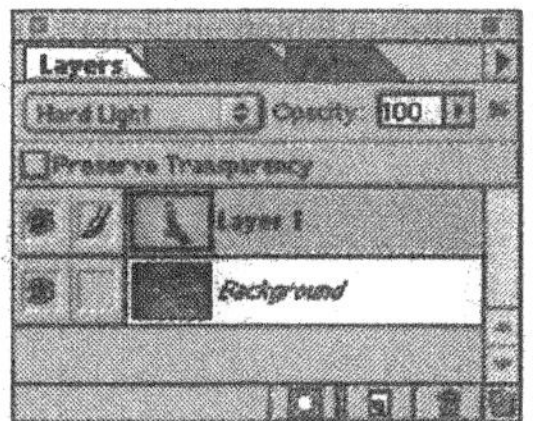

Here are the results from the blend modes: Multiply (C), Screen (D), Hard light (E) and Difference (F).

Layer masks

Layers provide flexibility because you can rearrange the position, blending mode and opacity of a layer at any time. Layer masks add another dimension – the ability to edit a layer's contents without permanently losing the image data. In other words, if you were to use the erase tool to scrub out part of a layer, there is no opportunity to restore that erasure other than using History.

Add a mask channel to the layer and one can 'paint out' the layer image by painting with a brush tool (the default will normally be set to black) on the layer mask. To undo the mask painting, paint the layer contents back in with white.

Basic steps

1 Go to the Layers palette and click on the Layer Mask button.

2 Make sure the Layer Mask icon is active.

3 Select the paintbrush from the tools palette with black as the foreground colour.

4 Apply the brush in the image window to remove the image layer as desired.

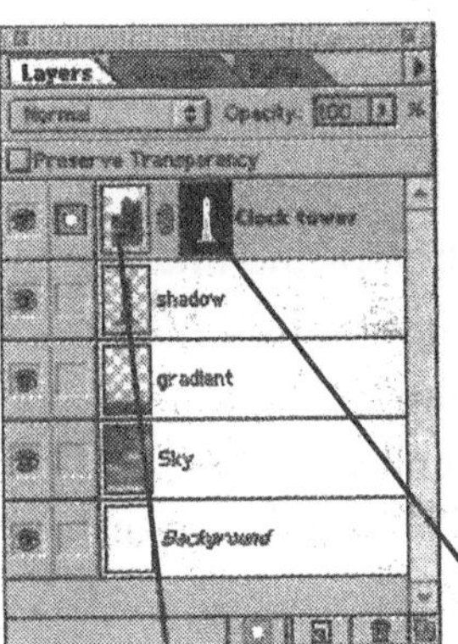

A prepared path of the monument outline was converted to a selection and by clicking on the Layer Mask button, instantly converted to a layer mask.

Preserve transparency

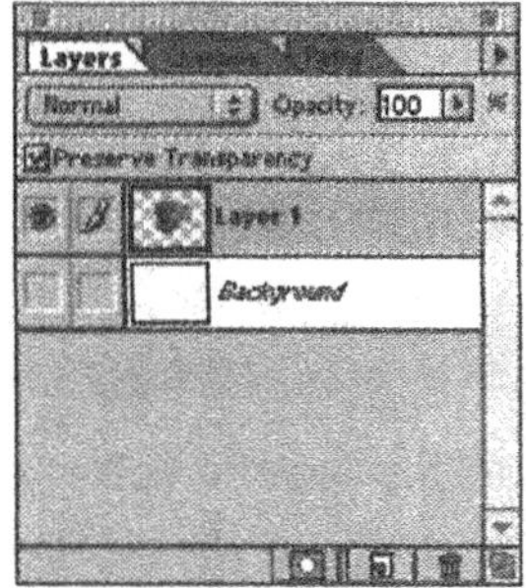

The empty areas of a layer are represented with a grey and white chequer pattern (the chequer appearance can be modified in Preferences), indicating transparency. There is a very useful item at the top of the Layers palette called 'Preserve Transparency' when this box is checked, the transparent areas are protected – you will not be able to work or paint on any area of the layer which is not opaque. There are a number of good uses for Preserve Transparency, like when you wish to fill the contents of a layer quickly, preserving the layer transparent areas, or, you wish to paint on a layer but not exceed the edge limits.

1 Normal image layer

Painting with Preserve Transparency switched off

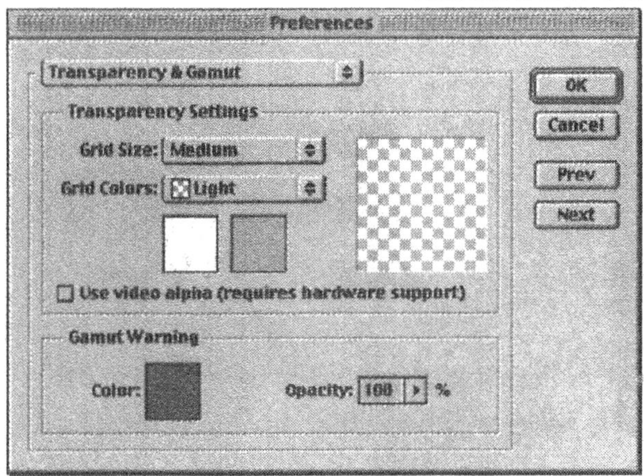

The transparency preferences dialog box

Painting with Preserve Transparency switched on

Clipping groups

You can make the contents of a layer act as a mask upon any layer or layers grouped above, by making them part of a clipping group. To link layers together this way, Option/Alt–click on the dividing line between the two layers. To undo a clipping group, Option/Alt–click the dividing line again. In the example below, a sunset layer was added above the background. A layer mask, masks the foreground. The second layer adds some more cloud. Because this second layer is linked as a clipping group it shares the sunset layer mask. Any modifications made to that mask will be shared by the two layers.

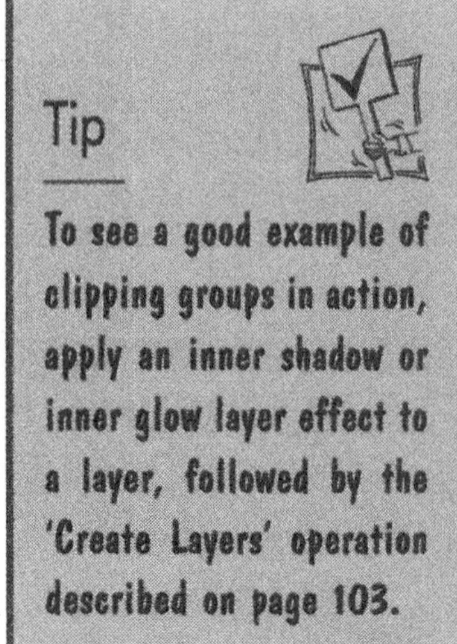
Tip

To see a good example of clipping groups in action, apply an inner shadow or inner glow layer effect to a layer, followed by the 'Create Layers' operation described on page 103.

Original image

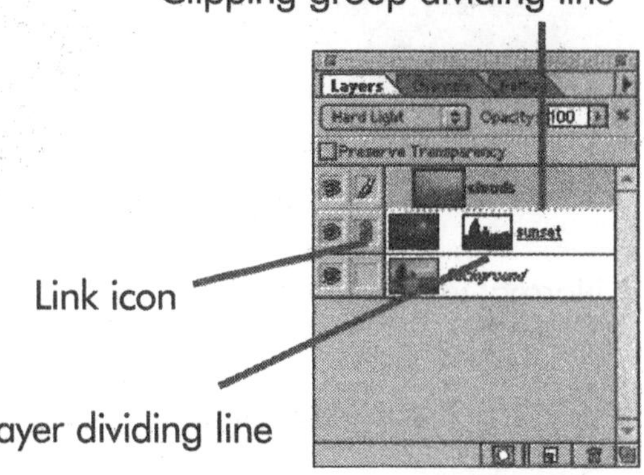

Final image showing two layers superimposed as a clipping group

Clipping group applied to an image above a type layer (text is editable)

Adjustment layers

Tip

Command/Ctrl click the New layer button at the bottom of the Layers palette as a shortcut to adding a new adjustment layer.

Whenever an image adjustment is applied, those changes are fixed once you start adding further steps in Photoshop to an image. Adjustment layers allow you to apply an image adjustment such as Levels, Curves or Hue/Saturation as a layer. Like image layers, adjustment layers share similar properties, they appear in the layer stack of the layers palette. Likewise, the opacity and Layer Options can be adjusted. You can remove an adjustment layer completely at a later time or you can edit the settings, just by double-clicking the adjustment layer.

Image adjustments always have a cumulatively destructive effect each time you apply an adjustment. With adjustment layers you can make as many image adjustments as you want, but the actual adjustment only occurs the once, when you merge the adjustment layers with the pixel layer.

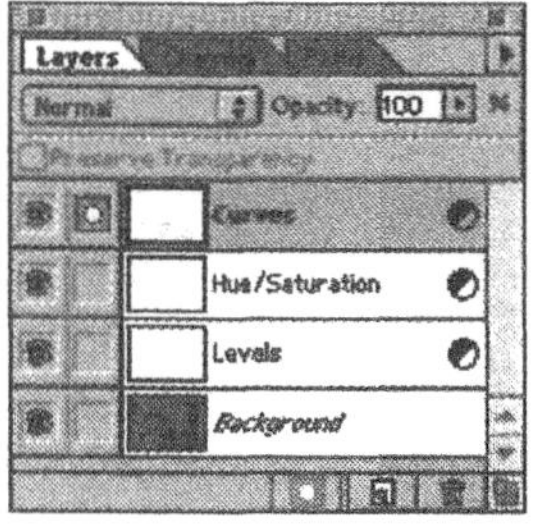

Multiple adjustment layers can be added and kept saved in a Photoshop document

A mask applied to the adjustment layer, masks the levels adjustment from being applied to the whole of the image area.

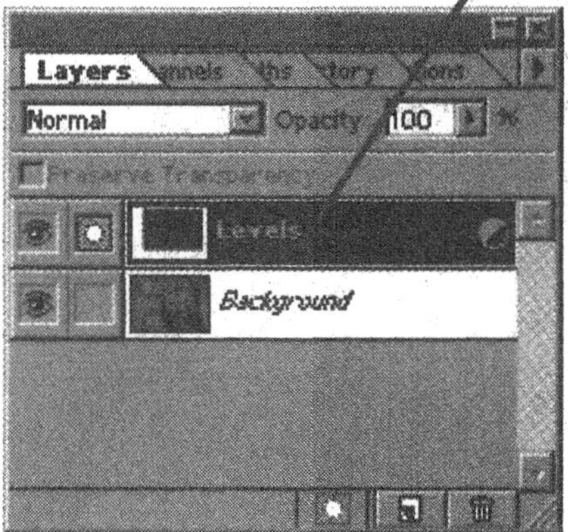

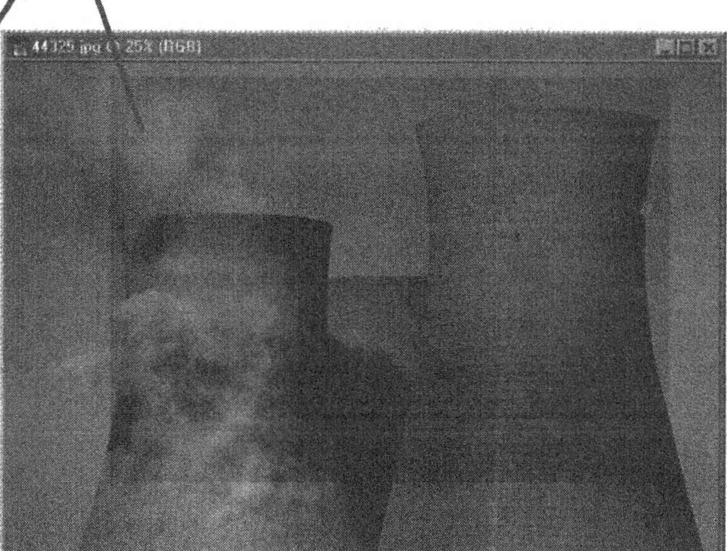

Align layers

Anyone who has used a drawing program like Illustrator, will be familiar with alignment controls, with which grouped objects can be orientated around a common axis point. In Photoshop 5.0 the alignment controls are to be found in the Layer menu and the Layer submenu gives visual hints of how the alignment will be applied. The basic principles are that the alignment command will take the highlighted layer as the reference point. First link the layers to be aligned, go to the Layers palette and click in the space to the right of the eye icon to switch on or off the link icon against the relevant layers and align all remaining layers accordingly: Top, Horizontal Center, Bottom or: Left, Vertical Center, Right.

Align – Top, will arrange all the layers so that their topmost edge will align with the topmost edge of the highlighted layer. The Vertical Center option will align all the layers vertical, central axis around that of the highlighted layer and so on.

Distribute layers

The distribute command will evenly distribute the layer spacing between the selected layers following similar rules to those outlined on the previous page. The Distribute Left command for example, will evenly distribute the layers, taking the left-most edge of each layer element as the reference point.

When the Align Layers and Distribute Layers commands are used in conjunction with each other, users can quickly group layers, evenly space them apart and make them align along an axis. The most obvious applications are in graphic design layouts and the construction of web pages. In particular, these layer controls are perfect for positioning text elements. For information on the how to use the type tool with type layers and type effects, see Chapter 7.

Basic steps

1 Select the layer to act as the reference point.

2 Go to the Layers palette and click beside the eye to link the layers to be aligned.

3 Open the Layer menu and select and Align or Distribute option.

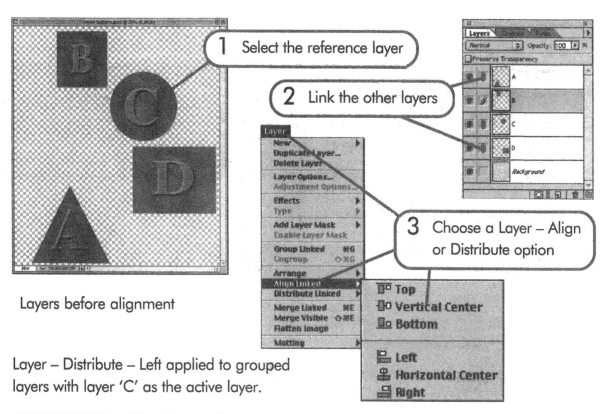

1 Select the reference layer

2 Link the other layers

3 Choose a Layer – Align or Distribute option

Layers before alignment

Layer – Distribute – Left applied to grouped layers with layer 'C' as the active layer.

Thin vertical lines show even spacing between leftmost edges of the layers.

Layer – Align – Align Horizontal Center applied with layer 'C' as the active layer.

Summary

- ❑ A layer is comparable to an acetate sheet floating above the background. A layer can be a complete image filling the whole frame or a small element surrounded by transparency.
- ❑ Changing the blending mode alters the way the layer pixel values combine with the pixels below.
- ❑ Normal, Multiply, Screen, Overlay, Soft Light, Hard Light, Darken, Lighten, Difference, Hue, Saturation and Color are the most useful blend modes.
- ❑ Layer masks enable you to edit a layer's visibility with unlimited undos and without permanently erasing data.
- ❑ The Preserve Transparency option helps you avoid painting or filling transparent areas.
- ❑ Clipping groups allow you to share layer masking between more than one layer.
- ❑ Adjustment layers are image adjustments applied as a removable layer, which can be altered or undone at any time.
- ❑ Align and Distribute layers adds Illustrator-like control to the alignment and distribution of grouped layers.

6 Retouch and paint

Painting tools

The **airbrush** and **paintbrush** are similar; the **eraser** can behave like either. The airbrush has a longer soft edge than the paintbrush, and can build its effect over time. A fast stroke has less colour than a slower one. The paintbrush can also have wet edges, where the colour builds up. All three brushes can fade over a given pixel distance. Fade simulates paint running out.

Using the paintbrush or airbrush will create a very smooth texture. If you need a suggestion of grain, try Filter – Noise – Add Noise (1to6%) or use the rubber stamp or pattern stamp tools (see page 112).

Blend modes allow you to set how the new painting is to react with the existing image. To darken a thin fringe of lightness at an edge, choosing Darken will only affect areas that are lighter than the colour you apply, allowing you considerable freedom.

- For a glow out of what is already there, choose Screen blend mode.
- If you need the detail, but a new colour, then select Color blend mode.
- Use the opacity slider for even finer control.
- The painting tools can also track along a path (page 47).

The range of options is limitless, do not be afraid to experiment. You do have multiple Undos!

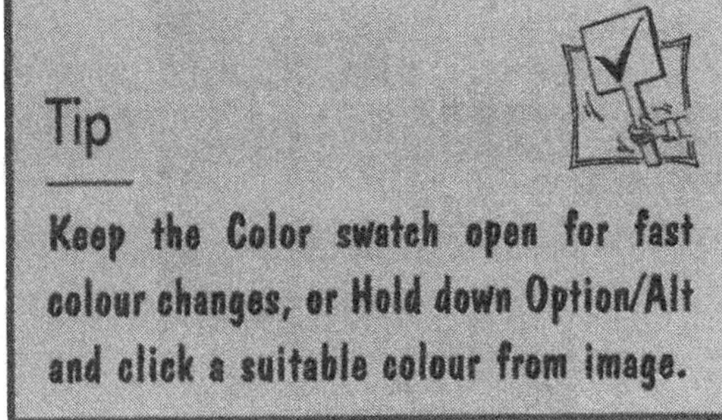

Tip
Keep the Color swatch open for fast colour changes, or Hold down Option/Alt and click a suitable colour from image.

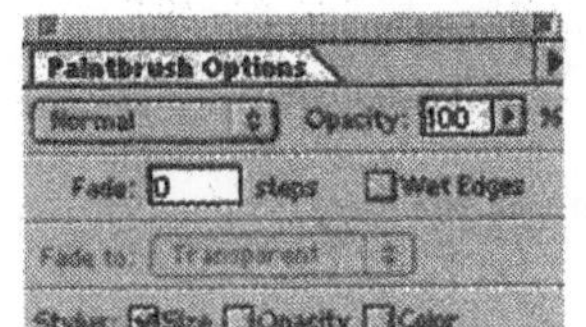

Paintbrush Options

Basic steps

❑ To remove an edge that is too light:

1 Select Airbrush.

2 Choose colour A as Foreground, and paint with a brush size slightly larger than the edge, with Blend mode Darken.

3 To retain a subtle lightness choose less Opacity than 100%.

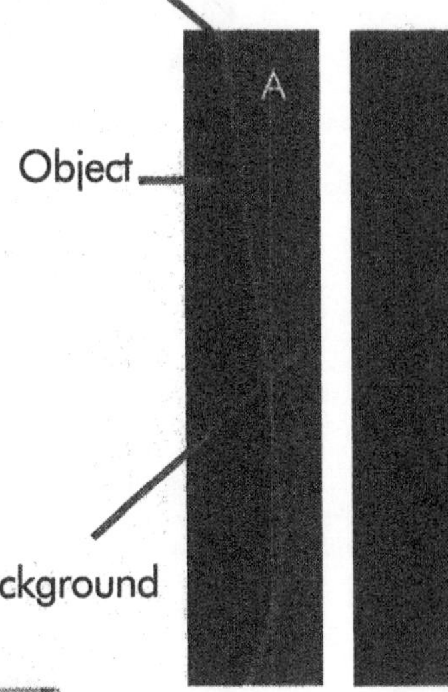

After

Using a digitising pen

Tip

Shortcut D gives you the default: black foreground, white background.

Shortcut X eXchanges background for foreground and back again.

There are three options specific to pressure-sensitive digitising pens; Color, Pressure, Size and Opacity (see Paintbrush Options on the previous page).

Color gives you the opportunity to paint with either the foreground or background colours dependent on the pressure you apply – press lightly to use the background colour, press harder for the foreground colour.

Pressure applies to the flow from the airbrush. **Size** and **Opacity** are available to the paintbrush – the less stylus pressure you apply, the smaller the brush size, and/or the opacity.

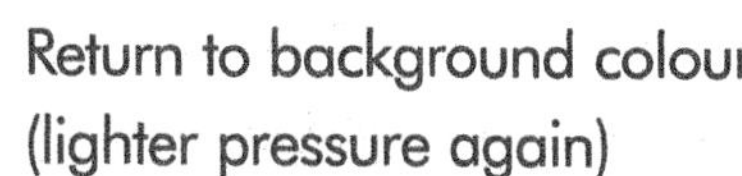

Foreground colour
(heavy pressure)

This airbrush line has been painted with the Color checkbox ticked, using a pressure-sensitive pen.

Take note

The eraser removes to clear on a layer, but to the background colour on the Background, or to a selected History state – that is the state against which the brush icon is set within the History palette (see page 87).

Tip

If you do not have a pressure-sensitive pen, avoid clicking on the stylus-related checkboxes, as you may find nothing happens when you paint!

The rubber stamp tool

Use this brush for 'cloning' – replicating an area.To remove a blemish, clone a matching nearby tone – Option/Alt-click this area with an appropriate sized brush, selecting opacity and blend mode to suit.

Cloning is smoother in Photoshop 5 than in earlier versions. The tool now only copies original areas, and does not repeat those from which you are copying (see also page 13).

You can clone from other open images; from just the current layer, from all the layers or from other layers in the same image – though this involves a lot of layer switching.

Cloning can be set aligned or non-aligned in the Options. If set to non-aligned, each time you lift your brush, the source will revert to the point that was Option/Alt-clicked. When aligned, the initial relationship between source and target is retained.

Too much cloning results in smooth areas compared to the original. Avoid this adding a small amount of gaussian noise afterwards (see page 112), trying to match the original texture – probably an amount between 3 and 6.

Basic steps

1 Select rubber stamp tool, then set the Brush size, Blend Mode, and Opacity to suit.

2 Hold down Option/Alt key to pick the source – and release.

3 Click where you want the clone, and drag to spread it, or

4 Release, select a new source and paint again

5 Repeat until you are satisfied with the effect.

Markings to be removed

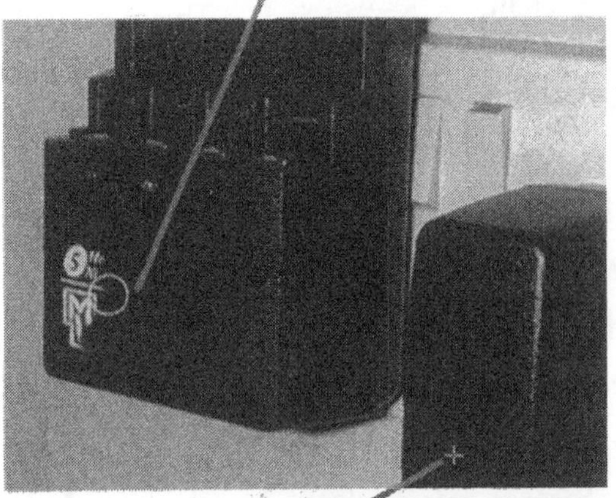

3 Paint the target area

2 Select the source area

Basic steps

1 Select a suitable rectangular area to define as your pattern.

2 From the Edit menu select Define Pattern.

3 Deselect the area.

4 Choose a large brush, relative to your pattern.

5 Try one pass, to see if the opacity is right – Undo and adjust as necessary.

6 Complete the action in one, longer pass.

Pattern stamp tool

A variant of the rubber stamp tool; to use it you must first have defined a pattern. After that you simply paint.

Any rectangular selection within open files can be designated as a Pattern from the Edit menu provided the selection does not have a feathered edge.

- The larger you can make the pattern the better the result
- Patterns carry texture, which flat colour does not
- Alignment is to itself
- Use in non-aligned mode with a large soft brush to avoid the worst side-effects of using a pattern – that of obvious repeats of the bounding rectangle edges

To complete this area of fishes, a rectangular selection is made as shown. It is then defined as a pattern in the Edit menu. In this case of a 10Mb file, a brush of 350-pixels was chosen, at 75% opacity and a very soft edge to complete the corner area. It was used with the Aligned checkbox ticked.

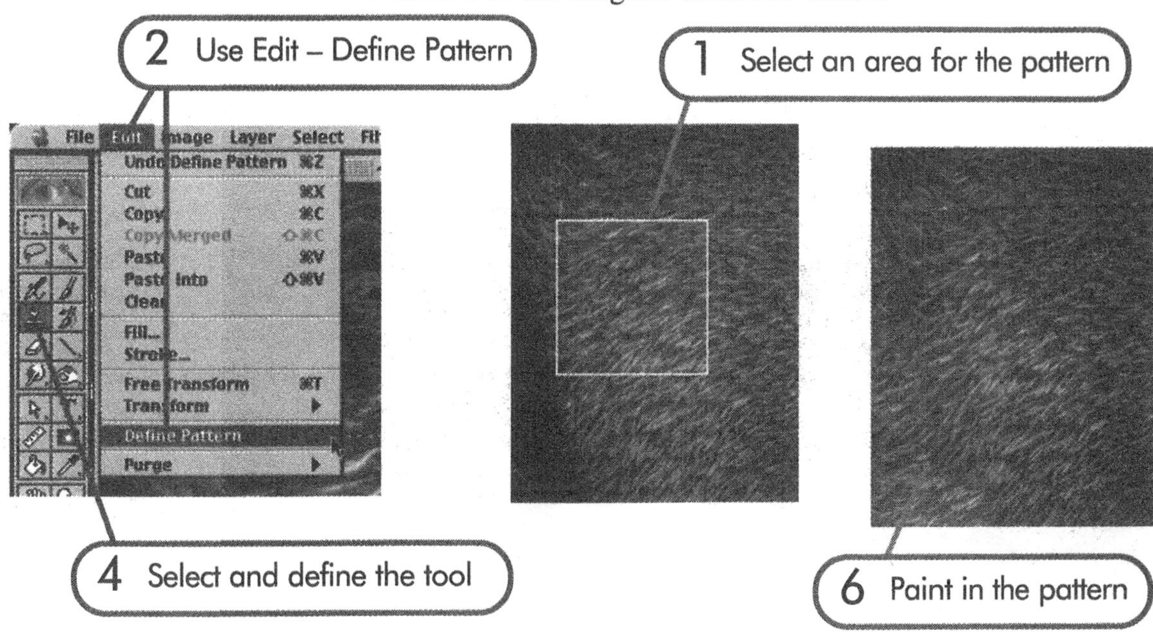

Dodge and burn tools

These direct photographic metaphors allow you to do local lightening, darkening and changes in colour saturation. For most work the percentage set should be very low (1 to 5%).

More texture is preserved using dodge/burn than by cloning with the rubber stamp, especially had it been used with a soft-edged brush.

- Set to display Brush Size, as opposed to the tool icon itself (Preferences–Display & Cursors)
- Use these tools slowly, building their effect gradually.
- Tolerance is greater in the midtones, but far less in the shadows and highlights, so beware of excessive use here.
- Use the dodge tool to lighten, the burn tool to darken.

Both leave the underlying texture intact, but used to excess can cause colour changes. Use the rubber stamp tool set to Color mode to correct this, by restoring colour from surrounding areas.

Basic steps

- ❑ Minimising wrinkles:

1. Select dodge tool with a small brush size relative to line, an amount of only 1 to 5, and midtones.
2. Run brush to and fro along dark part of line as needed.
3. Change to burn tool and repeat along highlight.

Tip

When working on large areas, use large brushes in single sweeps.

Minimising wrinkles, using dodge tool at 5%, midtones, and a 13-pixel brush.

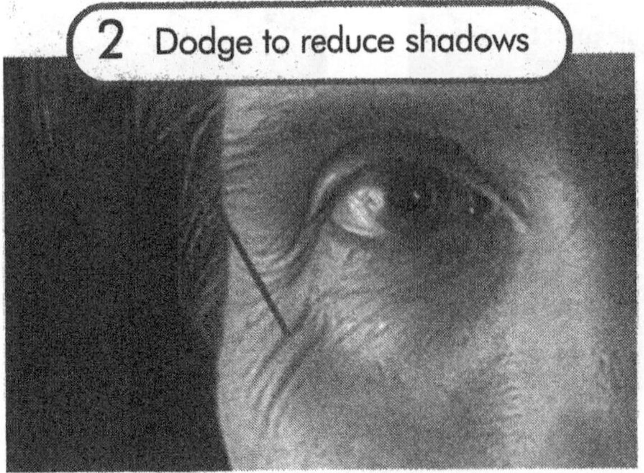

Before

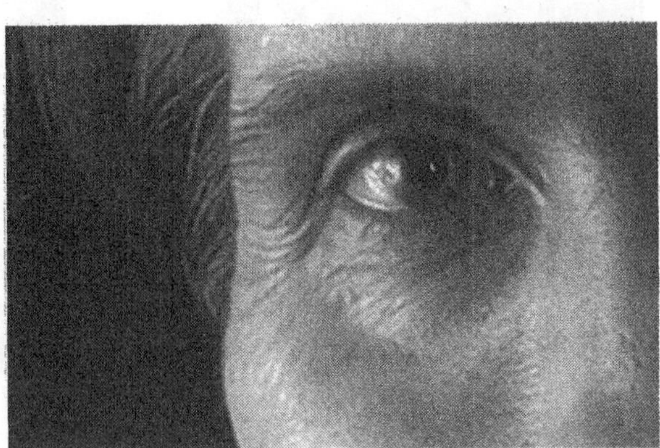

After

Sponge tool

Typical uses for these tools

- ❑ For creating highlights along surfaces – dodge tool
- ❑ For shading to the bottoms of images to 'seat' them better when putting a product into a new background – burn tool
- ❑ To lighten shadow areas in contrasty subjects to reveal more detail
- ❑ To create haloes, or vignettes to concentrate the eye upon the most important area of an image
- ❑ To lighten or darken the edge where elements meet, either to lessen or accentuate the boundary.

The sponge tool has two options; Saturate and Desaturate. These are used to either enhance the colour yet maintain the detail, or to tone down vivid colours.

Sponge only has the Options, Saturate and Desaturate and Pressure, unless you have a pressure sensitive pen which allows for variable Size and Exposure/Pressure.

Use the sponge tool set to Desaturate to bring colours within gamut if you are working on an RGB file destined to be converted to CMYK. (Turn on the View/Preview CMYK to show which colours will be out of gamut when the conversion takes place.)

Take the sponge tool, set it to Desaturate and an appropriate sized brush, and gently work at the areas that are outside the gamut, till they are no longer rejected by the Gamut Preview.

If the the colour then looks too dull, it may be possible to lighten or darken it with the dodge/burn tools.

Other uses for the sponge:

- enrichening blue skies
- enhancing the blush of a cheek

These do not lend themselves to being shown in black-and-white.

Use larger brush sizes in these cases to minimise patchiness. How large, depends on the size and resolution of the file.

The History palette

A Photoshop image is made up of tiles. History stores discreet stages in the creation of your images by storing only the changing states of these tiles as opposed to actual brushstrokes. This efficient use of memory means History only stores changed tiles, rather than the overall image, offering you the chance to restore localised areas of your image speedily and accurately.

Any open file creates an immediate Snapshot above the line in the History palette. Unlike history states it is not deleted when you reach the limit set in the maximum history states. You can save many Snapshots along the way which can give a much better indication of what your image looked like at those stages than the tool names or actions listed in History. The penalty is that scratch disk memory will be hit. You simply set the history brush to the Snapshot you wish to either fill from, or from where you want to paint. Remember that these items can be changed at any time. If at any stage you wish to create a new document this can be done from the menu or the left icon at the bottom of the palette. A snapshot is created by the righthand icon, or chosen from the menu.

There are two History Options: the number of undos (up to 99) and Allow Non-Linear History. With this last item set, clicking back to an earlier stage does not delete the intervening stages. This means that with certain limitations the history brush can paint from these ignored steps. With the non-linear function unset, History can be simply considered as a multiple undo.

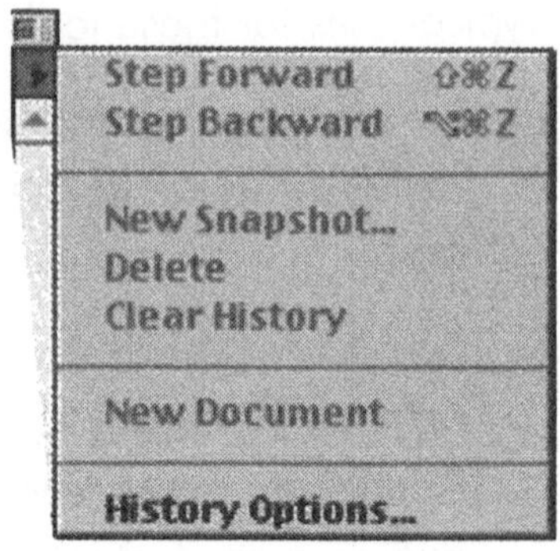

Step back a state at a time by using Command/Ctrl + Option/Alt+Z.

Step forward again with Shift +Command/Ctrl +Option/Alt+Z.

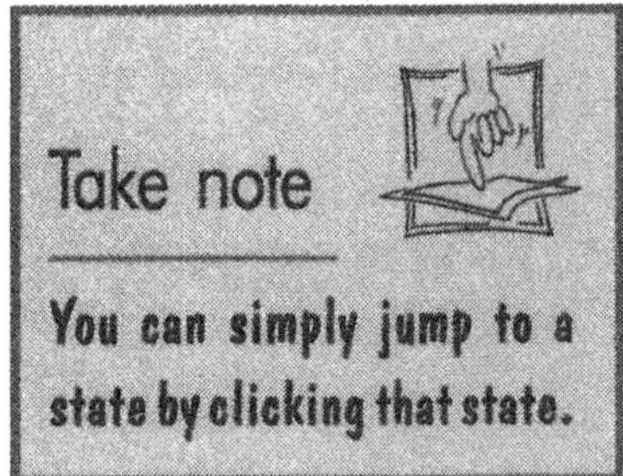

Take note
You can simply jump to a state by clicking that state.

Memory a problem?
Set a low Maximum States value and leave the box 'Automatically create first Snapshot' unchecked unless you need Snapshots

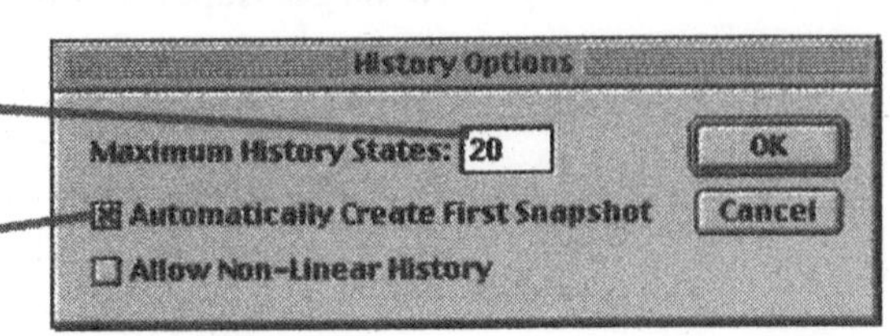

Basic steps

1 Select the History brush.

2 Click the History tab, behind Actions, to bring it to the front.

3 Click left column of State to paint from.

4 Paint the parts you need.

The history brush

The history brush has all the same attributes as for any other painting tool such as Size, Blend mode and Opacity.

Choosing the history brush from the Tools palette, you can paint from that state into your current state, or from any snapshot. The opacity and blend mode options are similar to the paintbrush.

The small pointer is the present state; this can be slid to any position in the list. If you opt to allow non-linear history, you won't lose the intermediate steps when you jump back.

2 Open the History Tab

3 Select the state

Current state

1 Select the History brush

4 Paint as needed

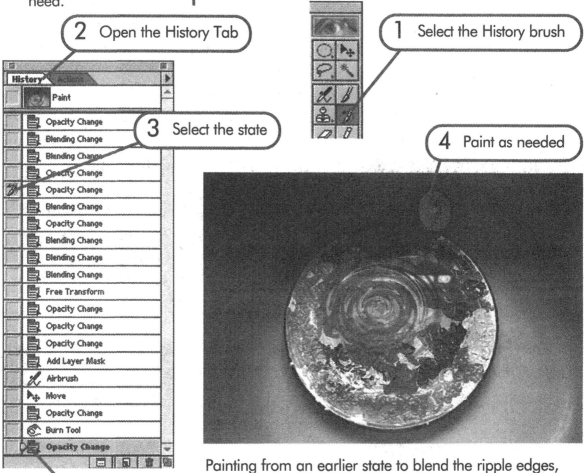

Painting from an earlier state to blend the ripple edges, with non-linear history set, did not lose the states between

Blur/sharpen/smudge

For very small areas of blurring, sharpening or smudging these tools are ideal. You can use them freehand or set a track for them using the pen tool, then stroke them along the path.

All three tools act exactly as you expect; the settings are similar to those for the paintbrush, with the option of fingerpainting with the smudge tool.

As you click and drag over the image, it will blur or sharpen according to the blend mode set and the pressure.

Beware the sharpen tool, it is easy to overdo its effect.

The smudge tool pulls the pixel's colour over others as you drag the mouse, using the colour which is underneath at the time. It can be slow, so avoid large brush sizes or large areas. Try to use less than 100% otherwise the end of your stroke will have the original brush area transplanted! The smudge tool can be used to simulate hair, by dragging outwards with a small brush.

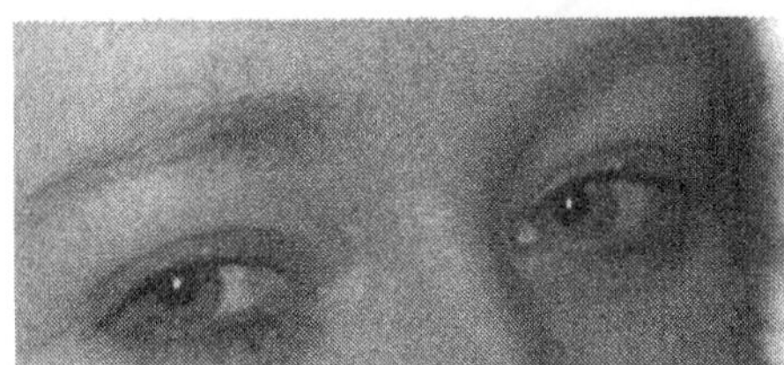

Section of original

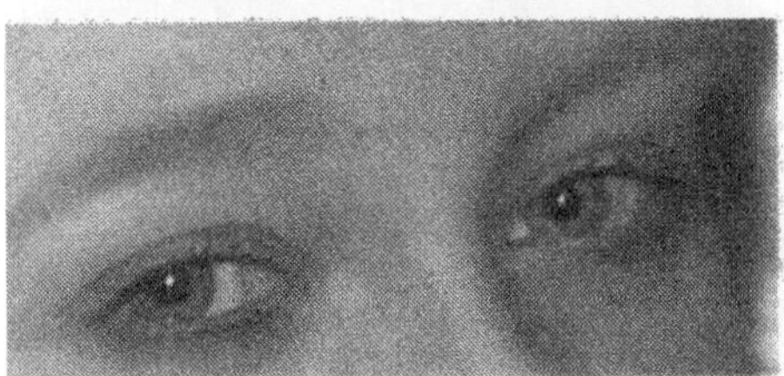

Same section with smudge applied

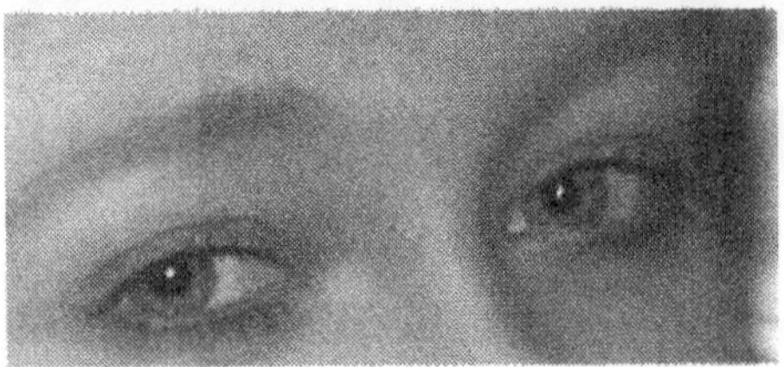

Eyes and brows restored with the history brush

Basic steps

- For skin with too much texture:

1 Set the smudge tool to 50%.

2 Using a large brush size, sweep across the skin areas, avoiding the eyebrows, eyes, etc.

3 Use the history brush to restore detail from main areas - result: skin as soft as a baby's bottom!

Take note

Finger Painting takes the foreground colour as its starting point for the smudge action.

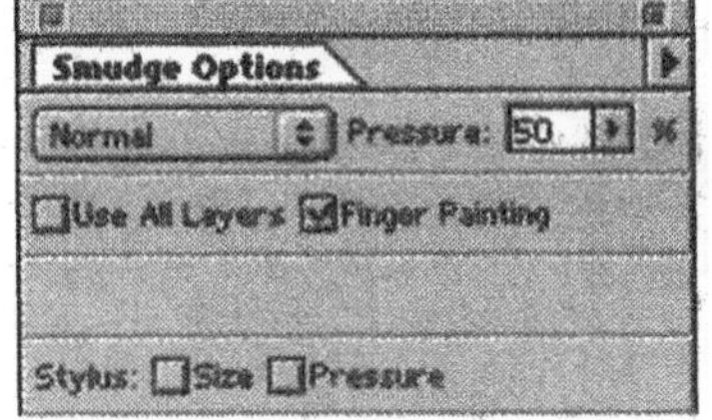

Tip

The blur and smudge tools can sometimes be used to lose spots, in place of the rubber stamp tool.

This will be when the result is more in keeping with a smoother texture.

Tip

Apply a small amount of noise (gaussian, 1 to 5) to smudged or blurred areas (see Noise, page 110).

Look carefully at the texture, and select Filter – Add Noise to match surrounding areas.

If there is a directional feel to it, try using the Filter–Blur–Motion Blur in a similar direction.

Before applying any of these brushes along a path, you must set up the brush and its properties. Create the path to the shape you need to follow, and go to the Paths palette to select Stroke Path/Subpath.

It is always easier to create a path with the Rubber Band box checked, so you can see where the path is, but if you want to end it without coming back to the beginning, it is annoying to be followed around the screen with this hanging off! To avoid this, when you have the path as long as is needed, just click once on the pen tool icon in the Tools palette to break the connection. It is now a subpath.

Use a Subpath to blur/sharpen just one part of an edge (this could be the image itself or on a layer mask edge).

If, when doing this you have too abrupt a beginning or end, then set the history brush back to just before this stage, and with a larger/softer brush just take back the ends.

Lastly, there is yet one more way in which you can extend your control over what you have done. If you go to the top of the Filter menu you can Fade the last effect you applied, and change the blend Mode.

The term Fade is used in two ways within Photoshop. One way is as decribed here, where you are reducing the effect you have just applied – this is found in the Filter menu. The other is where you set a brush to fade out over so many pixels as you use the tool – this is set in the tool's Options palette. (Pixel is short for picture cell, the smallest dot making up your image.)

Brushes

Basic steps

The characteristics of all the painting tools are set within the Brushes palette: these include size, shape, softness, opacity and blending mode. You can extend the range of brushes by the modification of existing brushes, or the creation or loading of new ones.

You can double-click an existing brush to edit it, or a blank cell at the bottom of the palette, or go to New Brush... from the menu triangle. Once created, they appear in the palette.

Their properties are set in Brush Options.

1. Either double-click on the brush icon, or go to Brush Options, via the triangle top right.
2. Set the values to define size, edge and angle of the brush.
3. Use the handles around the compass image to roate or reshape the brush.
4. Click OK.

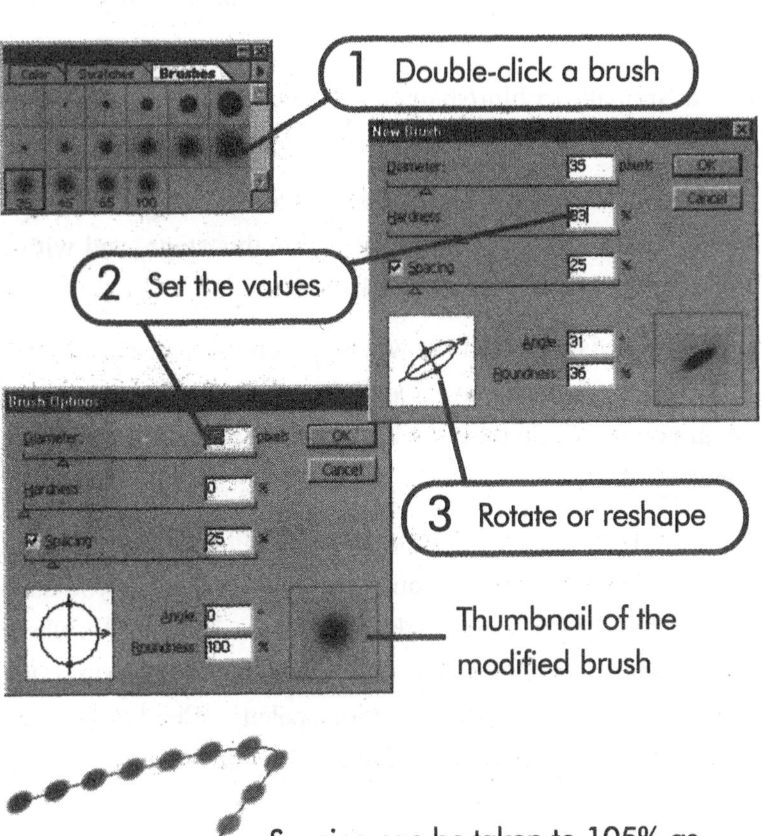

Spacing can be taken to 105% as here, and fade along the length

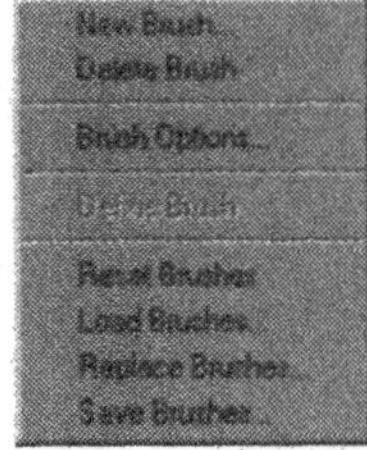

The definitions for a set of brushes can be saved, and reloaded later, via the menu

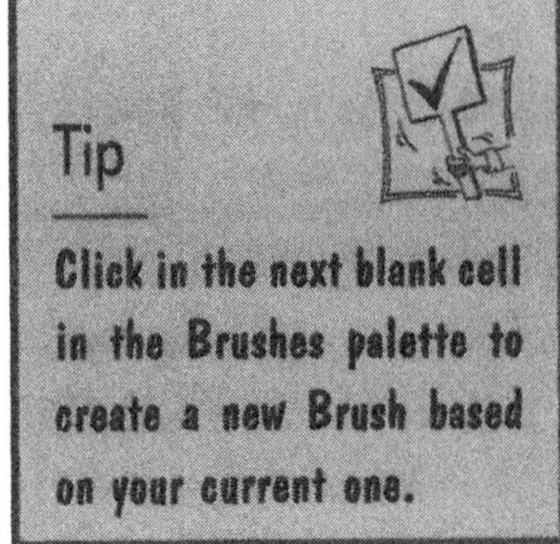

Tip

Click in the next blank cell in the Brushes palette to create a new Brush based on your current one.

Basic steps

1 Create your new brush shape as a black/ grayscale shape on a white background.

2 Select it and go to the top right triangle in the Brushes palette, and choose Define Brush. It will occupy the next available cell at the bottom of the table.

3 Select your new brush and paint your stars; or whatever shape you have drawn.

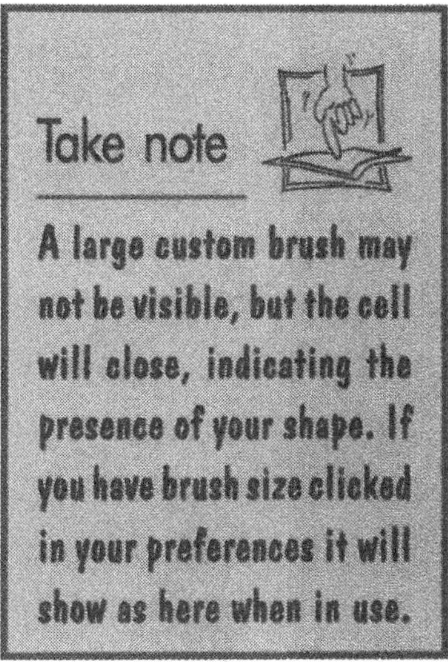

Take note

A large custom brush may not be visible, but the cell will close, indicating the presence of your shape. If you have brush size clicked in your preferences it will show as here when in use.

Custom brushes

The Photoshop CD contains a folder of alternative brushes that you can load,but it is fairly simple to create your own. The example here shows how you do it for a star shape.

Custom brushes once created, appear in the standard palette. They are made from any greyscale image where the background is white and the brush shape is defined by all pixels beyond 50% opacity. Maximum size is 1000-pixels square.

Custom brushes can be used to create patterns that can be spaced along a brushstroke where the spacing has been increased from the default of 25% so they no longer overlap. You can create a border this way.

The starting point for the star could either be a vector program or paths within Photoshop. Use these to create the greyscale brush. You could even scan in a contrasty star shape.

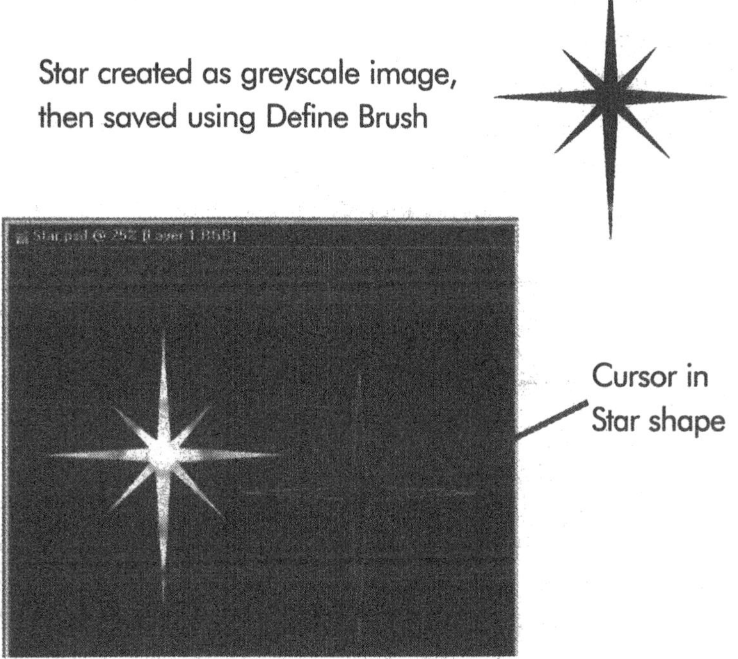

Star created as greyscale image, then saved using Define Brush

Cursor in Star shape

Star painted with white as the foreground colour

Pencil/line/paintbucket

The **pencil** tool is left over from the earliest days of computer painting with block graphics. It is really only ideal for the creation and modification of Icons. It has an Auto Erase function, which sets whether it starts in foreground or background colour; retaining it till you lift off. Due to its inherent speed, it does possess more subtlety with the latest pressure-sensitive pens.

The line tool is best for dimensioning and creating arrows, since all the tools are capable of drawing straight lines by clicking once, then holding down the Shift key and clicking again to draw a line directly between the two points. It is best to check the Anti-Alias box to avoid 'Jaggies' - the nasty stepped look.

The paintbucket is for flood-filling enclosed areas with flat colour, and comes into its own when creating masks or for creating cartoon images, as in the example. Before using the Paintbucket, check that the area is closed. If the boundary lacks contrast, the fill may 'leak'. Lowering the tolerance can help in such cases in the same way you might when using the magic wand tool. This tool is really just that; the magic wand followed by a Fill with foreground colour.

Basic steps

1 Draw the outlines with the pencil tool.

or

2 Scan in a sketch and open it in Photoshop, changing to RGB.

3 Select the paintbucket.

4 In the tool's Options, set Tolerance to 20.

5 Select colours by Option/Alt clicking from Swatches.

6 Click in each area to add colour.

7 Model with dodge and burn tools.

Take note

Anti-alias is the term used to describe the averaging of tones at hard edges to give smoothness.

Custom colours

You can choose colours:

- From the swatches at the bottom of the Toolbox
- In the Color palette
- In Swatches table
- Sampled from open Photoshop images

At the bottom of the Tools palette are two swatches; one overlaying the other. These are the foreground and background colours. Click in either to reach the Color Picker, allowing several different selection methods.

Numerous radio-buttons offer different ways to view colours. The Custom button takes you into several proprietary colour palettes, Pantone for one. Type your desired number while this palette is open and the colour will be displayed highlighted in the scrolling list. Choose Picker to return to the default Adobe Colour Picker.

Selected colour

Gamut warning

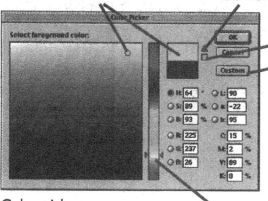

Closest in Gamut colour

Click to open the Custom colors dialog box

Color picker

Hue slider

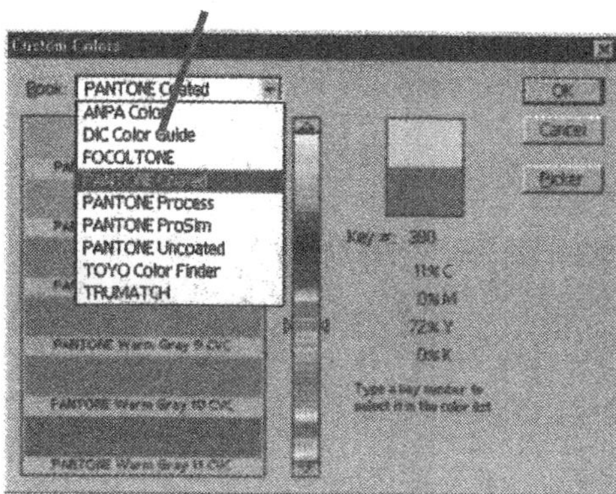

Custom colours (Pantone)

Take note

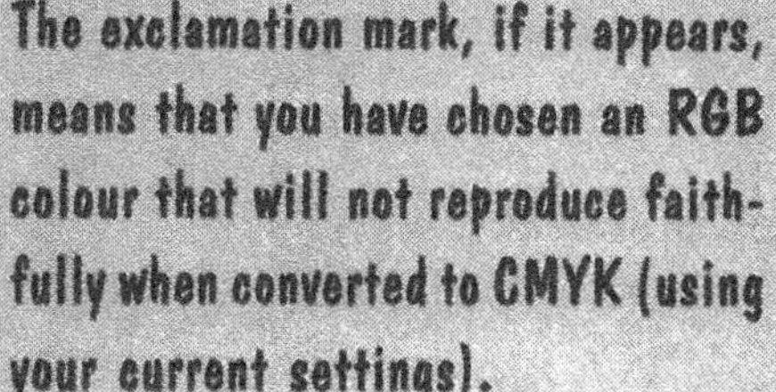

The exclamation mark, if it appears, means that you have chosen an RGB colour that will not reproduce faithfully when converted to CMYK (using your current settings).

Tip

When using spot colours, choose from Custom in the default Picker after clicking the Foreground swatch in the tools palette.

Gradients

Graduations, grads, ramps and vignettes all refer to the ability to fill areas starting at one colour and ending with another – sometimes adding a few more on the way! The simplest is Foreground to Background; all four variants are shown below. Having chosen one, you click to start and drag to where you wish to finish, and lift off. The gradient follows the direction.

A pulldown in Options has a choice of preset colours, but there is a nested dialog for fully editing the gradients in that box. Like any Fill you can also alter the opacity and blend modes.

Gradients can be applied in channels to give graded masks, as well as on layers, within selected areas, or overall. By starting and finishing slightly within your area, you keep a proportion of the full colours.

The midpoint can be moved away from centre, and when a gradient is within a channel, you can even apply curves to give more control (this is beyond the scope of this book).

Your first click and the lift-off define the start and end. Up to the click and beyond the lift remain 100% of your start and finish colours, in the direction of your dragged line.

Gradient variants

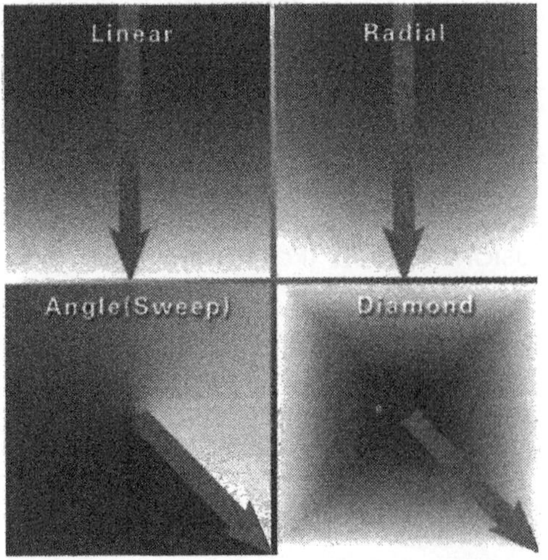

Single head arrows show the cursor's path

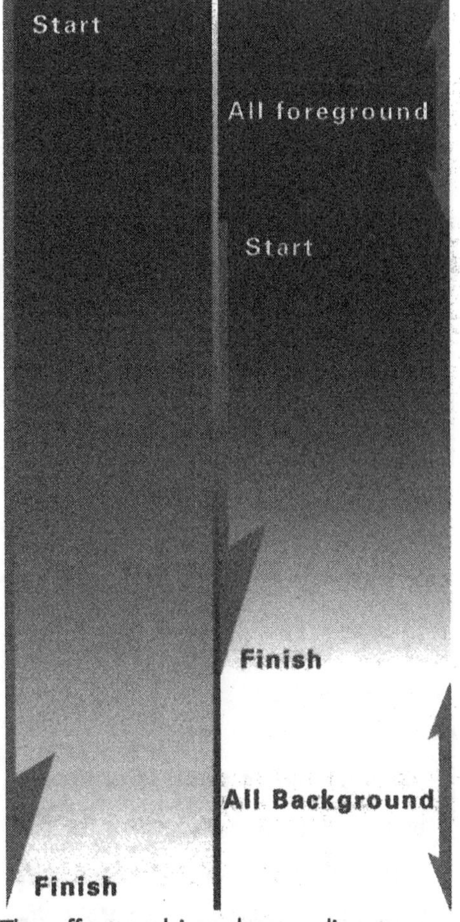

The effects achieved according to your start and finish points

Blend modes

After Normal, the most useful modes are Multiply, Screen, Lighten, Darken and Color.

Take note

The full technical description for each blend mode is provided in the User Guide, pages 205-207, with colour pictures on page 234.

When painting, filling or compositing one can apply in several modes (as shown on the left). Normal is self-evident.

Dissolve Breaks up the transition randomly, must be less than 100% to have an effect.

Multiply Accentuates the shadows and midtones, darkens

Screen Accentuates the midtones and burns out highlights, lightens

Overlay Modelling is maintained, colours merge

Soft Light At 50% and above lightens; below 50% darkens, subtly

Hard Light At 50% and above screens; below 50% multiplies, harsher

Color Dodge Brightens the colours

Color Burn Darkens the colours

Lighten Lightens darker colours and modelling

Darken Darkens lighter colours and modelling

Difference Tends to make a negative image

Exclusion Tends to make a negative image, but flatter

Hue Colours with blend colour, retains modelling

Saturation Affects the base image, only in the saturation

Color Maintains original modelling with new colour

Luminosity Retains original colour but modelling is from the blend colour

When using the line, paintbucket and stroke there are also **Clear** and **Behind**.

Summary

- If you need smooth tones, use the airbrush or paintbrush; if you need texture, use the rubber stamp or pattern stamp tools.
- Using a brush at 100 Opacity,will work faster than when set at less, or with a softer edge.
- To change the softness of the brush edge, double-click the brush-size cell, or make a new one by double-clicking at the end or choosing New Brush in the Options. Adjust the Hardness slider to suit.
- To swap between using the dodge and burn tools, temporarily hold the Option/Alt key. The action will change, but the icon in the Tools palette will not.
- The default number of states in History is 20, You can choose any number between 1 and 99. This will only adversely affect the amount of memory used if you carry out several global changes to the file.
- If you like a particular stage you have reached, click the right icon at the bottom of the History palette to take a Snapshot; it will appear at the top of the History palette above the line. Clicking on the left icon at the bottom makes a new document of that state, which can be saved as a separate file.
- If you need to paint in a straight line, click once at the start, hold down the Shift key and click at the end.
- Hitting X swaps between Foreground and Background. Hitting Q swaps between a selection and QuickMask.
- Choose Multiply as the blend mode when adding a gradation to a sky.

7 Type effects

The type tools

Photoshop is primarily an image editing program, yet with new improved type tools, Photoshop 5.0 provides the kind of flexibility normally only available in vector art drawing applications like Illustrator. They include: type, vertical type, type mask and vertical type mask. Select the type tool and click anywhere in the image window – the cursor changes to an I-beam pointer. There may be a slight delay while the fonts are being loaded, before you see the main dialog window appear.

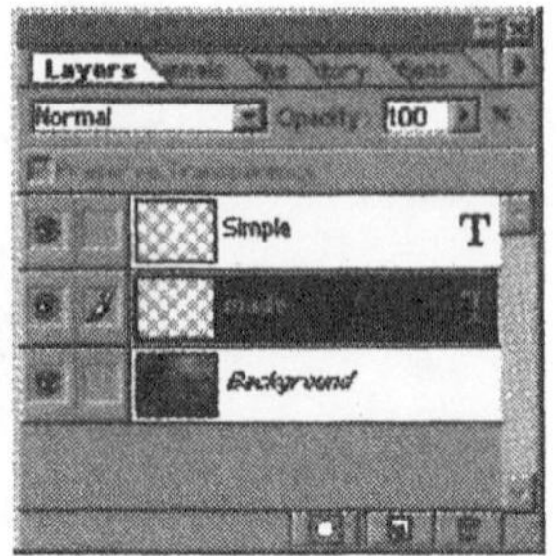

Font

Font style

Alignment

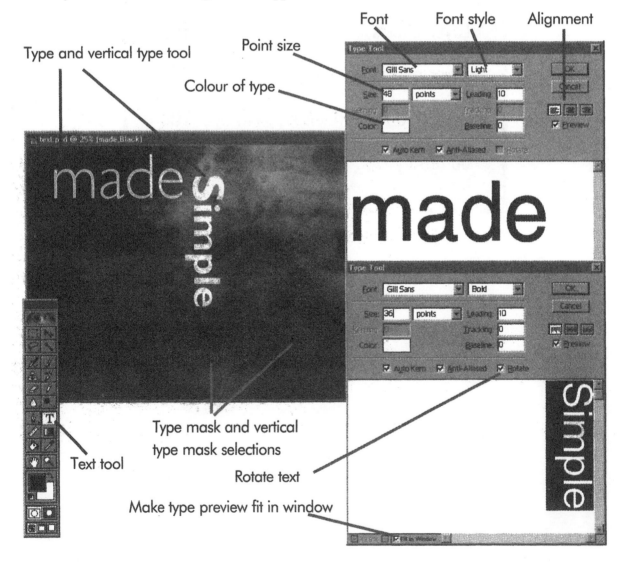

Type and vertical type tool

Point size

Colour of type

Type mask and vertical type mask selections

Text tool

Rotate text

Make type preview fit in window

Type interface

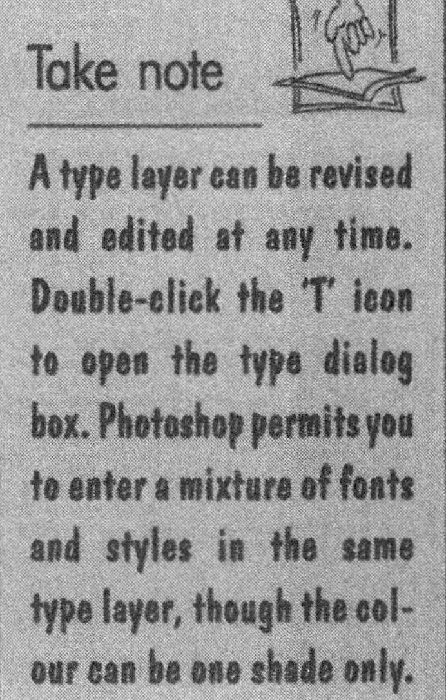

Take note

A type layer can be revised and edited at any time. Double-click the 'T' icon to open the type dialog box. Photoshop permits you to enter a mixture of fonts and styles in the same type layer, though the colour can be one shade only.

Enter text in the main window and drag the cursor over it to highlight it and change any of the text attributes, such as the font, point size or leading. When either of the type tools are used, they create a type layer. These layers are fully editable – the text is stored in vector art form and can be enlarged to any size without the text becoming pixelated. The type mask tools generate a type selection which can be used like any other selection tool.

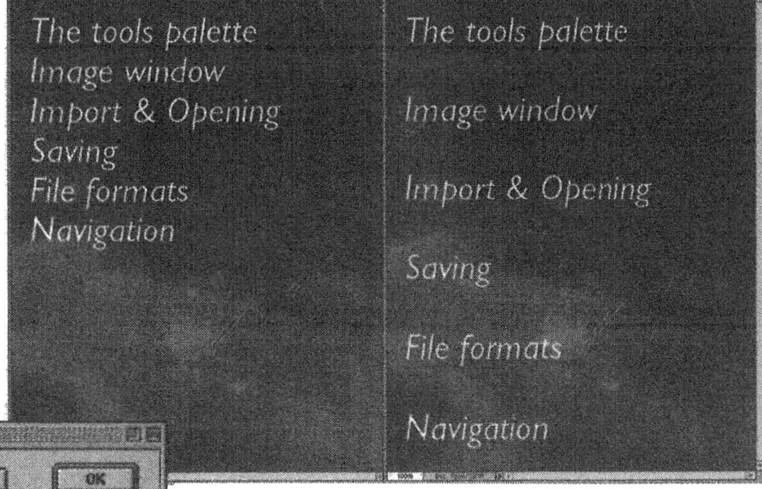

Enter leading

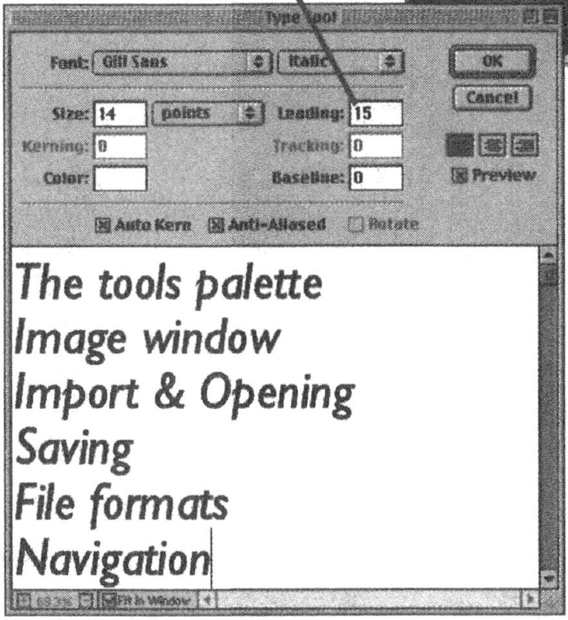

Leading refers to the space between rows of type. For example, in the above illustration, the leading is set to 15 points in the left-hand and 30 points in the right-hand window. Note that when the Fit in Window box is checked, the dialog box type preview will show not the actual size, but a scaled preview of how the text appears in the image.

Layer effects

Layer effects are another new feature found in Photoshop 5.0. Once one had to read up on how to create a drop shadow or emboss effect and manually add the necessary layers. Layer effects now make the process direct and easy for anyone to use. The full range of effects includes: Drop Shadow; Inner Shadow; Outer Glow; Inner Glow; Bevel and Emboss. Leave the preset parameters as they are, though you will probably want to experiment with using different angle settings. While this dialog box is open, you can access any of the other effects from the pop-up menu without having to select an effect via the Layer menu each time.

Basic steps

1. Select Layer – Effects – Bevel and Emboss...
2. Set the Angle (and other parameters) as required and check the Apply box.
3. Try a different layer effects from the pop-up menu.
4. Click OK to close.
5. Double click the *f* which indicates a layer is active, to edit its effects.

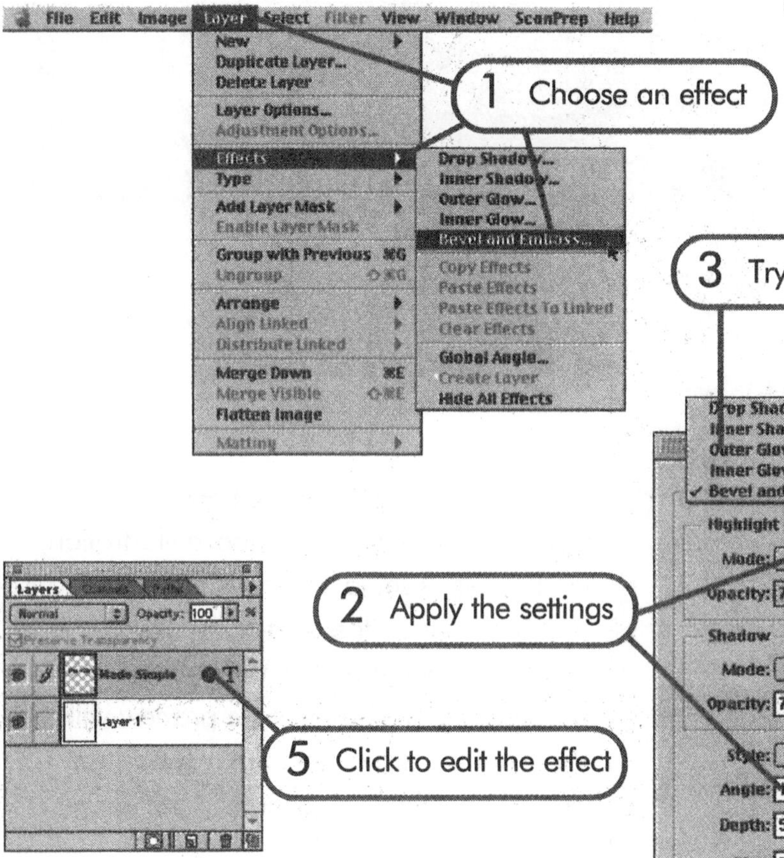

1 Choose an effect

3 Try a different effect

4 Click OK

2 Apply the settings

5 Click to edit the effect

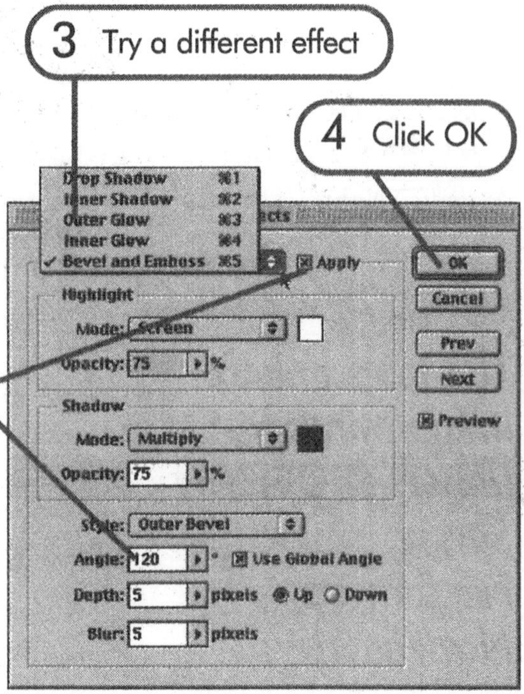

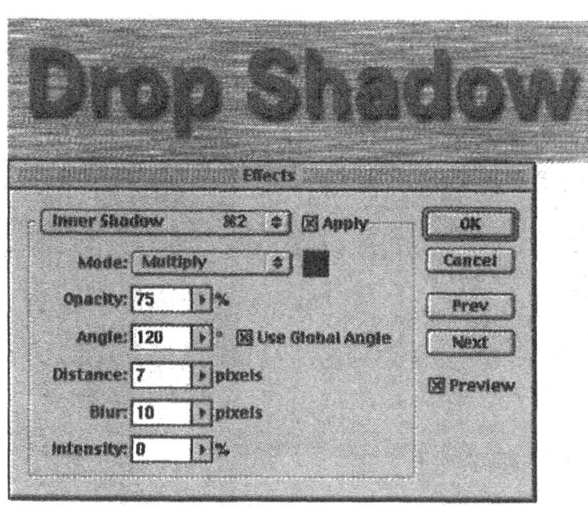
Drop Shadow
Effects
Inner Shadow ⌘2
Apply
OK
Cancel
Prev
Next
Preview
Mode: Multiply
Opacity: 75 %
Angle: 120 ° Use Global Angle
Distance: 7 pixels
Blur: 10 pixels
Intensity: 0 %

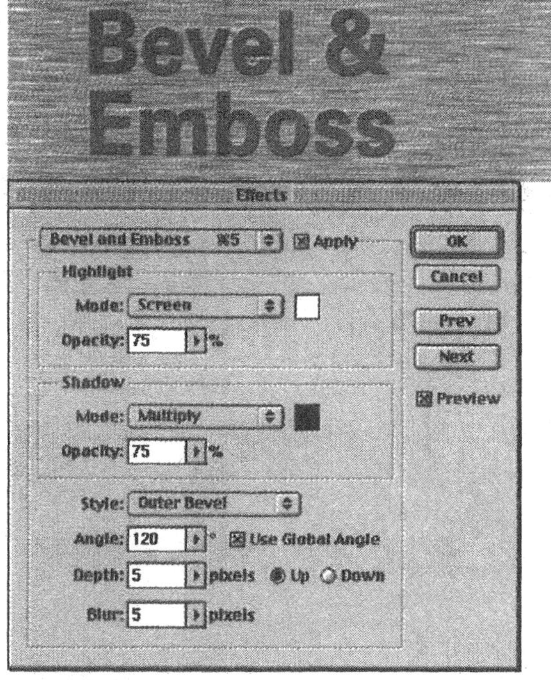
Bevel & Emboss
Effects
Bevel and Emboss ⌘5
Apply
OK
Cancel
Prev
Next
Preview
Highlight
Mode: Screen
Opacity: 75 %
Shadow
Mode: Multiply
Opacity: 75 %
Style: Outer Bevel
Angle: 120 ° Use Global Angle
Depth: 5 pixels Up Down
Blur: 5 pixels

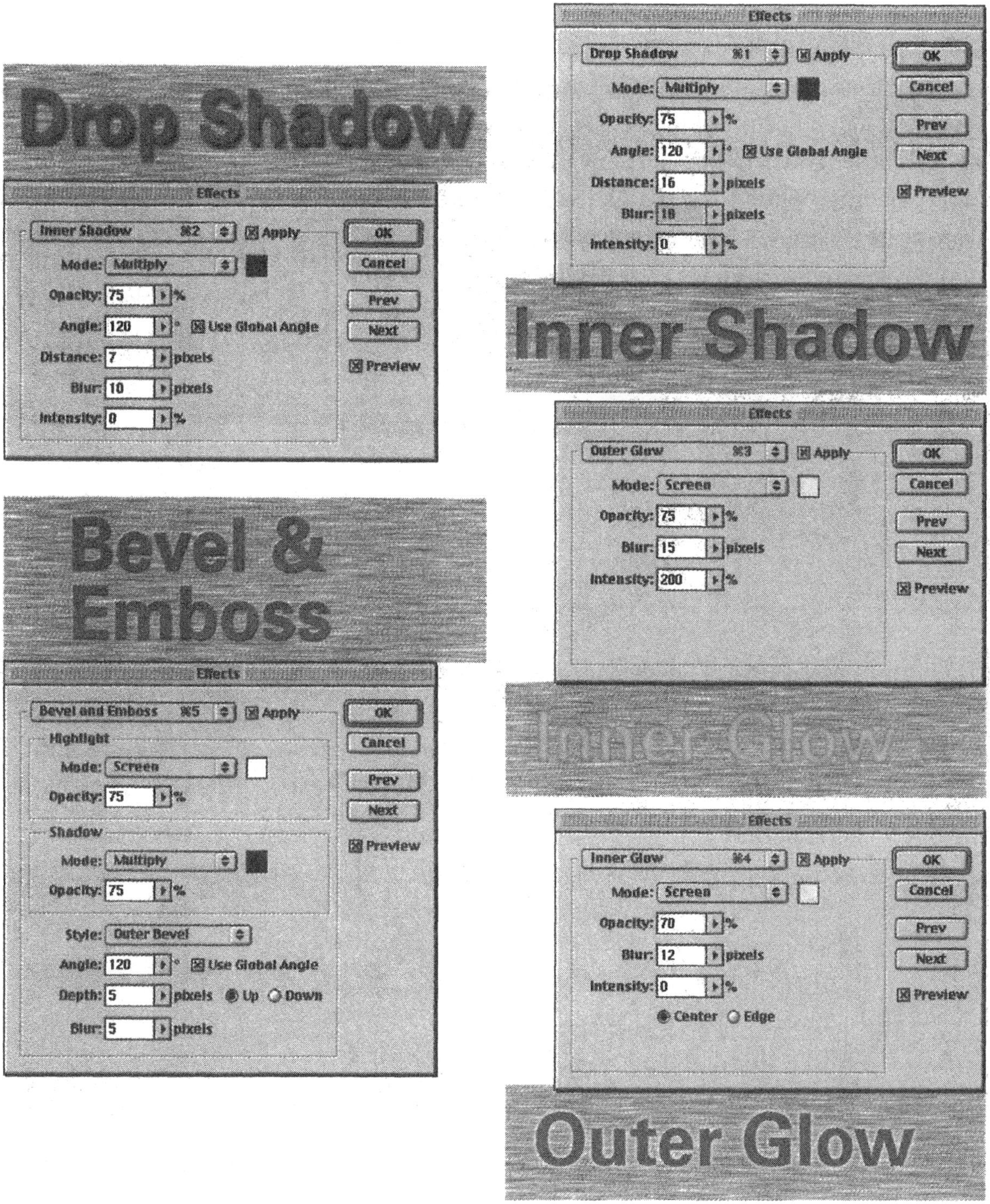

Effects
Drop Shadow ⌘1
Apply
OK
Cancel
Prev
Next
Preview
Mode: Multiply
Opacity: 75 %
Angle: 120 ° Use Global Angle
Distance: 16 pixels
Blur: 10 pixels
Intensity: 0 %
Inner Shadow

Effects
Outer Glow ⌘3
Apply
OK
Cancel
Prev
Next
Preview
Mode: Screen
Opacity: 75 %
Blur: 15 pixels
Intensity: 200 %
Inner Glow

Effects
Inner Glow ⌘4
Apply
OK
Cancel
Prev
Next
Preview
Mode: Screen
Opacity: 70 %
Blur: 12 pixels
Intensity: 0 %
Center Edge
Outer Glow

Layer effects on images

Basic steps

While this chapter discusses the application of layer effects to type layers, you can in fact, apply layer effects to an image layer too. The method used is exactly the same. Just as text layer effects are fully editable and follow any changes you make to the text, there are interesting possibilities to be found when editing an image which has a layer effect applied to it. In the example on this page, a layer mask has been added and when you erase the layer contents the layer effects will adapt to follow the new outline shape.

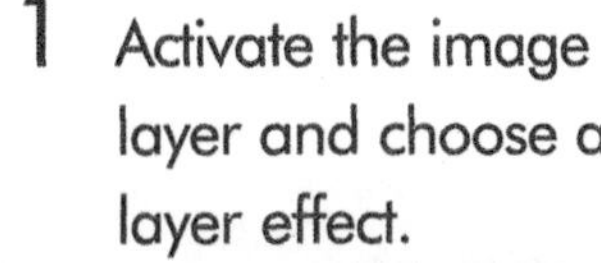

1 Activate the image layer and choose a layer effect.

2 Click the add layer mask button in the layers palette and select a brush tool.

3 Paint with black in the layer mask to mask out portions of the image layer.

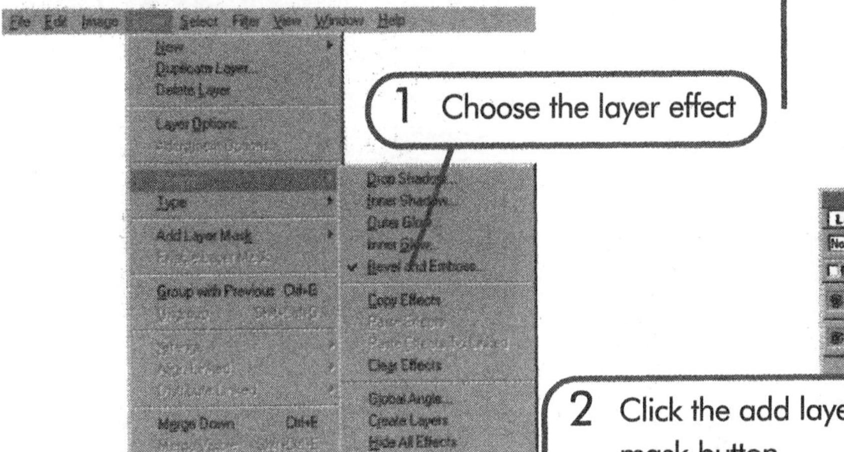
1 Choose the layer effect
2 Click the add layer mask button

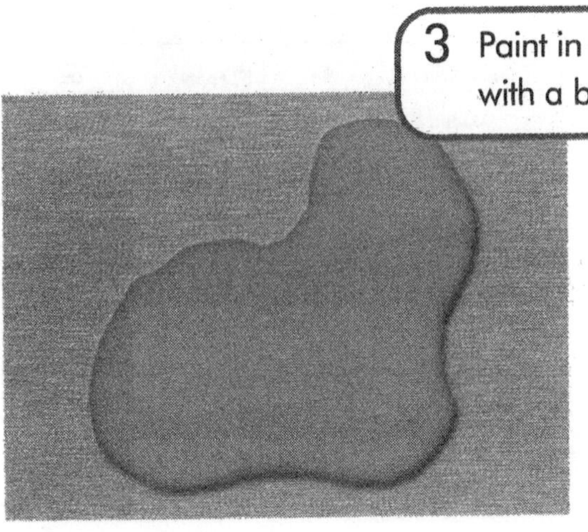
3 Paint in the layer mask with a black brush

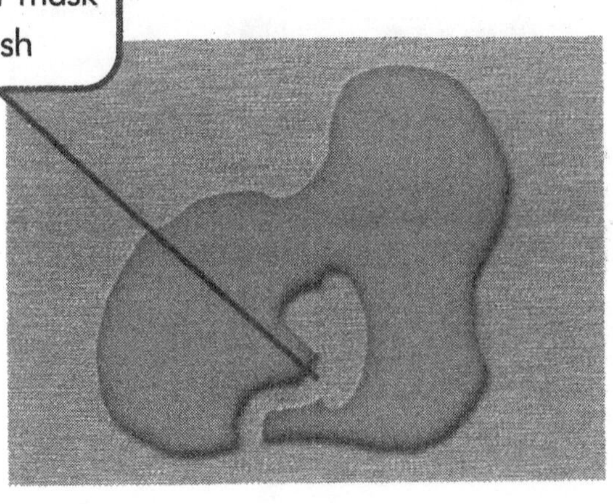

Textured text

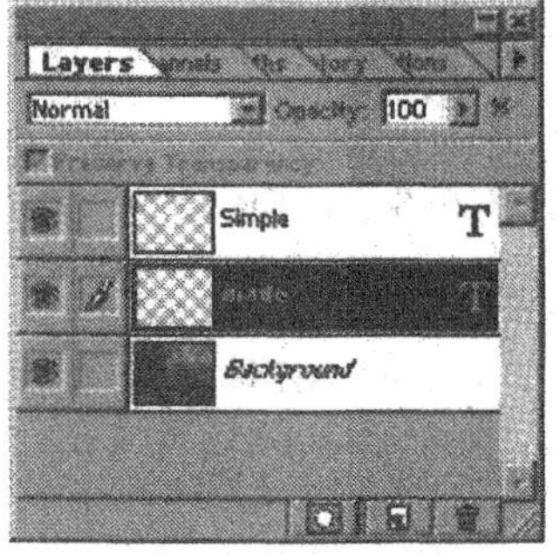

Layer clipping groups were described earlier in chapter 5. Clipping groups form the basis of a little known technique for adding texture to text in Photoshop. If you have two layers and Option/Alt click on the divide between them, the uppermost layer will always be masked by the underneath layer's contents. Therefore, if you place an image texture layer above a type layer and create a clipping group, it will mask the layer above. In the example here, we have a textured background, a type layer and above that another texture layer (incidentally, the texture was created using the Kai's Power Tools 3 plug-in). The type layer also has some layer effects applied to it. The beauty of this setup, is that in Photoshop 5.0, you can change text content or font, point size etc. and the layer effects and texture will adjust to match the new type layer contents.

Tip

You can deconstruct a layer effect using the Create Layers option in the Layer menu. This command will convert the layer effect into actual image layers. Once done, the image layers are rendered and fixed. The effect can no longer be edited as before.

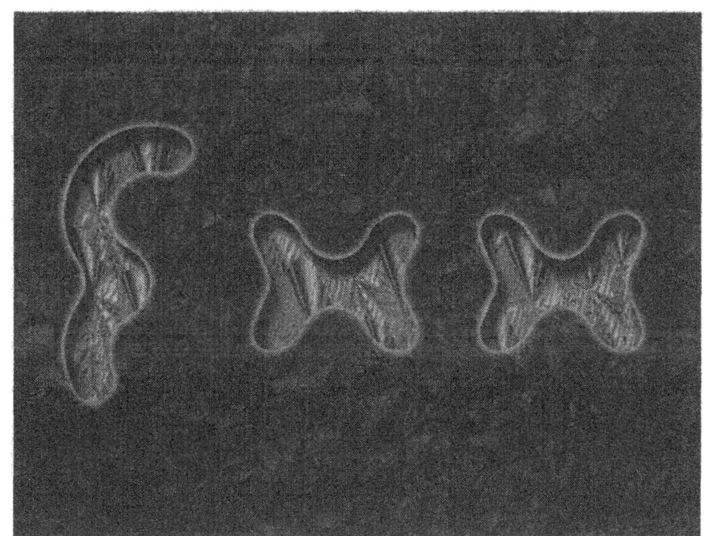

The above text effect was created by adding a texture image layer above the text layer and creating a clipping group. This masked the top texture layer with the text.

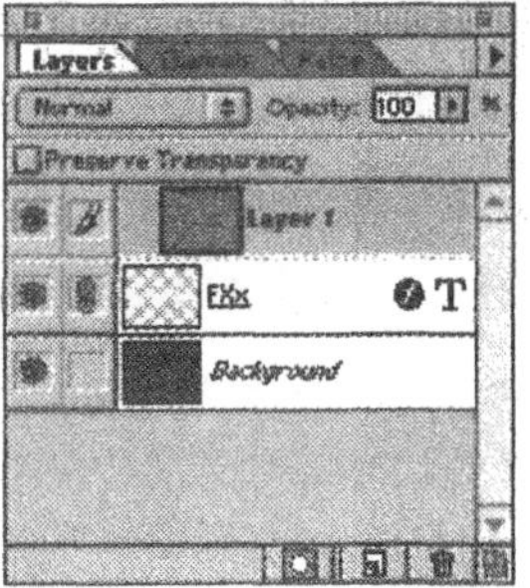

Spot colour channels

Basic steps

Spot colours are used when it is important that the printed colour conforms to a known standard and for the printing of small type (below 24 point) and graphics in colour. A four-colour process mix can be used when printing larger non-serif point sizes, but not for fine type and lines as the slightest mis-registration will make the edges appear fuzzy. Spot colours can be added to images as part of the graphic design or as a means of accomplishing a colour not available in the CMYK gamut, like metallic 'specials'.

1. Choose New Spot Channel.
2. Click on the Color box.
3. Choose from the installed custom colours.
4. Back in the New Spot Channel dialog, enter a solidity percentage to match the solidity of the custom color (in this case, 100% – see Tip).

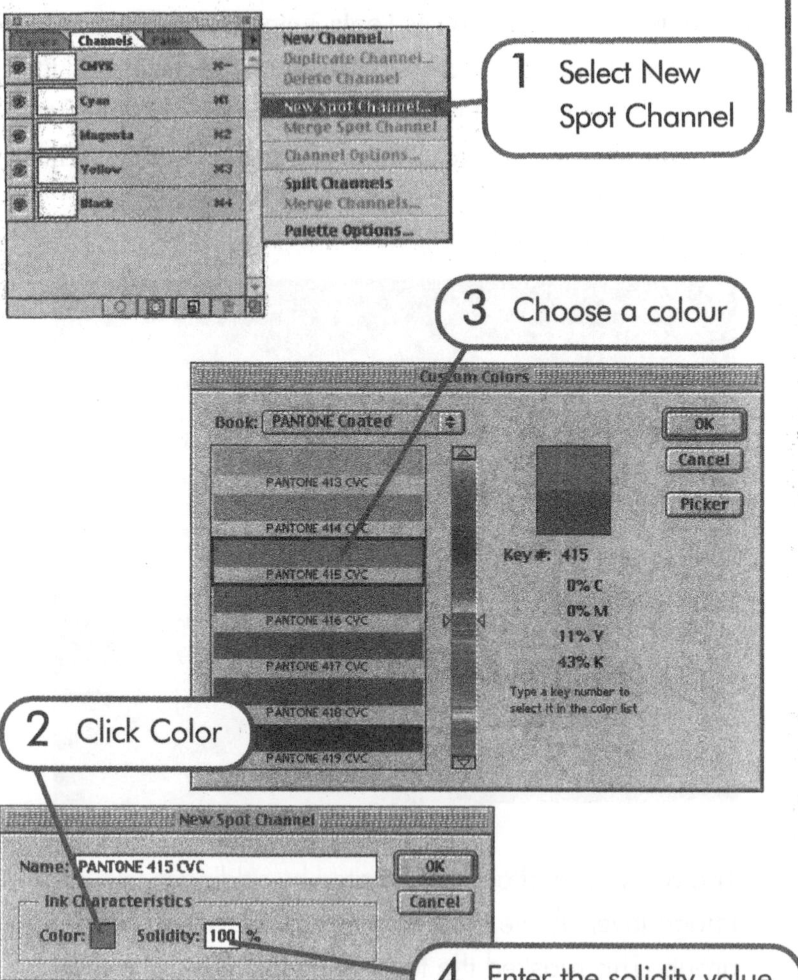

Tip

When you change the solidity of the custom color, the effect is simulated in the image preview, matching the ink characteristics. Most custom colours are opaque (100%), whilst varnish colours are translucent. To produce a faint tint, lower the opacity in the spot channel.

5 With the new spot channel active, select the type selection tool, enter text and fill with black.

6 Use Image – Adjust – Brightness command (or Levels) to adjust spot colour tint opacity.

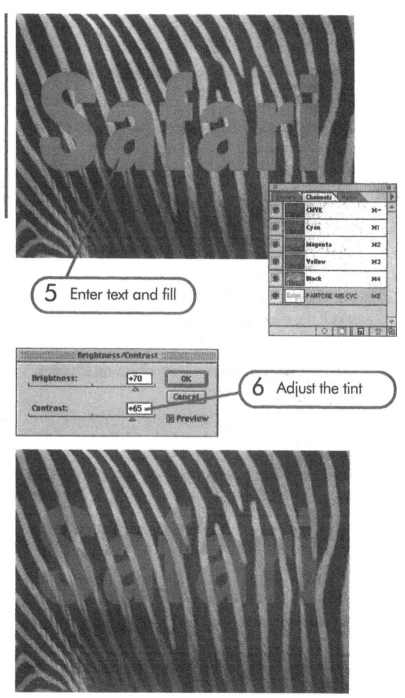

5 Enter text and fill

6 Adjust the tint

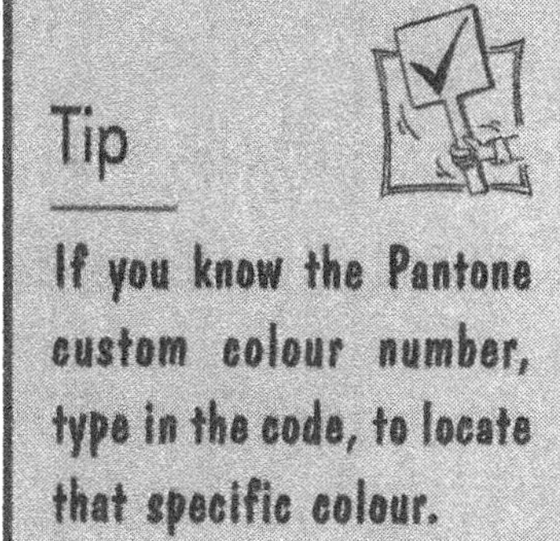

Tip

If you know the Pantone custom colour number, type in the code, to locate that specific colour.

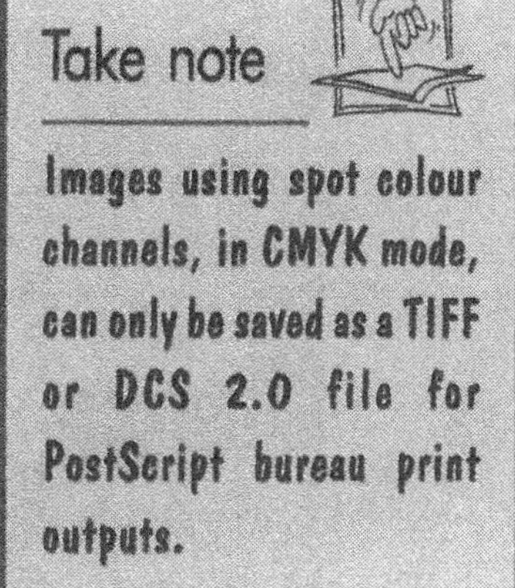

Take note

Images using spot colour channels, in CMYK mode, can only be saved as a TIFF or DCS 2.0 file for PostScript bureau print outputs.

Finished image preview with spot channel

Summary

- Type added using the new type tool in Photoshop 5, is fully editable.
- Type can be set vertically or horizontally and either as type layers or as a type selection.
- The type attributes like font and point size, etc. can all be set in the type tool dialog box and can be revised at any time.
- Layer effects automate the process of adding effects like Drop Shadow, Inner Shadow, Outer Glow, Inner Glow, Bevel and Emboss. Like type layers, layer effects are fully editable.
- Layer effects can be applied to image layers. When applied, the effect will always adapt to follow any revisions to the layer outline.
- Create Layers... renders the layer effects as a layer or group of layers.
- Once rendered, the type and effect layers can no longer be edited as before.
- Textured text can be made by adding a layer clipping group above the type layer.
- Spot colours are used by designers in preference to a process colour mix for fine line graphics and small point size type.
- Type added to a Spot colour channel is always added as a type selection only.

8 Graphic Effects

Blur

Basic steps

Blur can be used to make parts of an image stand out. To keep realism, also add Noise.

First isolate the main subject, by whichever selection method seems most appropriate (see Chapter 3), and ideally create a separate layer for the background. The background can then be blurred without affecting the subject.

Each subject will be different, so what happens at the edge is up to you. Here is an example which uses Filter–Blur–Radial Blur, then a touch of Filter–Noise–Add Noise then a lesser amount of radial blur. The idea here is to lessen the impact the canopy has upon the shot and give a greater impression of speed. The figure will remain untouched yet still seem part of the whole.

Blur and noise used together are a powerful way to lose the artificiality of computer work in images.

1 Loosely lasso the figure, coming closer where there are abrupt contrast changes.

2 Use Select – Feather to apply a feather of 15 pixels.

3 Hold down the Command/Ctrl Key + J or use Layer – New – Layer by Copy to create a layer with only the man.

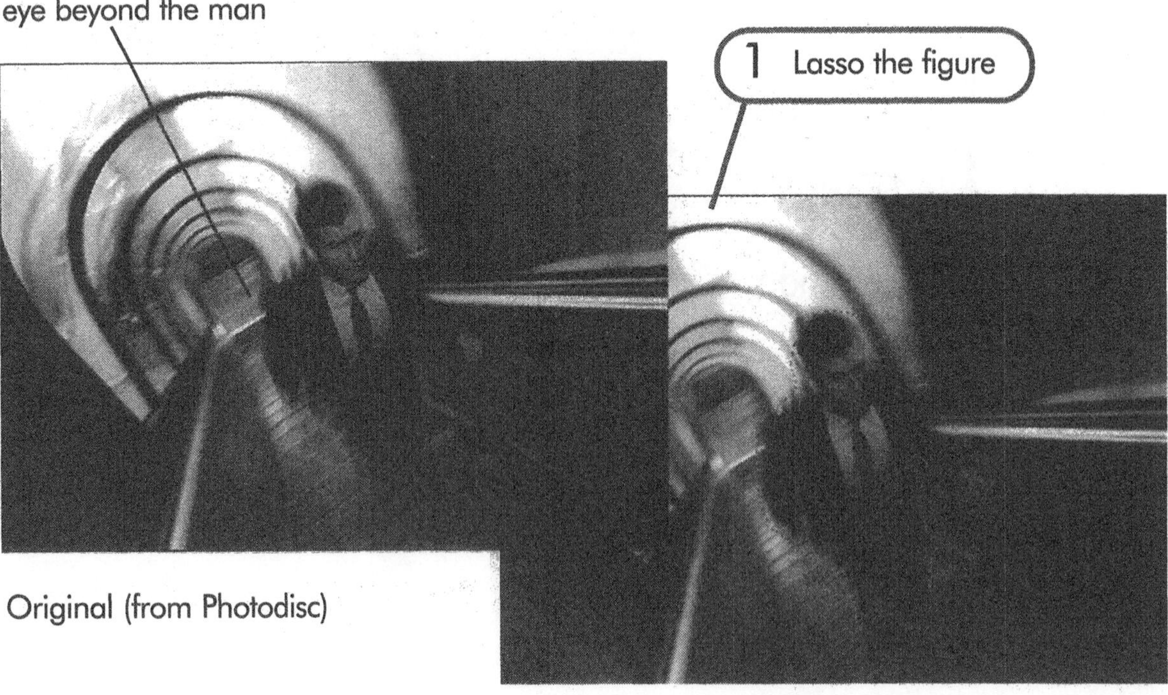

The contrast and repetition draw the eye beyond the man
1 Lasso the figure

Original (from Photodisc)

4 In the Layers palette, select the Background.

5 Use Filter – Blur – Radial Blur, set an amount of 50 and drag the centrepoint to suit the image.

6 Select Zoom and Draft and click OK.

7 Open the Filter menu and choose Noise–Add Noise, setting the Amount to 15 and the Distribution to Uniform, then click OK.

8 Use Filter – Blur – Radial Blur again and set a new value of 4 to add a zoom effect to the noise.

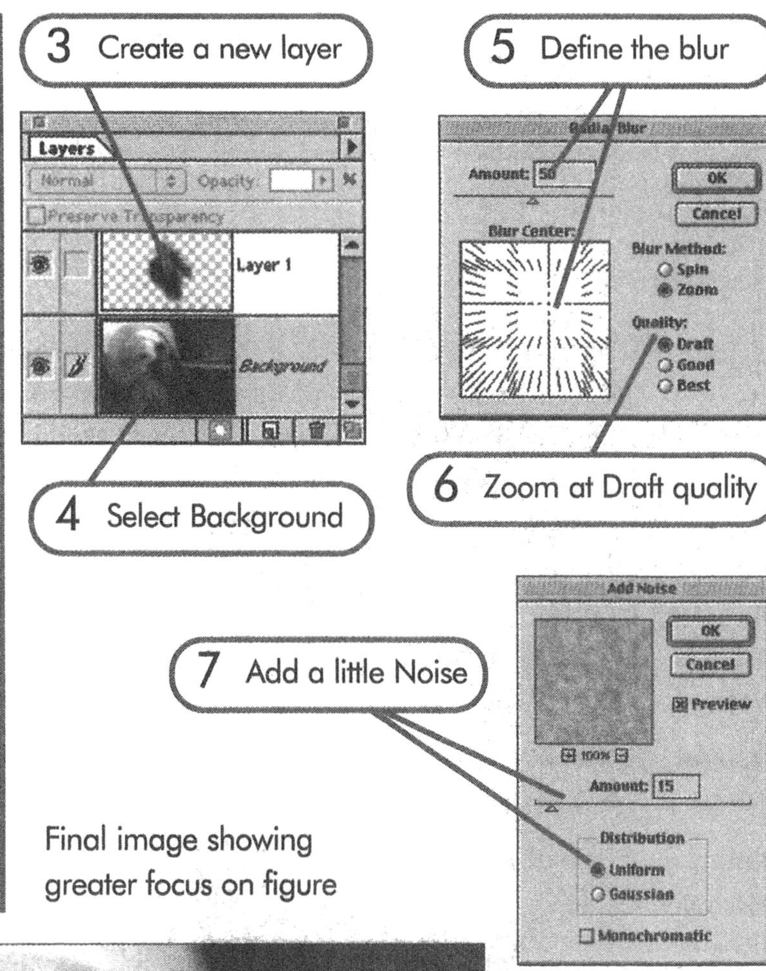

Final image showing greater focus on figure

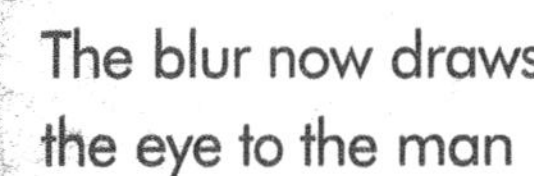

The blur now draws the eye to the man

Sharpen

Here is a button which does as it says. Sophisticated or subtle it is not. If that effect was not enough there is another preset Sharpen More. The advantage of this pair of filters is that they do not ask you to understand what they do, and they are reasonably quick.

Unsharp mask (USM)

To bring out detail from some areas and leave what should be flat areas untouched then use the unsharp mask filter. The name stems from a well-established photographic masking technique which masks the main areas and flattens the contrast there, whilst with an unsharp edge, it opens gaps where all your fine detail is present. The overall contrast is then increased to restore the correct contrast. This means that the edges are all over-enhanced. This technique translates well to computers, but does require some understanding of what is happening.

Amount refers to the amount of extra contrast you put into the fine detail.

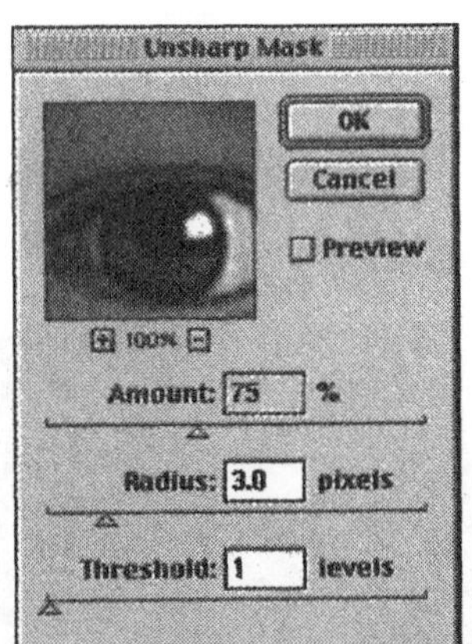

Radius is the size of the gap through which you see the original detail, the larger the radius the bigger the detail can be to be affected.

Threshold controls the starting point; the higher the threshold, the less the blander areas are affected.

The **Preview** checkbox refers to whether you update your image; not the window within the dialog box. To gain speed leave this unchecked.

- ❑ The best way to enhance detail, is to use unsharp masking (USM), also change to Image–Mode–Lab Color mode (Lightness, a and b).
- ❑ Select the lightness channel, and filter only this channel. This will create fewer artefsacts, and should translate well to CMYK.
- ❑ Use USM locally with soft-edged selections, so feather first
- ❑ Leave USM to the end of editing. If sharpening globally, it is best done at the same time as CMYK conversion.

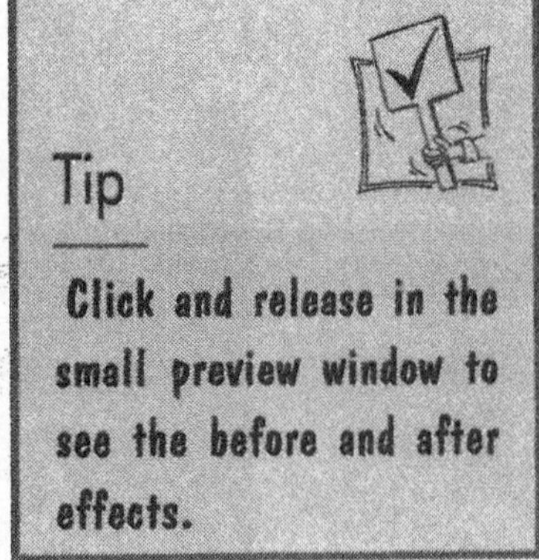

Tip

Click and release in the small preview window to see the before and after effects.

Basic steps

1 Use Filter – Sharpen – Unsharp Mask.

2 Start with an Amount of 75%, Radius of 2 or 3 and a Threshold of 0.

3 Widen the Radius – if artefacts appear in smooth areas, reduce it a little.

4 Balance Amount against Threshold.

Sharpen Edges is the preset version of the real sharpening tool - UnSharp Mask (USM). The Threshold slider allows you to limit the action of this tool to fine detail, but for use in sharpening faces, it is only half the answer.

In a portrait, it is the eyes, eyelashes, teeth and lips which need sharpness, unless you are trying to bring out the hardened leather texture of an old sailor or steelworker. Pictures of children and gorgeous girls or the thirty-something mother need soft skin and bright eyes.

To help this along it is worth isolating the areas that need sharpening with a soft-edged selection before applying the filter, you can then achieve the best of both worlds!

In the example shown the effect has been done overall; note the girl's eyes and the enlarged weave (Threshold=3).

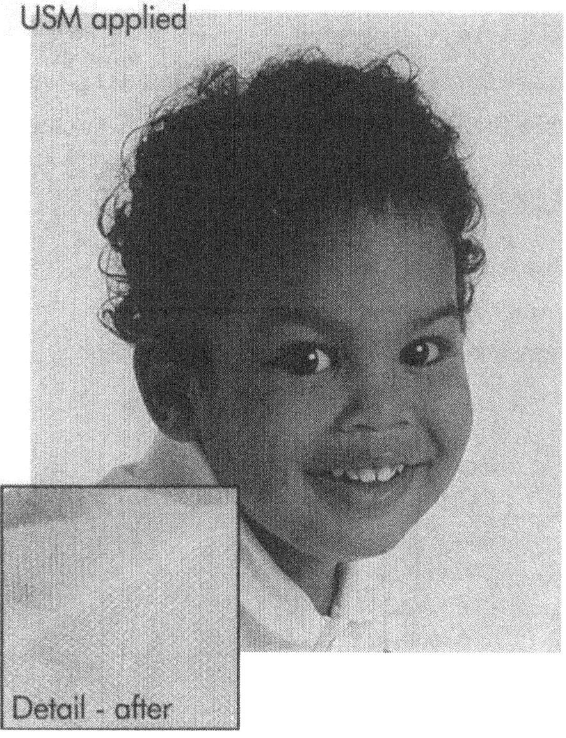

Add Noise filter

In the example on pages 108 to 109, noise was used to give the filter something to blur. Adding noise can improve areas that are too smooth due to overcloning, or painting a flat colour into an area which contained a texture. When adding gradients to photographic images, it becomes almost essential that one adds noise to the colour to avoid banding. This is also true of shadows whose edges have been obtained using soft edge vignettes.

Make the noise match what exists. When trying to blend in a new patch of colour take a look at the differing amounts of natural noise which exist in each channel, then try to simulate this individually.

From a digital camera, a file may show marked noise within the Blue channel, therefore if you are to replace a small patch, look to see what amount of noise is needed. The area may need about 8 in the blue channel, yet only 1 in the red and 2 in the green.

Gaussian distribution is more random than *Uniform*. Use differing amounts in each channel as well as varying the distribution, when simulating natural textures.

Creating a texture

Noise can also be used to create texture, either by itself or by using the Filter–Render–Lighting Effects filter. For example, here's how to create the texture of orange peel.

Tip

Try blurring text to use as the texture Channel. A Texture Channel that has been blurred often helps realism.

Basic steps

1. Use File – New to create a document of, say, 640 x 480 pixels.
2. Click on the Foreground swatch and make a colour, setting Red = 230, Green =160 and B = 75.
3. Use Filter – Noise – Add Noise and set an Amount of 16, with Gaussian Distribution.
4. Duplicate the red channel, then select it in the Channels palette.
5. Select Filter – Blur – Gaussian Blur, at 1.2.
6. Reselect RGB.
7. Open Filter – Render – Lighting Effects and set the new channel as the Texture Channel – this is known as the 'bump map'.
8. Experiment with the parameters and the lighting angle
9. Click OK to finish.

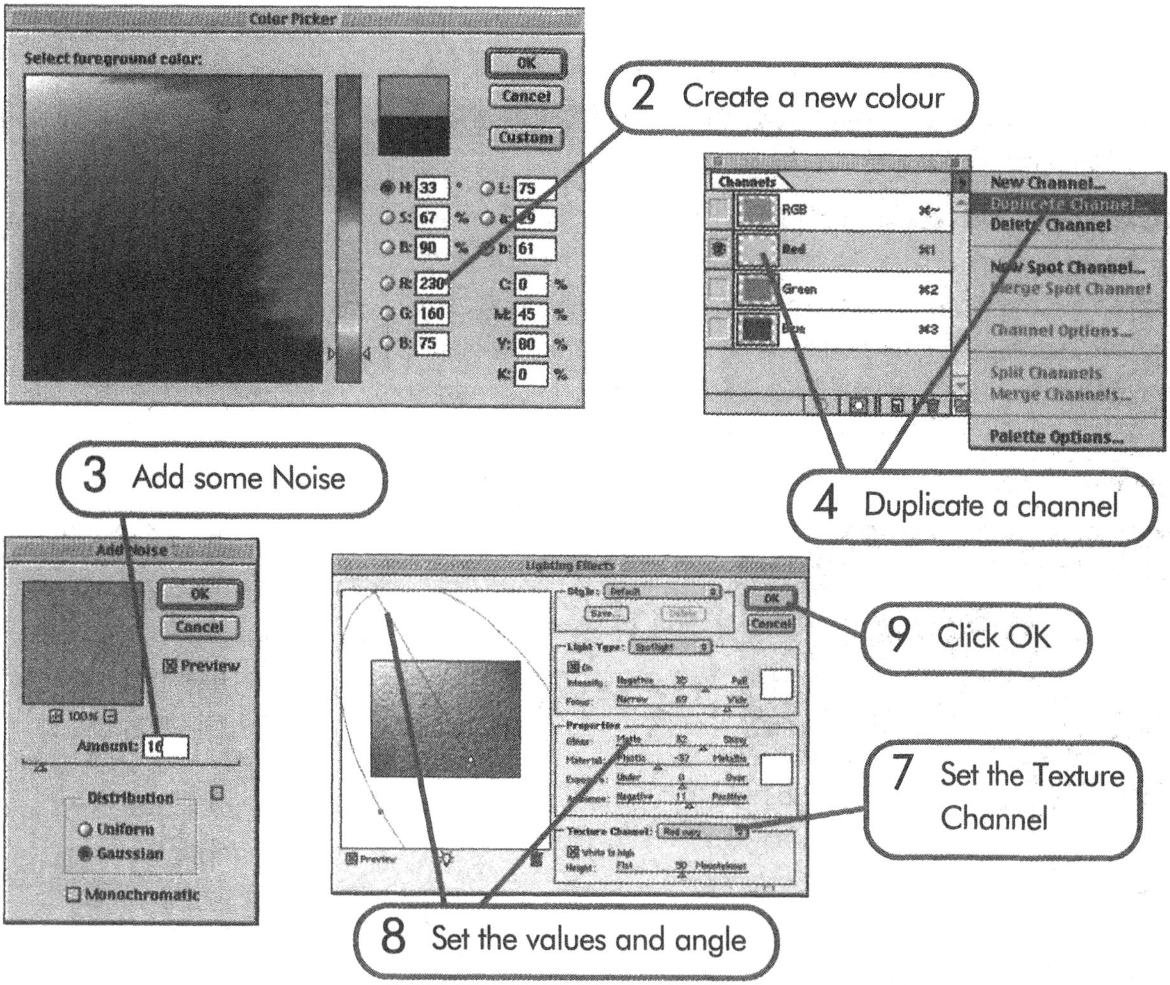

2 Create a new colour

4 Duplicate a channel

3 Add some Noise

9 Click OK

7 Set the Texture Channel

8 Set the values and angle

The final orange peel texture

Take note
Lighting Effects only works in RGB. If you want the same texture but a different colour, choose a new colour and fill with Color blend mode set.

Clouds

Basic steps

The Clouds filter used straight is somewhat unconvincing, but is a good starting point. The way to get the most from it is to understand what is missing. It is a feeling of depth; perspective and the gradient provide this.

The points to remember are: create your sky larger than you need, as it is going to be heavily distorted; try different gradients, and zoom out to give yourself room to manoeuvre. It is worth learning shortcuts such as D to ensure that the background colour is white, and free transform where every option is available via modifier keys. The sky you create can now be used as a background for other images.

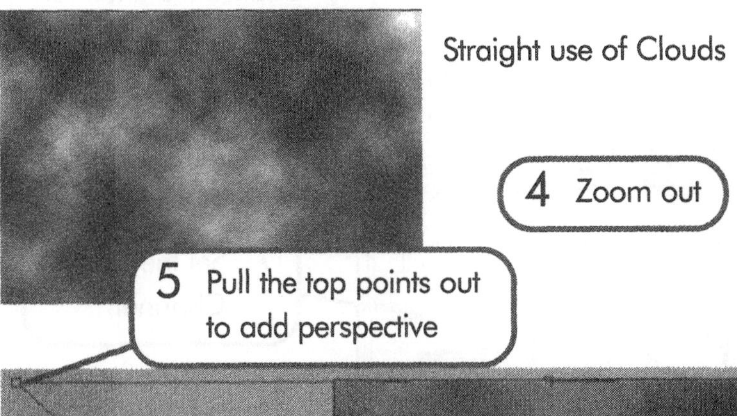

Straight use of Clouds

4 Zoom out

5 Pull the top points out to add perspective

You can now see the reason for starting from a larger file!

6 Set a dark to light gradient

With darker top, and the perspective change, the sky now has depth and looks real.

1 Create an area twice the size needed.

2 Hit D, and choose a sky blue Foreground.

3 Select Filter – Render – Clouds, then Select All.

4 Select Edit – Transform – Perspective, then zoom out.

5 Pull the top points outwards press Enter.

6 Make the foreground colour darker. With the linear gradient tool, the blend mode set to Multiply and opacity at 40%, click and drag from top to bottom.

Basic steps

1. Create a realistic texture, as shown opposite and Select All.
2. Apply Render – Difference Clouds an even number of times – the new pattern should have more complexity.
3. Select Filter – Render – Lighting Effects, and experiment with the settings to create added depth (see page 113).
4. Try changing the overall colour by filling with blend mode set to Color, or more locally by painting with the airbrush in the same mode.

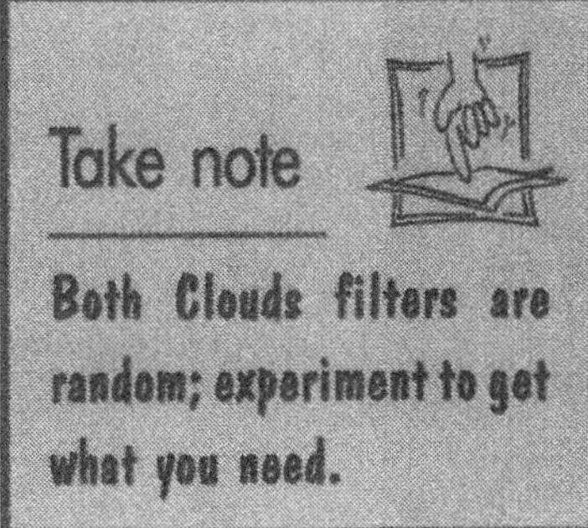

Take note
Both Clouds filters are random; experiment to get what you need.

Clouds as texture

The Clouds filter within the Render menu can be used to render a random pattern when creating textures using any foreground and background colours. As we discussed with noise earlier, you can use this with Lighting Effects to great effect. Provided that the sky or texture is created slightly oversize, it can easily be introduced into another image.

Difference Clouds creates an inverse of the colours set, which can be a good starting point in the creation of a more random effect. Try choosing this item repeatedly: this is of more use when creating textures than cloudy skies.

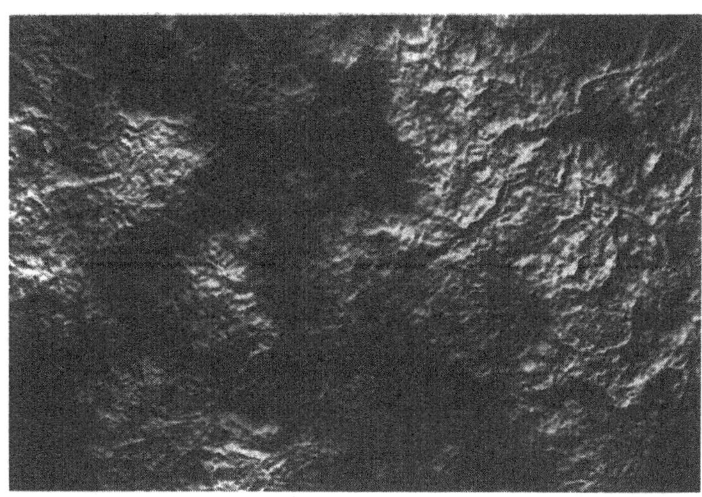

Image created from the sky on the opposite page with four repeats of Difference Clouds and the use of Lighting Effects.

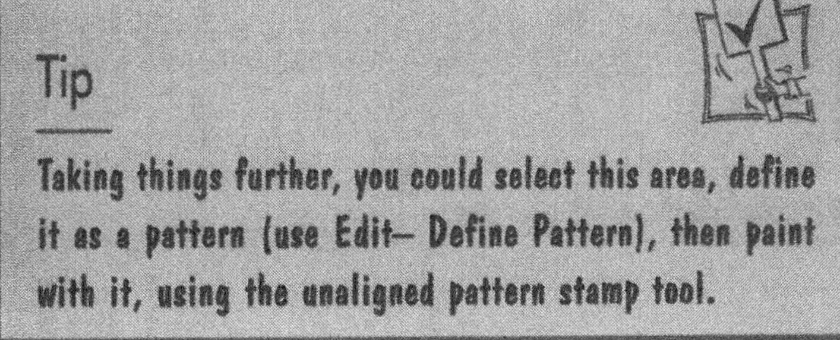

Tip
Taking things further, you could select this area, define it as a pattern (use Edit– Define Pattern), then paint with it, using the unaligned pattern stamp tool.

Zig-Zag

Need a ripple as if a stone had been dropped into a pond, or cream spinning in coffee? This is the filter!

Using the pattern that was created from the clouds filter earlier is a good start as it shows the use of layers as well.

A ripple would overlay the bottom of a pond, yet be made from that view. It is therefore natural to take a soft elliptical selection of the texture to the layer above and rippling only this layer. You now have a ripple which looks as if it is on the surface. To add realism, you can do a perspective distortion (as was shown for the sky) on the background layer to make it look wider in the foreground. This is part of the reason for choosing a large feathered edge.

Basic steps

1 Create a very soft edge to a selection of the background – use Filter – Blur – Gaussian Blur, set at 3 pixels.

2 Deselect and make a new large ellipse Marquee with a 25 pixel feather.

3 Make this into a new layer with Command/ Ctrl+J.

4 Use Filter – Distort – Zig-Zag, setting at 75% and 5 ridges, Around Centre.

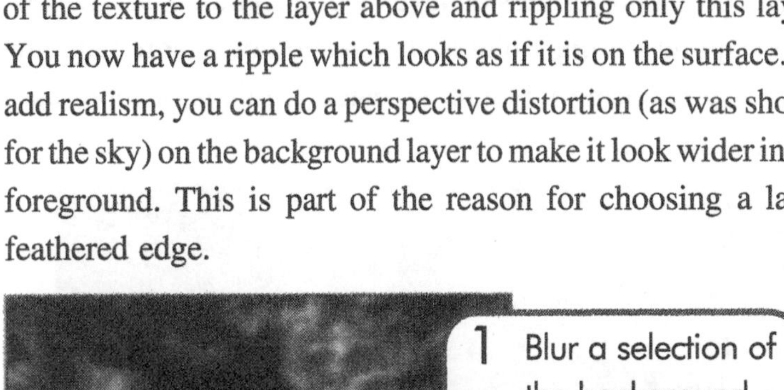

1 Blur a selection of the background

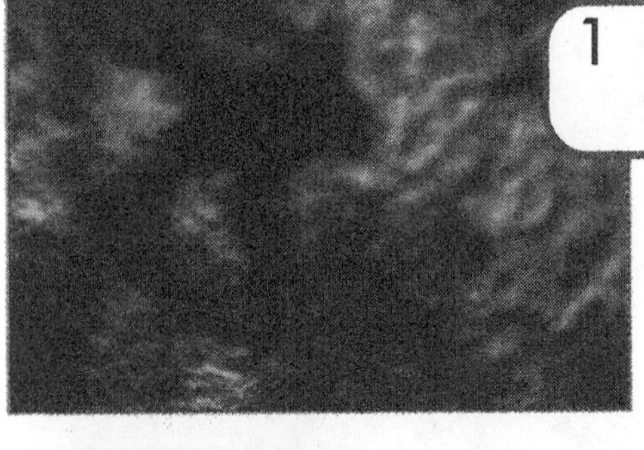

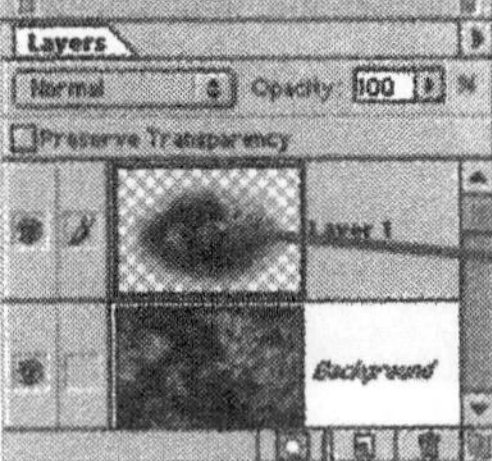

3 Make the ellipse into a layer

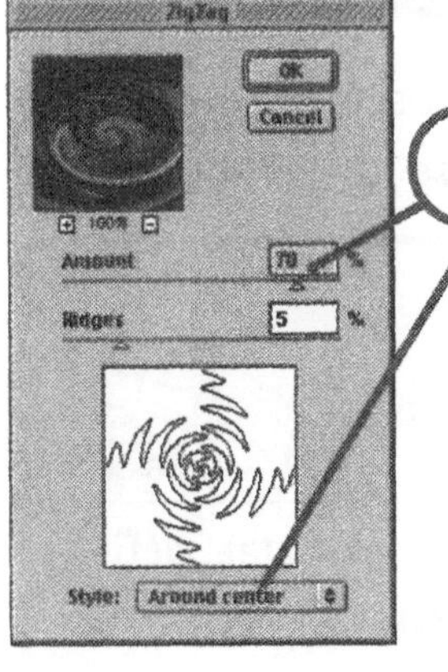

4 Define the Zig-Zag filter

Tip

Add another layer of an upturned sky set to Screen blend mode.

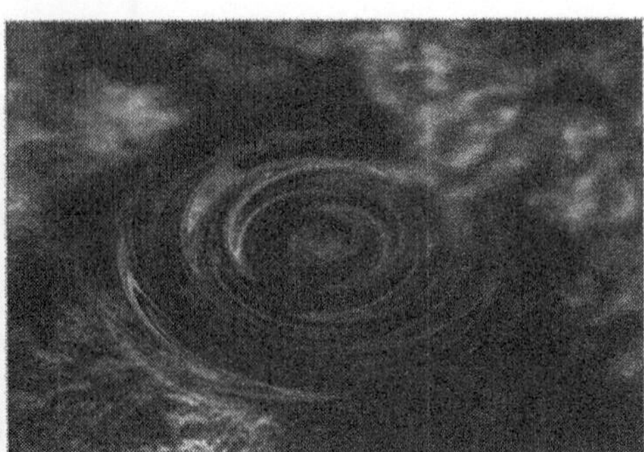

Final surface ripple

Basic steps

Twirl

1 Make a selection, generally the ellipse.

2 Feather this selection with a minimum of 25 pixels.

3 Within the Twirl dialog box zoom out, so that the full picture can be seen.

> **Take note**
>
> **Unlike Zig-Zag, Twirl is often best on the same layer.**

To explore abstract art possibilities, this filter should prove a useful starting point. This series of horizontal gradients is an Illustrator EPS to give a feel for what this filter can do. File/ Import brings it in. The elliptical selection is made using the ellipse marquee, with a large feather (64 in the image shown) – this avoids a harsh transition. The amount of twirl was 211°.

Before creating the twirl, try lightening the centre of the image with the burn tool set very large and for the midtones, this adds a feeling of the third dimension.

Original file with light and shade added using Levels or the dodge/ burn tools to enhance the feeling of depth

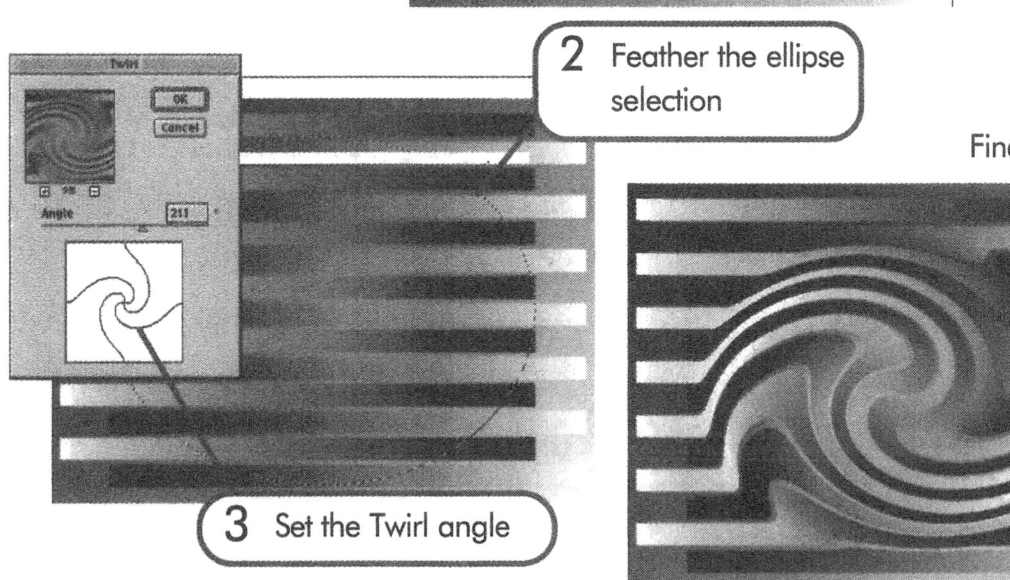

Final twirl

3D Transform

Basic steps

This tool converts a known 3D shape in a 2D scene, into a new viewpoint of that object. First use one of the three wireframe primitives; the cube, cylinder or sphere. In this case, the cube. It gives you four control points and you edit with these and the Field of View slider.

The tool draws from one side, and expands when dragged. Align the points with the hollow arrow.

Make the wireframe cube lock to the shape and perspective of the phonebox. Then use the two viewpoint tools, the **Pan camera** and **Trackball** to move the object to your new view.

The **Field of View** slider controls the perspective; the **Dolly** controls the distance from the subject, and therefore the size of the image.

Planes that were originally hidden will contain no data, and be rendered as a flat grey. If you take images this far, you may well merge other images to these planes or redraw them, to complete the effect.

1 Copy telephone box to new Layer.
2 Select an area beyond the phonebox.
3 Use Filter – Render – 3D Transform and select the cube.
4 Align the wireframe points to the object.
5 Use the Field of View to align the top and sides.
6 Use Pan and Trackball tools to transform.
7 Click OK to finish.

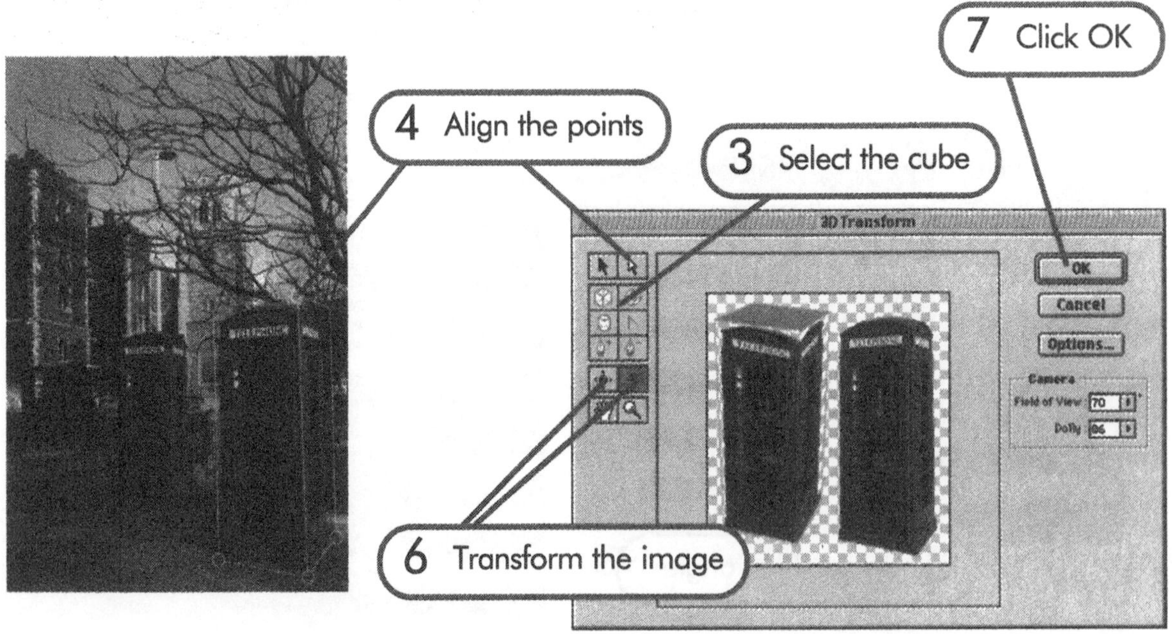

Effects filters

Take note

Filters can be faded after application, and used in different blend modes. You can apply one over another or apply the same filter in differing amounts to different areas.

Adobe used to bundle the Gallery Effects Filters as separate Plug Ins, now they are integrated, and seem faster. Space only allows a brief introduction to some of them. They invariably rely on a fair amount of RAM, so use globally only when you have substantial memory, otherwise, in small selections.

Another point to watch; several of these filters use the foreground and background colours for their effect, so choose these before using the filter.

Remember also that the plus and minus signs beneath the preview image allow you to zoom in or out.

Here are a few applied effects to the same original:

Original

1

2

3

4

5

6

1 Sketch/Graphic Pen

2 Artistic/Cutout

3 Texture/Patchwork

4 Sketch/Water Paper - faded (90%-Normal)

5 Sketch/Stamp

6 Other/High Pass

Summary

- Excessive blurring, or cloning of your image may not look real because it is too smooth, add some noise within a soft-edged selection.
- When you need to make extensive use of a filter effect, rather than make one large hit, try repeating the effect, using lesser amounts.
- Any texture (in fact any rectangular selection!) can be tiled to fill a larger area (RAM-dependent). Choose non-aligned to minimise the effects of obvious repeats.
- If you need to disguise a gradation created within Photoshop, do not use blur alone. Add noise, or add a large amount of noise, then blur, then add a small amount of noise.
- Uniform noise is likely to look smoother than Gaussian noise.
- A simple texture can be created by adding noise to an area, then applying Motion Blur.
- If you plan to create a texture that has depth use the Transform/Perspective Tool to give a perspective distortion – widen the foreground to make it seem nearer. Create the texture in a larger document than needed to allow for this distortion.
- Try using different foreground and background colours than blue and white when using the Clouds filter, or add additional colours after initial creation.
- Experiment – filters are the Photoshop playground.

9 Printing

Printer selection

In the image window, at the bottom left (Mac), or the Windows Info bar in a similar position, is an area which when clicked, reveals an outline of the image in its relation to the page size you have set within Page Setup (See the image on page 124).

What printer to choose for use with Photoshop is another matter, and this decision will vary according to the depth of your pocket and the use to which you will be putting the prints. For economic personal use, Inkjet technology provides probably the best option, rising through thermal wax, dye sublimation, laser copy, Pictrography™ and Iris™.

If the print output is intended for proofing purposes, then the acceptable tolerance must be tight, equating to costly. If on the other hand the work is for yourself, whatever machine that prints satisfactory colour for your budget becomes your criteria. If you need photographic style colour output, high end Inkjets, Pictrography™ and Dye Sublimation are the tops.

Today the economically priced inkjets printing on specialist glossy paper are hard to fault. The giveaway is that the weight of the paper tends to be less than that of photographic paper.

There are also a few printers that write directly to photographic paper and the quality is superb, but at a price. In many instances there is no need for a really good printer at home, because for the occasions you need the quality, you can take your data to a bureau and take your pick of the technologies available!

Printers provide the means to show a hardcopy of your work. To be acceptable as a proof of your data, both your system and the proof printer need to be calibrated to agreed standards. (Proofing is beyond the scope of this book.)

- ❑ If your images from Photoshop are to be used in page layouts, then your actual printing program is not Photoshop, but a DTP application such as PageMaker or Quark Xpress. These may require the use of a RIP (Raster Image Processor). It will be the DTP program not Photoshop that defines your choice of printer.
- ❑ Photoshop itself does not require a RIP, but once exported to a DTP program, it is stored in a manner that does have this requirement.

Resolution

Jargon

Pixellation describes a file that has too little resolution and shows individual pixels – the 'Jaggies'.

Interpolation is where a file of, say, 150ppi is resampled to take it to 300ppi, and Photoshop guesses what values it puts between the known ones.

Tip

The general rule to determine a suitable resolution is to multiply the lines per inch used by the printer by a factor of 1.5 or 2. A magazine using a 150lpi screen would need between 225 and 300ppi.

Picture cells – pixels – are the smallest square points in your image. They are a finite size, but their ultimate size will depend on how many you pack in. Pixels per inch (ppi) is a linear measurement. If you pack seventy-two pixels into each dimension, it will be 72ppi. Resolution is not concerned with the particular size of the pixels, but the density to which they are packed. All pixels in any one image are of equal size.

If you open two 6x4 inch image files, one scanned at 300ppi and another at 150ppi, and drag the one with fewer pixels per inch it will seem smaller and will fit into the new canvas. They are no longer the same size – what has happened is that since the file is concerned with pixels, and pixels are all the same size, scanning at 150ppi has created a smaller sized picture.

The resolution needed for a picture to look smooth and sharp, depends on whether you are looking at it on screen, as ink on paper from an inkjet printer or as a colour transparency. The file resolutions you might need are:

- Monitor screen publishing – between 72ppi and 96ppi
- A Pictrograph™ will print at either 267ppi or 400ppi
- Inkjet printing needs around 200–300ppi
- For magazine reproduction, about 225–300ppi
- For output back to transparency, around 1000ppi
- For newspapers, with their very large screens, a file need only be 160ppi.

Photoshop assumes a screen resolution of 72ppi, so viewing at 100% may not be quite exact.

Page Setup, Print dialogs

Having made the selection of printer, you can set up your file for output. The options will vary for each printer, but basically, you are able to set the paper size; the orientation, (portrait or landscape); and if in colour, which colour management system you are using. Some printers will offer more than one resolution, and this can be set from either the Page Setup or the print dialog boxes.

Once Page Setup is complete, go to File – Print, where you can select the number of copies, and sometimes items like a border or background colour, and even a scaling factor. The dialogs you see are sometimes generic system-wide layouts, but may well be overridden because they offer printer-specific options. Little general guidance can be given here.

A check on your settings can be made from the Info bar at the bottom left of the screen (PC) or of the image window (Mac). The image will always be centred on the page. If you need to place the picture in a specific area of the page, you will must import your image into a page layout or illustration program. The clumsy method to do this in Photoshop would be to set Canvas size to your Page size and move your image into position, making your file much larger.

Although to print ink onto paper, the colours will be CMYK, the printer itself may well carry out the conversion, thereby requiring the file to be in RGB. This is typically the case with most Epson inkjet printers.

- ❑ Make sure printer drivers are loaded and up-to-date.
- ❑ Ensure your printer is connected to the correct port.
- ❑ Ensure you have set the correct paper size. Specially coated paper must be the right way round.
- ❑ In Page Setup double-check all the settings, then and only then go to 'Print'.
- ❑ Always save your image before printing.

Printable area

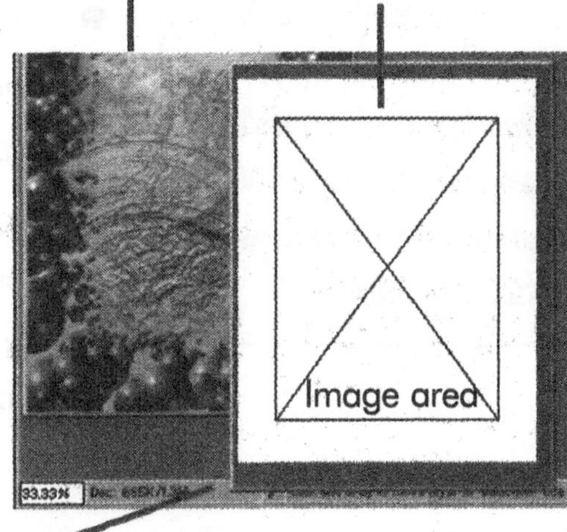

Click here for the preview to pop up

Image preview window

Out to print

- Create and keep a native Photoshop file for editing. Files you save for going to print via a DTP (page layout) program should be saved as either TIFFs, EPS or DCS 2.0
- These formats allow the file to contain information that can be recognised as masks (clipping paths) or in some cases allow colours to be edited
- Files can also contain precise halftone screen details, but this is somewhat rarer
- Acrobat files can be made from your images, either individually or via PageMaker or Quark Xpress, which can also be used by some printers

This is not the same as printing. This is where the files you create are to appear in the pages of a brochure or advertisement and although you may also make copies on your own printer, the files you create in Photoshop are to go into page layout programs such as Quark Xpress and PageMaker.

Your master editable file may well still be in native (.psd) Photoshop format, but the flattened file will likely be an EPS or TIFF file. It could be either in RGB or CMYK, but never both in the same page layout program.

With the introduction of Level 3 Postscript RIPs (Raster Image Processors) it may be that you can supply RGB files in either EPS or TIFF or even Acrobat files (.pdf). Opinion is divided here, but conversions to CMYK rely on your knowing important information about the intended processes and equipment that are to handle your files, so submitting RGB files will give the end user more scope.

Many times the decisions are not yours to make, and as circumstances vary widely, we will make no recommendations as to the best methods here beyond observations which help you decide.

If you intend your files for Web use or for output to slides and large format transparencies, then work in RGB throughout. Overall unsharp masking is best done at the time of conversion; this can be handled by the RIP, so could be another reason to stay in RGB. If the scans you receive to work upon are CMYK, then keep everything in CMYK, unless a required filter is unavailable to CMYK. If you know the printers' settings then set these in the preferences before conversion. If you need an idea of how colours will translate then Select View/Preview/CMYK, (only accurate if the CMYK parameters are set).

Image and canvas sizes

When first opening an image, the dimensions for both are the same. The image fills the canvas. The difference comes when you want to make the picture smaller than the total area or want to add some space around the existing image to allow for a background or another picture. Both these circumstances bring about an effective reduction of the existing image or an increase in the canvas area.

Which actually happens depends upon the resolution of the image. If the resolution is not to change, then the canvas can be made larger. If the resolution is changed, which can only be done with the **Image Size** dialog box, then the canvas will also. When you open an image, you need to make a decision as to how you intend using it.

Suppose your picture is currently 15cm wide, but needs to be 15.3cm – the current image size is not to change, but extra background is needed to make the width, you would then go to **Canvas Size** and make the change there. Let us assume the picture was to be on the left, with the extra area to the right. In the the small diagram at the bottom simply click in the middle left box, set the new width,then hit OK. The area beyond your image will take on the background colour. It is this extra area of canvas you now need to fill, naturally if this was to be a flat colour you could have selected your background before this action, but it is more likely you will fill this area with an extension of your first image or another picture.

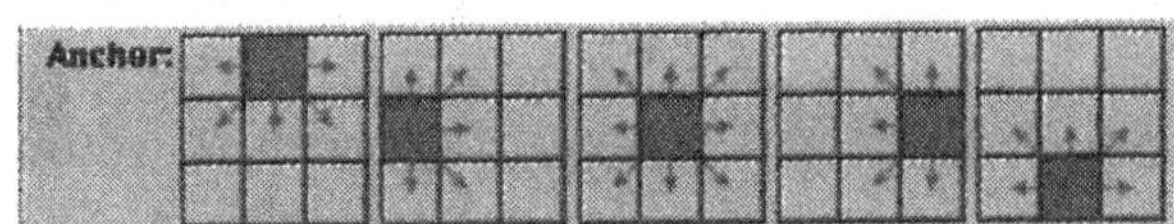

Four of the nine possible ways to increase the Canvas size of an image. The dark grey is the existing area. You can also use this method to crop an image.

- ❑ Image size can be changed whilst retaining the link to resolution, by ensuring that no resampling takes place. As size goes up resolution goes down, and vice versa.
- ❑ The aspect ratio is maintained by checking the Constrain Proportions box. Unchecking, allows you to shrink or stretch one dimension.
- ❑ To change just the resolution, check the Resample box. Where possible do such changes in multiples (72,144,288...), this makes interpolation more accurate.

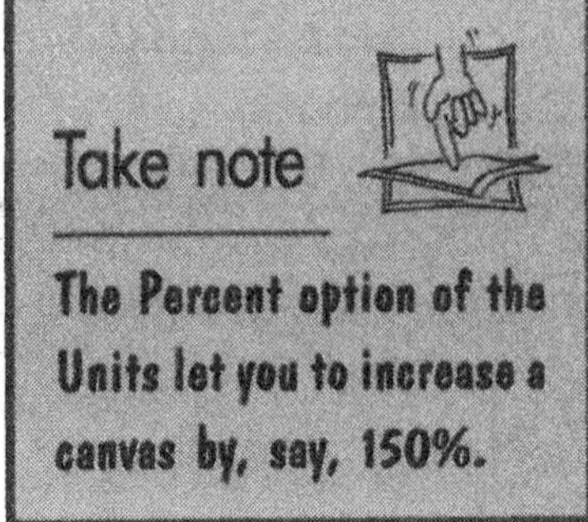

The Percent option of the Units let you to increase a canvas by, say, 150%.

RGB versus CMYK?

- The Adobe RGB (1998) workspace is not as large as that of a transparency, but does fairly fully cover the CMYK gamut, but it is evident how small the CMYK gamut is.
- The diagram below in black-and-white is not an easy way to show the relationship between RGB and CMYK.

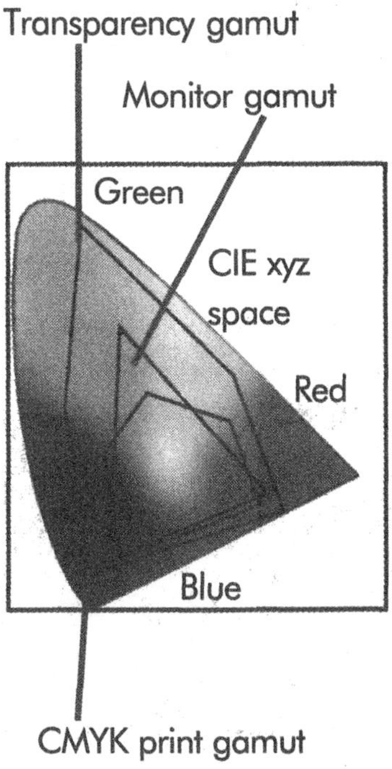

Transparency gamut

Monitor gamut

Green

CIE xyz space

Red

Blue

CMYK print gamut

RGB (red, green and blue) are the primary colours used to display full continuous colour on your monitor, to show images on the World Wide Web, to re-create transparencies. It is the base file of digital cameras and scanners.

CMYK (Cyan, Magenta, Yellow and Key) are the colours which when applied to paper in tight groups of dots give us an impression of smooth colour in magazines, brochures, book jackets and packaging.

The colours we are capable of seeing are well-encompassed by RGB; less well by CMYK. Many filters within Photoshop will only operate in the RGB domain.

Due to the advent of digital cameras and because the files very often need to be converted in different ways depending on the processes or hardware, many manufacturers of RIPs (Raster Image Processors) are taking the RGB route, so that CMYK conversions with differing characteristics can be output in the same workflow incorporating different USM (UnSharp Masking) and different screen resolutions all from the same master file.

Adobe themselves are seeing a steeper takeup of Acrobat which can hold both RGB and CMYK in the same file and so it seems that the benefits of this approach will make it more likely that files will remain in the RGB domain further along the path to print than hitherto. Epson, who make colour printers, have certainly decided that they can give the public better colour if you send the printer RGB files and let the software in the printer do the tricky stuff.

Your authors are divided on this subject, but if you wish to try your hand at CMYK then be prepared for hours of reading and a steep learning curve.

Indexed colour

An indexed colour file is single channel and contains no Layers; it has a limited palette of 256 colours. The palette can contain a variable choice of specified colours, which allows them to be tailored to the range within the image, thus making smaller files than their 24-bit equivalent. The range can be reduced further to 216 colours for use on the World Wide Web for greater speed. In this form it is said to be Web-safe. The GIF format uses indexed colour, and also has the option to select a colour to become transparent, allowing you to create a non-rectangular cropped object, by surrounding it with the transparent colour.

The GIF format has another option; that of interlacing, which allows the image to be presented gradually on a Web page, building the page in horizontal slices, thus giving an impression of the image fairly quickly, then interlacing further slices to build to the full resolution. The JPEG format has a similar function known as progressive JPEG.

Indexing the colours of an image is the last stage; the original image will have been created in full-colour then reduced to Indexed Color mode, as no filtering can be done, and the brushes are hard-edged.

- ❑ Indexed Colour is used where small size is far more important than the need for accurate colour.
- ❑ Indexed Colour mode is ideal for screen-based presentations, or for use on the web when saved as a GIF.
- ❑ Buttons on web pages are often in GIF format for reasons of size and speed.

Taking an RGB image to Indexed Color via Image – Mode reduces the range of colours and thus the file size

Indexed colour palette showing the full range of colours in the file

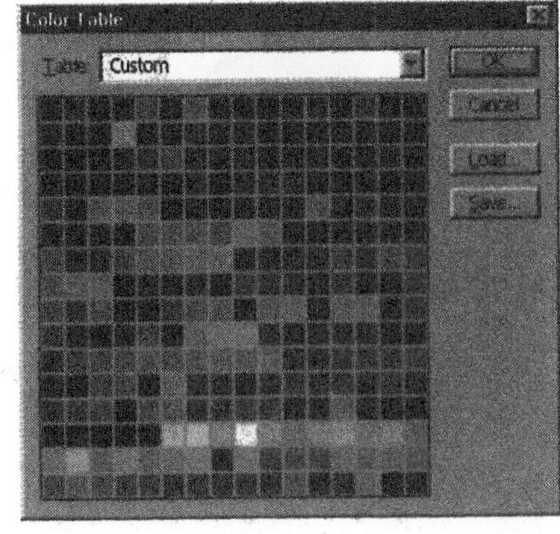

Bitmaps

- Scanning in images such as logos as bitmaps will contain only black and white.
- Going from bitmap to greyscale gives far more scope for editing.

Greyscale original

This correctly refers to files which contain only black and white pixels, where each pixel is either black (a value of 0) or white (a value of 1). However, it is often somewhat erroneously used to refer to files containing pixels as opposed to vectors. These should be referred to as pixelmaps.

Bitmap mode in Photoshop is a mode in which a picture is made up of only black or white pixels. Any effect of tone is created by clustering – sparsely clustered dots of black will simulate light grey; densely packed will seem like dark grey.

There are several options available when translating from greyscale to bitmap mode, ranging from the 50% threshold which will make no attempt at holding greys to the printers' style screen options.

The .bmp file format known as bitmap is really the PC equivalent of the Mac PICT format, in that it can contain files at several bit depths. Both these two formats simply grew out of the original true bitmap.

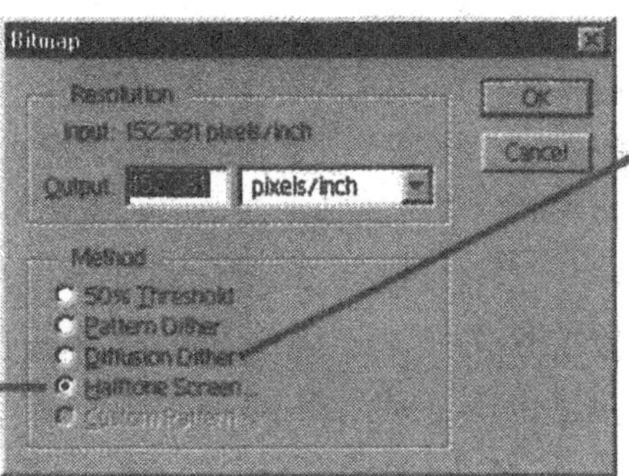

Diffusion Dither gives the effect shown below

Halftone screen is best for holding greyscale detail – set the Frequency to match the output media

Halftone Screen

Frequency: lines/inch

Angle: 45 degrees

Shape: Diamond

OK | Cancel | Load... | Save...

Convert with Image – Mode – Bitmap, setting a Method option

Greyscale

Generally described as black-and-white, the term is used to denote that there is one channel and it is capable of storing values of black from solid black to no black, that is white!

Using greyscale images well is quite a skill. Original black and white photos give a clue as to how well they work as images from Photoshop. If you start from a colour picture, you need to have an image that does not solely rely on colour contrast. Also, unless you have a good high resolution printer, it will be your printer which lets you down. Older 300dpi laser printers are not a good means of printing from Photoshop. Most current colour printers will give you better results.

When deciding to use greyscale, make sure you have an image which has good blacks, clean whites in the highlights, yet good separation of tones in the midtones (faces and any areas of prime interest). Shades of red and green may separate well in colour but merge completely when in greyscale. Be prepared to use the Curves, Levels or the Channel Mixer before your conversion.

You can scan direct to greyscale from black and white originals or scan to colour then change to greyscale. If the range of tones is long, then there can be distinct advantages of scanning in colour, and although we think of greyscale as black-and-white, there are many times when black is too cold and the toning of this to another colour will give more atmosphere to the image.

Take note

Many output devices require you convert a greyscale to colour – generally RGB TIFF.

- ❑ As a form of primer for duotones, try experimenting with reshaping Curves individually after converting a Greyscale Image to RGB Colour.
- ❑ Your finished work can have the look of a Duotone, but will still be an RGB file. If the colours are not too whacky, you should be able to convert to CMYK if necessary; this does not reduce the cost of printing down to that of a true duotone.

Duotones

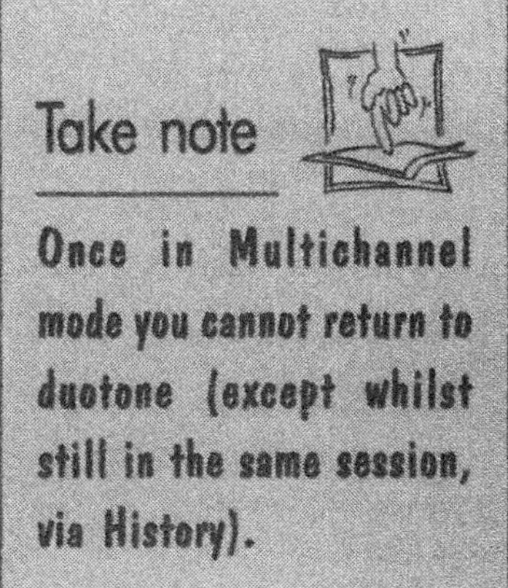

Duotone mode encompasses monotones, tritones and quadtones. The process is the substitution of a colour for a greyscale image. The basic duotone is where a curve is set for the black ink to cover the shadows, and the selected second colour is used for the midtones and highlights. The others are variants are of this basic process. Duotone is a good way of preserving a long range of tones in print. It can also add mood or retain a feel of colour without the added expense of four-colour printing.

The starting point is a greyscale image. The colours used are often Pantone colours – there are a range of presets for each category. There is great scope for experimentation once you have mastered the basics using the examples on the CD-ROM.

Clicking on the graph box allows you to manipulate the curve defining the chosen Ink colour. Clicking on the colour box goes to Colour selection.

Duotone mode has only one channel; however if you need separate channels, change to Multichannel mode from the Image/Mode menu. Save the file in DCS 2.0 format with the type of preview you need, in either single or multiple file form.

Curves and colours are reflected in their icons

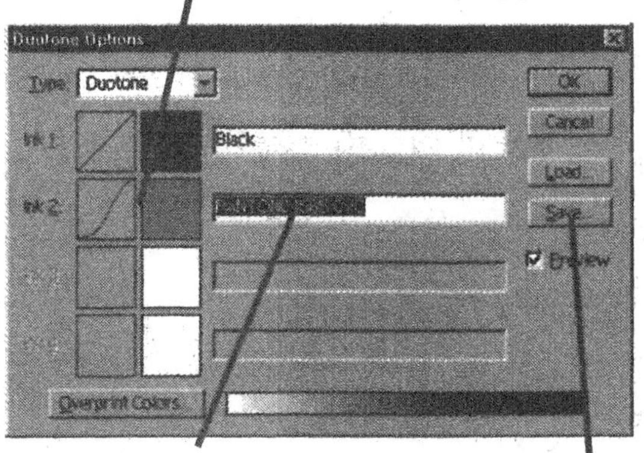

Duotone Options dialog

Be sure colour references match the printer's, exactly

Settings for one image can be saved for use on others

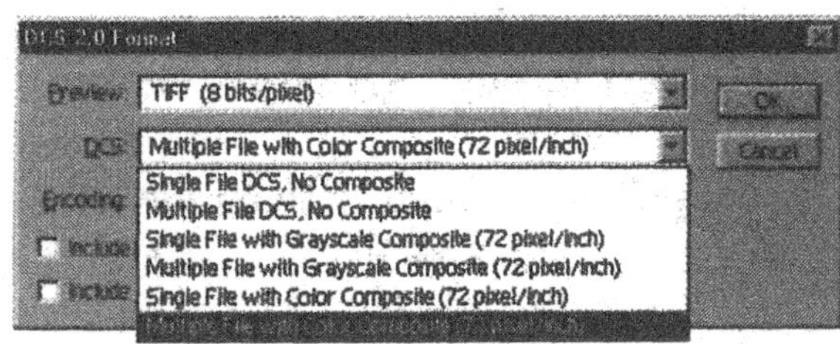

DCS 2.0 file saving options

TWAIN, File Info

Although originally an acronym humourously designated **T**echnology **W**ithout **A**n **I**nteresting **N**ame, Hewlett Packard insisted it was where two technologies met (the Twain!). The TWAIN interface is a popular cross-platform way for scanners to communicate with computers.

Photoshop incorporates a TWAIN interface Plug-in, so that you can go to **File – Import – Select TWAIN_32 Source** to select the driver for the particular device. If you have only one TWAIN device, you need do this once only. After that you may go straight to your device and you will see your specific driver interface. It is here that you make such selections as Resolution, Size, Crop, Exposure, Negative, Slide, Sharpness, etc.

- ❑ TWAIN allows developers to keep costs down, because it is cross-platform, and this means supplying just a plug-In rather than a full program

Windows Import

Mac Import

File Info

This is primarily for newspapers and magazines, and gives an opportunity to enter directly into the file information for later use with picture databases and search engines, and information regarding the image's construction or techniques, or values used in the creation of a vignette.

Use the pull-down menu to jump through the various categories or use the Next and Previous commands. Use Append when adding from an earlier File Info.

File Info dialog box

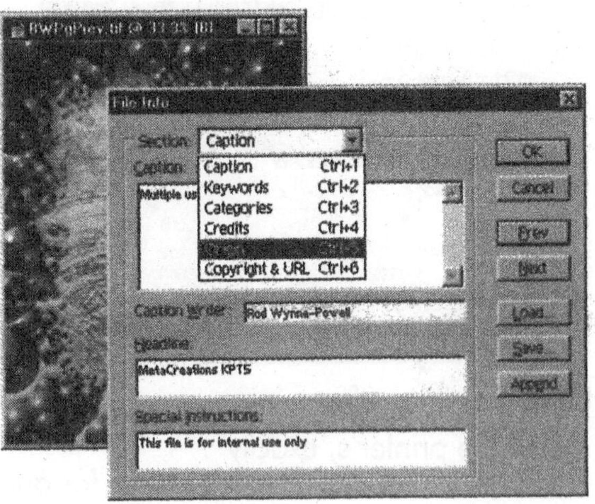

Output to Epson inkjets

The Epson range of printers have become extremely popular due to their price and quality, but the dialogs can be daunting to use. Many users only see the front page, little realising the control they can exercise over the quality of the output. With the colour control offered by Photoshop 5, it is good to know the printer is aware of your settings.

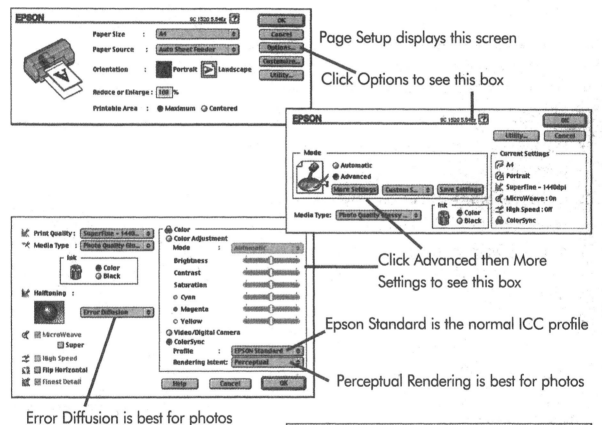

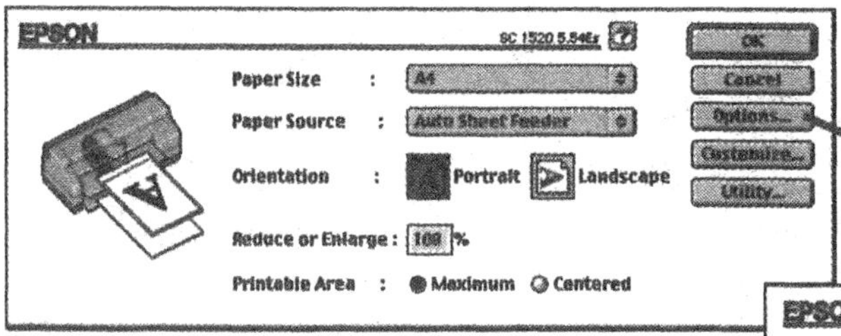

Page Setup displays this screen

Click Options to see this box

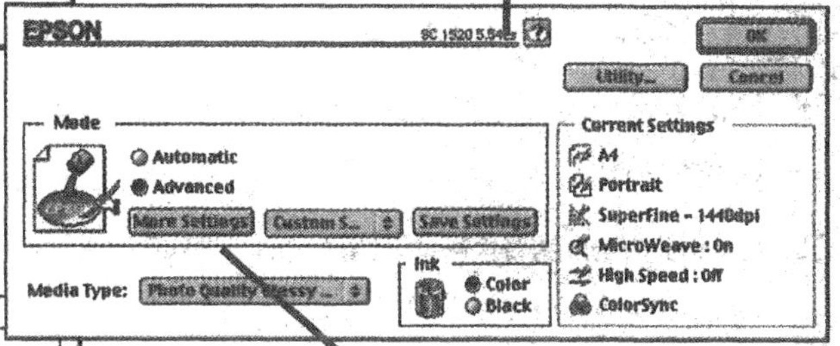

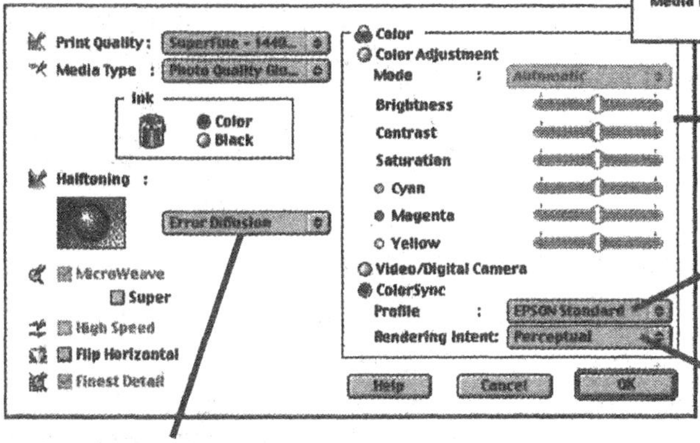

Click Advanced then More Settings to see this box

Epson Standard is the normal ICC profile

Perceptual Rendering is best for photos

Error Diffusion is best for photos

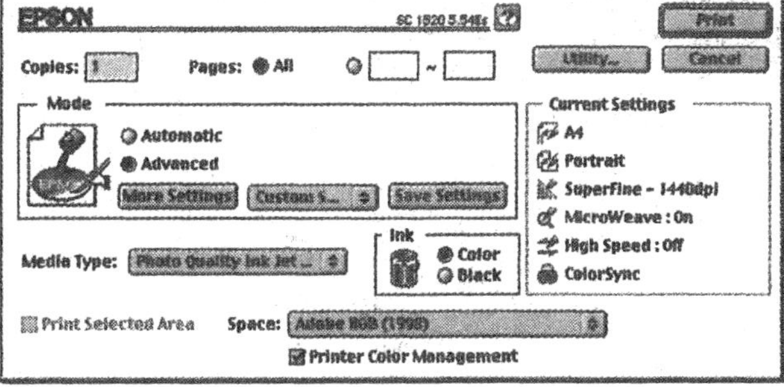

The print dialog has the Color Management as well as the Copies and Pages selection options

Summary

- When using your own printer, your files can be printed from your native Photoshop file (.psd on PC). Any text you type has to fall within your total picture area.
- If you have PageMaker or some other page layout program, then you could lay pictures exactly where you want on the page, and text can be partly over pictures if need be.
- Files for the latter use, or for use in DTP, will need to be in the less editable file formats of TIFF or EPS, but it would still be best to keep the editable Photoshop file.
- Use RGB, Indexed colour and GIF for Web work.
- Use bitmaps if you want to colour up logos in a DTP program.
- Use duotones where black and white alone would lack warmth or mood.
- Keep in RGB mode for as long as possible, because you can use all of the filters, and your file should be smaller.
- Use EPS files for clipping paths, where you want to have an image cut out around its edge as opposed to a rectangular box.

Tip

There's a Wizard for creating the cutouts for web and print. It is located in the Help menu as Export Transparent Image. It will take you through the steps for a clipping path for print and a transparent GIF for use on the World Wide Web.

10 Automation & Help

Automated plug-ins

The reason Photoshop contains so many different features, is that it is designed to cater for the demands of many types of customer. Since most people happily access only a small proportion of Photoshop's functions, it can therefore sometimes be hard for the novice to remember the exact procedures to use each time, or know where to look up the relevant instructions in the user guide. The fundamental concept behind automated plug-ins, is to make Photoshop more accessible to users of all skill levels.

Automated plug-ins are a wizard facility which incorporate some useful clues and tips to help you make correct choices as you follow the step-by-step instructions. In future, it is likely that third-party developers will develop more automated plug-ins, these will make Photoshop even easier for the typical user to master. Some of the automated plug-ins like Resize Image are found in the Help menu and others like Fit Image, Multi-page PDF to PSD and the Contact Sheet feature are located in the File – Automate menu.

Fit Image wizard

This allows you to specify the pixel dimensions you want an image to fit into. For example, if you have an exact area to fill and you don't want the picture to exceed either the maximum width or height.

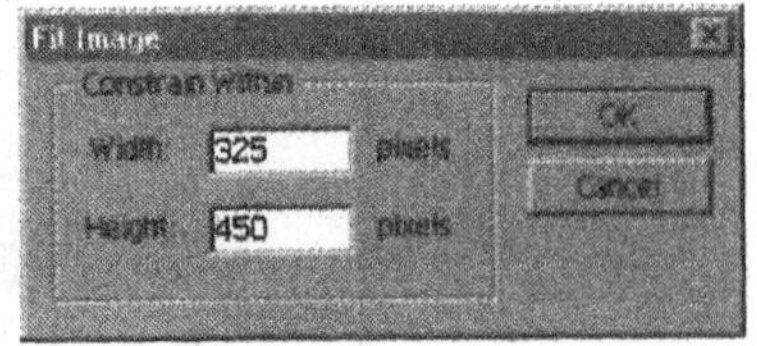

The Contact Sheet wizard

This will enable you to build a single printout file from the contents of a folder. Choose a source folder and enter the output requirements. Photoshop will automatically generate a contact sheet from the images inside the selected folder.

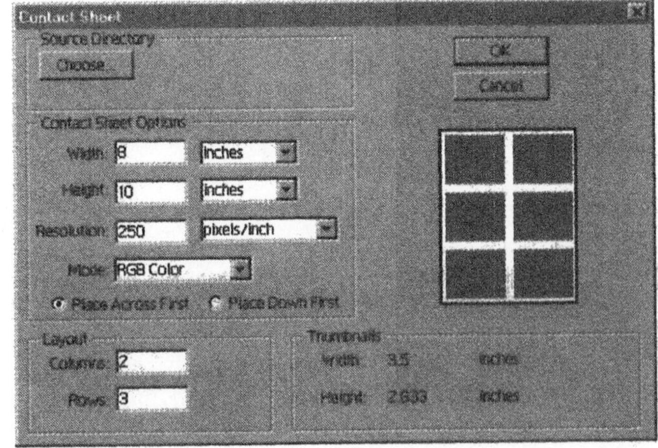

Export Transparency wizard

Original image

Transparent GIF

The illustrations show the stages of producing a transparent GIF from an image, through the wizard. All you have to do is respond to the prompts and click Next at each stage.

- You are first asked if you have made a selection of the area to be transparent – if not, it can be selected at that point.
- You then select the output mode – graphics or online use.
- The wizard then completes the processing to export the image as a transparent GIF

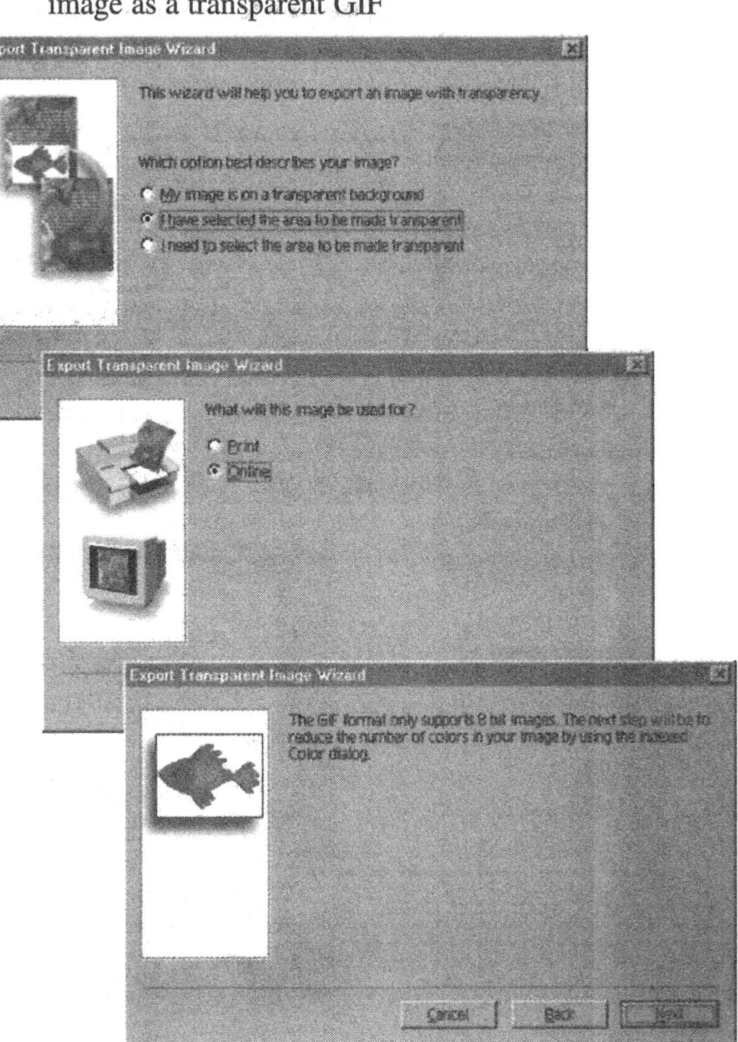

Tip

Actions are another essential Photoshop automating feature for repeated tasks. See page 138 for more information on recording an Action and the use of Batch Actions.

Recording actions

Actions allow the user to create their own Photoshop shortcuts. Most, but not all Photoshop operations are scriptable. Exceptions include use of the painting tools and drawing pen paths. Otherwise, most Photoshop commands can be recorded and replayed in sequence.

Playing back an action is simple – select the action and click on the play button. You can also assign a custom key combination. Double-click the action name and choose a keyboard key or key combination. In Button mode (see palette fly-out menu), clicking on the action name will launch it.

Basic steps

1 Click on the New action button in the Actions palette to start recording.

2 Give the action you are about to record a name and assign a hot key if you like.

3 Click Record and perform the sequence of actions.

4 At the end, click the Stop button.

5 The list view can be expanded to show the individual action commands. These can be edited if need be.

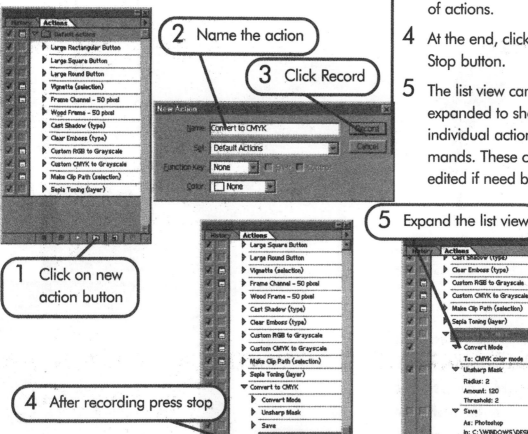

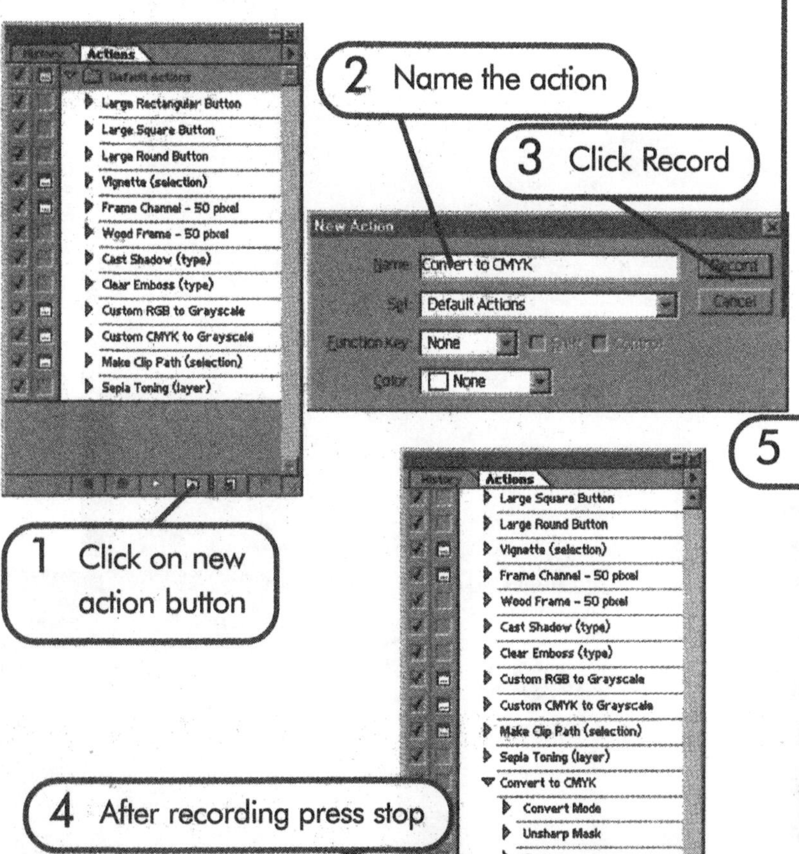

Batch actions

Tip

A basic set of Actions will have been installed with Photoshop. Many more are available in the Goodies folder on the Photoshop Deluxe CD-ROM.

To load an action, go to the Actions palette fly-out menu and select Load Actions... Once an Action has been recorded or installed, you can apply an action to a batch of images. The files to be 'actioned' must all be located in the same folder or subset of folders. The Batch option can be found under the File – Automate menu. Choose the action from the 'Play' section and select the folder to process in the 'Source' section. If the Batch command won't process a folder as expected, then you may need to check the Override Action 'Open' commands and take a look at the Destination options. Save and Close will overwrite the original, but you may prefer to choose a separate destination folder to write the modified files to.

Select Action from pop-up menu

Image Source folder options

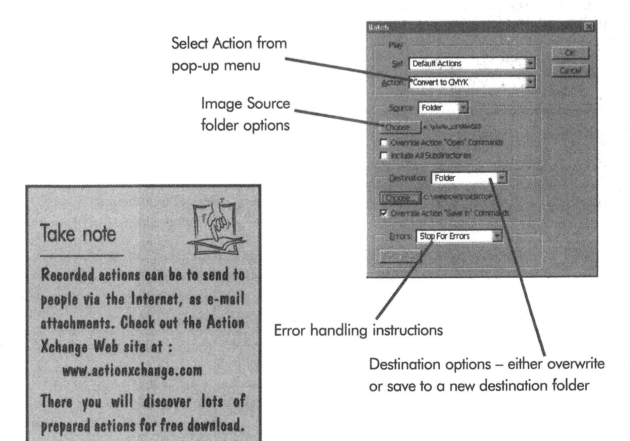

Error handling instructions

Destination options – either overwrite or save to a new destination folder

Take note

Recorded actions can be to send to people via the Internet, as e-mail attachments. Check out the Action Xchange Web site at :

www.actionxchange.com

There you will discover lots of prepared actions for free download.

Troubleshooting

Hardware

When trying to pinpoint a problem that doesn't seem to be described in the manuals, consider first if this is maybe due to a hardware or operating system fault. Third party Video cards are a notorious source of trouble, especially on the Windows PC system. For example, many cards or the driver software are known to conflict with Photoshop 5.0 and the colour management monitor calibration process. Other likely sources of trouble can easily be discounted by removing them one by one. The SCSI chain may be too long or a SCSI cable is faulty. SCSI problems could cause drives to not mount or be the cause of frequent system crashes. Disconnect all the SCSI devices and if that cures things, reconnect them again. Ensure you use only the shortest/best quality cables available. Check also that each attached device has its own unique SCSI ID number.

Extension conflicts

More often, a problem like a computer crash or freeze may be due to an extension conflict. As extensions and control panels are added to the operating system, something that has recently been added – like a new utility – will conflict with the current order of extensions. Try restarting the computer with all the extensions switched off, or only have the extensions essential to Photoshop switched on. A helpful utility application called Conflict Catcher (Mac) will help pinpoint such conflicts and resolve these by allowing you to re-list the order in which the system extensions load at startup. It could even be that the Photoshop preferences file has become corrupted. The file is now located inside the Adobe Photoshop Settings folder inside the Photoshop application folder. Keep a backup copy of your customised settings and preferences, so that if the preference

Quicktips

Failed operation
If you get an annoying alert sound when trying to perform a Photoshop operation, double-click with the mouse to call up a dialog message explaining why the operation cannot be carried out.

Startup preferences
Hold down the Command/ Ctrl and Option/Alt key whilst Photoshop is loading and you can first set the scratch disk and if then held down again after, locate the plug-ins folder on start-up.

Pasteboard colour
Shift click with the bucket tool to fill the pasteboard with a custom foreground colour (version 4.0 also).

Slow redraws
Multiple adjustment layers save on file size and memory usage, but may significantly slow down the screen redraws. If this happens, switch them off temporarily to regain screen refresh speed.

Transform Again
Command/Ctrl+Shift–T will repeat a transform. Command/Ctrl+ Option/Alt–T will duplicate the current layer and allow you to perform a transform. Command/Ctrl+ Option/Alt+Shift–T will duplicate the layer and repeat the last transform.

Preference shortcuts
Double-click the rulers to call up the Units & Rulers Preferences. Double-click a guide with the Move tool, to edit the Guides & Grids settings.

file does need to be dumped, you simply replace it instead of having to reconfigure everything all over again.

Colour management

The most common problems people experience, concern the new Photoshop 5.0 colour management system. For this reason, Adobe included a colour management wizard with the new 5.0.2 update. This is launched automatically when you first load Photoshop after installing the application. The setting up process is described more fully in Chapter 1 of this book, but any time you wish to use the wizard to reconfigure Photoshop's colour settings, it can be reached through the Help menu.

Memory

Editing large image files in Photoshop can put an enormous strain on the resources of an underpowered computer system. To use Photoshop effectively, you need a recent computer with a fast chip clock speed, enough video memory or a special (compatible) video card to ensure rapid screen redraws and a display in thousands or preferably, millions of colours. RAM memory is very important – a base RAM specification of 32 Mb is just about enough to run the operating system these days plus a few other standard applications. Photoshop will perform best with at least 32 Mb of RAM all to itself and even that will only permit editing of low resolution images. To work on larger sized files, it is sensible to upgrade the 32 Mb to something like at least 96 Mb, or more if your machine will allow it. When making a new computer purchase, one of the things to look out for is the number of empty RAM slots available. If there is only one slot, then the maximum amount of RAM you can have will be just 128 Mb. With three slots you can expand up to 384 Mb or even higher with the latest 256 Mb modules.

Hard disk space

When memory runs low, hard disk space is used as virtual memory or as it's known in Photoshop, a 'scratch disk'. In fact, there must be at least as much contiguous megabyte space in free hard disk space as RAM memory to make use of all the RAM memory first. If you keep getting 'Sorry, the Primary scratch disk is full' error messages, you will need to find more disk space. Installing a separate dedicated 2 Gb drive, internally or externally is a fine investment. Keep this disk empty and use it solely as a Photoshop scratch disk and you'll never have to see those messages again. This should definitely provide a noticeable performance boost. There are various Hard drives to choose from and the most important specification to look out for is the sustained data transfer speed. A Zip drive has a sustained transfer rate of just over 1 Mb per second, a SCSI AV drive, around 3 Mb per second. Faster drives, like Ultra SCSI RAID systems are available. These require a special accelerating PCI card, but the data transfer rate is a lot higher: around 20 Mb per second or faster.

Over a period of time, the computer's hard disks will get fragmented and this can lead to reduced performance, especially if the Startup disk is also used as the primary scratch disk. Overall, a computer performance will slow after a month's heavy use. Defragmenting the drive using a custom utility like Norton Speed Disk, will help keep the disks in order. The Norton Utilities suite of programs will also take care of maintaining the disk – checking for disk errors and repairing them as well as offering the ability to recover lost data. Don't forget to regularly rebuild the desktop files once every two weeks or so. On the Macintosh, hold down the Command and Option keys at startup to force the system to rebuild your disk desktop files. This will also help clear the decks so to speak!

Quick tips

Scaled actions
If you set the ruler units to 'percent' before recording an action, coordinate sensitive operations recorded in the action will work to scale on any size of image.

Unsave
An accidental save, like overwriting the high-res master, can easily be undone using the history palette to go back a step.

Beginners' pen paths
In the pen tool Options palette, switch on the Rubber band option. This will help newcomers understand better how to draw with the pen path tool.

Clipboard memory

Whilst editing in Photoshop, keep an eye on the amount of memory used. If working on a particularly large file, it does help to reduce the number of histories down to three and bear in mind that when you copy something to the clipboard, the contents will be held until the next copy operation. The Edit > Purge menu is useful as a means of clearing items like the clipboard or history. Use this whenever performance noticeably decreases.

SOS

Follow through the above hardware and system setup tips and you should find Photoshop will be a very stable program to use. Anything that can go wrong will go wrong of course and there is nothing that can be done when a crash in another program causes Photoshop to crash with it too. For these reasons, follow the well advised mantra: SOS (Save Often Stupid). Always keep you Photoshop files backed up and stored safely on recordable media disks and have these stored safely away from heat, direct sunlight and electromagnetic radiation.

Photoshop is a very powerful, professional tool, but it is also a fun program to play with. The umpteen third-party plug-ins available for Photoshop provide a dazzling array of special effects and texture generation. The only limits to what you can in Photoshop are those of your imagination!

Summary

- Automated plug-ins are designed to help user access and use Photoshop efficiently and correctly to carry out specific tasks.
- Automated plug-ins like the Resize Image Wizard, will offer different options for Web design and graphics use.
- Export transparency will convert a selection of the masked are to make a transparent GIF or create a clipping path for a TIFF file.
- Actions are Photoshop scripts you can record yourself or download from various web sites.
- Automated plug-ins can also be recorded as part of an Action script.
- Batch actions can be used to automatically repeat an action on a large number of images.
- Help is available via the Help menu. There is also an extensive Adobe on-line support facility for people with Internet access.
- Many Photoshop problems can be traced to a hard-ware fault like a video card or SCSI chain problem.
- If you suffer persistent system crashes, try running Photoshop with a minimal extensions set and the preferences file deleted.
- Editing large image files requires extra RAM memory and ideally a separate hard drive allocated as a scratch disk.

Appendix: shortcut tips

Tip

Rules for working out the Macintosh keyboard equivalents are simple:

The Alt key is equivalent to the Option key and is located to the right of the Control key. Where the list has 'Control', use the Command key.

The Control key on the Macintosh is used instead of a PC right mouse click.

The accompanying table contains a brief summary of some essential shortcuts The key commands shown here are for Windows PC.

Keyboard shortcut	Function
Control–O	File – Open File
Control–P	File – Print File
Control+Shift–P	File – Page Setup
Control–Q	File – Quit
Control–S	File – Save
Control+Shift–S	File – Save As
Control–W	File – Close
Control–C	Edit – Copy
Control–V	Edit – Paste
Control–X	Edit – Cut
Control–Z	Edit – Undo last operation
Esc/Control–Period (.)	Cancel or abort function (System command)
Control–R	View – Show/Hide Rulers
Control+Spacebar	Zoom in
Alt+Spacebar	Zoom out
Control–plus	View – Zoom in with window resizing
Control+Alt–plus	View – Zoom in without window resize
Control–minus	View – Zoom out with window resizing
Control+Alt–minus	View – Zoom out without window resize
Double-click hand tool	View – Fit To Screen
Double-click zoom tool	View – Actual pixels at 100%
Tab key	Hide/show palettes and toolbox
Shift+Tab key	Hide/show all palettes except toolbox
Spacebar	Access hand tool
Control key	Access move tool (excepting pen tool)

Keyboard shortcut	Function
Control-B	Image > Adjust > Color Balance
Control-L	Image > Adjust > Levels
Control-M	Image > Adjust > Curves
Control-U	Image > Adjust > Hue/Saturation
Control+Shift-N	Layer > New Layer
Control- J	Layer > New > Layer Via Copy
Control-E	Layer > Merge Down
Control-A	Select > Select All
Control-D	Select > Select None
Control+Shift-D	Select > Reselect
Control+Alt-D	Select > Feather
Control+Shift-I	Select > Invert Selection
Control-F	Filter > Apply last filter used
Control+Shift-F	Filter > Fade filter
Tab key	Hide/show palettes and toolbox
Shift+Tab key	Hide/show all palettes except toolbox
Control-Period (.)	Cancel or abort operation
Esc	Cancel operation (Crop/Transform/Save)
Tab key	Jump to next setting in any active dialog
Alt click Cancel button	Change Cancel button in dialog boxes to Reset
Control click channel	Load channel as a selection
Control-1	Activate channel-1, e.g. red or cyan channel and so on
Control- ~	Activate composite channel, e.g. RGB/CMYK

Take note

The majority of keyboard shortcuts remained the same between versions 4.0 and 5.0. If you use other Adobe products, you will now find a lot of common features in terms of the interface layout and shortcuts.

Tip

The Contextual menu can always be accessed by holding down the right mouse button (PC) or Control key (Mac). This will pop up a list of options associated with the currently selected tool.

Index

Symbols

A

B

C

D

E

M

N

O

P

Q

R

ROUTLEDGE Routledge
Taylor & Francis Group
LONDON AND NEW YORK

Printed and bound by CPI Group (UK) Ltd, Croydon, CR0 4YY
22/10/2024
01777637-0009